CW00377168

BREXIT

BREXIT

DEMOCRACY IN CRISIS

By

ANTHONY WESTON BREWSTER

CONTENTS

Winston Churchill, Zurich, September 1946

In September 1946 in Zurich, Winston Churchill surprised the world with his appeal for the creation of a United States of Europe. It gave rise to the European Movement and the process that led to the creation of the Council of Europe and the European Convention and the European Court of Human Rights. However, the memoirs of Belgian socialist politician, Paul-Henry Spaak, one of the architects of European integration, wrote of Churchill's speech in Zurich, that whilst Churchill wanted Britain to promote the creation of a united Europe, he did not want Britain to be part of it. Incidentally, as far back as 1930, Churchill had written in favour of European unity but qualified his support by adding: "We are with Europe but not of it… we are interested but not associated."

The Schuman Declaration of 9ᵗʰ May 1950

"Europe will not be made all at once or according to a single plan... The coming together of the nations of Europe... It proposes that Franco-German production of coal and steel... be placed under a common High Authority, within the framework of an organisation, open to the participation of other countries of Europe. The pooling of coal and steel production should... provide for the setting-up of common foundations for economic development as a first step in the federation of Europe."

The above declaration was by Robert Schuman, the French Foreign Minister, known as the architect of European integration.

"Europe's nations should be guided towards the superstate, without their people understanding what is happening. This can be accomplished by successive steps, each disguised as having an economic purpose, but which will eventually and irreversibly lead to federation (of Europe)."

Attributed to the French economist Jean Monnet, one of the founding fathers of the European Union, 30ᵗʰ April 1952.

Mikhail Gorbachev

"The most puzzling development in politics, during the last decade, is the apparent determination of Western European leaders, to recreate the Soviet Union in Western Europe."

Attributed to Mikhail Gorbachev, General Secretary of the Communist Party (Soviet Union) between 1985 and 1991.

The 'Will of the People'

"*The will of the people is the only legitimate foundation of any government and to protect its free expression should be our first objective.*"

Thomas Jefferson, President of the USA (1801-1809).

Note: These words characterise a 'people's democracy' not a 'parliamentary democracy'.

'Government of the People, by the People, for the People'

"The nation was conceived in liberty and dedicated to the proposition that all men are equal and that the future of democracy in the world would be assured that 'government of the people, by the people, for the people', shall not perish from the earth."

The Gettysburg Speech (1863) of President Abraham Lincoln (USA)

Note: These words legitimise the concept of a 'people's democracy'.

PREFACE

The purpose of writing *Brexit Means Brexit, Democracy In Crisis* was for the author, a former senior police officer and senior police advisor to the government, to undertake a 'search for the truth' and provide the people with a candid 'view from the street', amidst all the disturbing political and media obfuscation, to support the 17,410,742 people who voted to 'leave' and better inform the 16,141,241 people who voted to 'remain', in the Brexit referendum of 23rd June 2016, which has divided our country.

Having suffered the media frenzy and parliamentary shenanigans since the Brexit referendum, the author was motivated to chart the journey of the Brussels to Strasbourg Express, an extension of the lavish Orient Express, as the European political elite 'wine-and-dine' at our expense.

The main motivation of the author was to inform the ardent 'remain' voters, those who want a second referendum, those who cannot accept the result of the first referendum, about the harsh reality of our membership of the European Union 'juggernaut' as it 'thunders' towards its ultimate destination of a country called Europe or a United States of Europe.

It was, also, to support the much maligned 'leave' voters, who were characterised as uneducated, xenophobic, racist and elderly, by the liberal media and the political elite, vociferously campaigning for a second referendum or a 'People's Vote', to overturn the inconvenient result of the first referendum, which was, of course, a vote of the people.

Furthermore, the author cannot accept the brazen attack on our liberal democracy by our elected representatives, those we select and elect to represent us in parliament, who have vociferously demanded a second referendum and think they know better than the 'wisdom of the crowd'.

We, the people, elect our fellow citizens to represent us in the 'corridors of power', and we expect them to respect the 'will of the people', when the people have spoken in a referendum. This reasonable expectation is non-negotiable, as the electorate don't expect them to demand a second referendum, to overturn the inconvenient result of the first referendum.

The European political elite, in their Brussels and Strasbourg 'ivory towers' have developed a reputation for demanding a second referendum, when a first referendum did not achieve the required result, and this is profoundly undemocratic. The rejection of the result of a first referendum and the demand for a second referendum, raises the ridiculous concept of the 'best of three', which would be a disaster for our liberal democracy.

When our elected representatives, in our national parliament, asked the British electorate for their decision, on such an important constitutional matter as our continued membership of the European Union, they should have accepted the majority decision of the electorate, unconditionally.

Every elected representative, regardless of their personal views, should respect the 'will of the people', expressed in a public referendum, and deliver on their decision, not disregard the decision of the people and demand a second referendum, to change the result. We, the people, have no influence, beyond our single vote, in an election or referendum, and should that single vote be ignored by those we elect to represent us in the 'corridors of power', our respected liberal democracy is virtually dead.

This is a constitutional battle between the 'will of the people' and those they elect to represent them in the 'corridors of power'. This is a battle between the 'sovereignty' of parliamentary and the concept of a 'people's democracy', particularly when the 'people have spoken' in a plebiscite.

It's also apparent that the people have been misled by the political elite, about the real nature of the European Union, and its journey from the European Economic Community (EEC) or the Common Market to the European Union, and the ultimate 'clandestine' destination of a federal country called Europe or a United States of Europe and the author wants to inform the British people that they have been deliberately deceived.

It's, therefore, important to reveal the words of one of the founding fathers of the European Union, Jean Monnet, on 30th April 1952, who, according to the book *Britain and the European Union: Alternative Futures* written by Mark Baimbridge, Brian Burkitt and Philip Whyman, and published by the 'Campaign for an Independent Britain' 2005, said: "Europe's nations should be guided towards the superstate without their people understanding what is happening. This can be accomplished by successive steps, each disguised as having an economic purpose, but which will eventually and irreversibly lead to federation."

This quote is deeply disturbing and very little to do with the principles of our endangered liberal western democracy. Do the people, who want to remain in the European Union super-state, know that we've been misled by the European political elite from the start of their grand project?

Perhaps, we should reconsider the wise words of Thomas Jefferson, the President of the United States of America (1801-1809), who said: "The will of the people is the only legitimate foundation of any government and to protect its free expression should be our first objective." These words characterise a 'people's democracy', not a 'parliamentary democracy'.

When the people are selecting their political representatives, they must consider the 'primacy' of the people or those they elect to represent them in the House of Commons. Why would the people elect representatives who put their own views above the views of those who elevate them to power? Parliament may be 'sovereign', but our elected representatives must respect and accept the 'will of the people', expressed in a plebiscite, called by parliament, specifically to ascertain the views of the people.

The first attack on our valued liberal western democracy, was when the Conservatives took us into the European Economic Community (EEC) or the Common Market in 1972, without reference to the people. However, our membership was later confirmed in a referendum in 1975, called by a Labour Government, but were the unsuspecting people informed that the ultimate 'clandestine' destination was a federal United States of Europe?

The question is, therefore, before the people voted to remain in the European Economic Community (EEC) or the Common Market, were they made aware of the views of Jean Monnet, a founding father of the European Union, who had developed a plan for the unification of Europe by stages? First there would be a modest beginning, by pooling Western Europe's iron, coal and steel resources, then step by step, the whole of Europe's economic resources... would be pooled in a common market. Lastly, but some way off, a United States of Europe would emerge.

Furthermore, before the unsuspecting British people voted to remain in the European Economic Community (EEC) or the Common Market, were they made aware of the 'Schuman Declaration' of 9th May 1950, which is believed to be the founding text of European integration, which was delivered by Robert Schuman, an architect of European integration?

The 'Schuman Declaration', inspired by Jean Monet, the first Planning Commissioner, included the following: "Europe will not be made all at once, or according to a single plan. It will be built through concrete achievements, which create solidarity... It proposes that Franco-German production of coal and steel be placed under common High Authority, within the framework of an organisation open to the participation of the other countries of Europe. The pooling of coal and steel production should immediately provide for the setting-up of common foundations for economic development, as a first step in the federation of Europe."

The main question, therefore, is that when we joined the European Economic Community or the Common Market (1972) and confirmed membership in a public referendum (1975), did the British people know that the ultimate destination of the economic community was a federal European super-state, which would involve the loss of sovereignty and independence?

Furthermore, according to the publication *A Nation Is a Nation Is a Nation* by John Murray, published by Carnegie Publishing (1995), some major figures in the Conservative Party were economical with the truth, as follows: "In 1960, Prime Minister, Heath, expressed the view to his Cabinet that the dangers of supranational aspects of entry were being exaggerated but not all members of the Cabinet agreed and he was instructed (by them) to seek an authoritative legal opinion from the Lord Chancellor, who said: 'Adherence to the Treaty of Rome would, in my opinion, affect our sovereignty in three ways: (a) Parliament would be required to surrender some of its functions to the Community (European Economic Community). (b) the Crown would be called on to transfer part of its treaty-making power to these organs. (c) Our courts of law would sacrifice some degree of independence by becoming subordinate in certain respects to the European Court of Justice'."

The question is, therefore, was the legal advice of the Lord Chancellor, about the loss of sovereignty, given to the people when they were asked to confirm membership of the European Economic Community or Common Market, by Prime Minister Harold Wilson, in the 1975 referendum?

Furthermore, if the following statement by Mikhail Gorbachev, General Secretary of the Communist Party (USSR), between 1985 and 1991, is to be believed, the British people were right to vote to 'leave' in the Brexit referendum (2016): "The most puzzling development in politics, during the last decade, is the apparent determination of Western European leaders to re-create the Soviet Union in Western Europe."

It is, of course, important to note that the views of Mikhail Gorbachev were probably made well before the European Union hoovered up so many former communist satellite states, which were part of the former Soviet Union (Kremlin) or Union of Soviet Socialist Republics (USSR), which served to endorse or confirm his rather radical observations.

However, now that the British people have spoken in a referendum, it is the duty of their political representatives to deliver on their promises, in their manifestos, before the 2017 General Election, and get the United Kingdom out of the European Union, before it reaches a federal Europe, which the much respected President Mikhail Gorbachev (USSR) thought was the political re-creation of another Soviet Union in Western Europe.

Sadly, we have been exposed to the Liberal Democrats, vociferously campaigning to 'Stop Brexit', and the unsavoury spectacle of socialist Labour 'sitting on the fence', hoping for the worst, wanting a general election, and emerging as a 'Remainer' party, ready to impose a Marxist agenda on our unsuspecting people. This could be so much worse for our valued liberal western democracy, than leaving the European Union.

The leader of the Labour Party, Jeremy Corbyn, has led an opposition party, which has undermined the government, since they negotiated the Withdrawal Agreement, yet he has always been a staunch Eurosceptic.

He voted against our country joining the Common Market (1973) and campaigned to leave in the referendum (1975) to confirm membership. He also voted against every EU treaty ever considered by parliament.

Being such a staunch Eurosceptic, why would he not show leadership, and support the government's withdrawal arrangements, if it wasn't to achieve political advantage, rather than the interests of the nation?

This is a classic example of political hypocrisy on a grand scale.

The latest revelations about this militant Eurosceptic were reported in the *Daily Mail* on 6th February 2019, under the heading 'Fury of Labour Remainers after Corbyn's attack on EU Frankenstein' which included: "Jeremy Corbyn faced a furious backlash from Labour Remainers last night, after a newly unearthed video exposed his loathing of the EU. Shot in 2009, it showed (him) attacking the idea of the Irish holding a second referendum on the Lisbon Treaty… The video, which was published by Labour gossip website, The Red Roar' shows (him) mocking the concept of holding repeated votes on the same issue. He was addressing an audience of Irish activists, the year after they rejected the controversial Lisbon Treaty by 53.4% to 46.6%, which created the first president of Europe and a European foreign minister. He said: 'Don't scrap your posters, don't recycle them, because you're going to need them for a third referendum. Because I've got a feeling they're going to keep on voting until they get the answer they want' and 'If you succeed in getting a no vote here, that will be such a boost to people like us, all over Europe, who do not want to live in a European empire of the 21st century. I'm pleased you're having a referendum. I wish we were having (one) in Britain'."

Sir Keir Starmer, a member of the Labour Shadow Cabinet, when being interviewed by Sky News on 12ᵗʰ November 2018, suggested that Brexit could be stopped and should the deal (withdrawal agreement) fail, all options must be on the table, including an option of a public vote. He made this divisive statement, despite the fact that his great leader, Jeremy Corbyn, when being interviewed by the German magazine *Der Spiegel*, in November 2018, claimed that Labour can't stop Brexit and urged his party (members) to recognise the reasons why the people voted to leave.

Incidentally, the Labour manifesto for the 2017 General Election, said: "Labour accepts the referendum result and a Labour government will put the national interest first. We'll seek to unite the country around a Brexit deal that works for every community. Labour recognises that leaving the EU with no-deal is the worst possible deal and would do damage to our economy and trade. We'll reject no-deal as a viable option and negotiate transitional arrangements to avoid a cliff-edge for the economy."

Did the inept Labour leadership not know that when parliament invoked Article 50 of the Lisbon Treaty (2009), it provided for a long period of negotiations, to produce a Withdrawal Agreement, to be followed by a transition period, to negotiate our future relationship and a trade deal, or should an agreement not be reached, the alternative of leaving without an agreement (no-deal) and trading under World Trade Organisation rules?

Well parliament had the opportunity on 15ᵗʰ January 2019 to vote on the negotiated Withdrawal Agreement, which included a framework for our future relationship, including our trading relationship, and the majority of Labour, the Liberals and the Scottish Nationalists, voted against the agreement, which plunged our nation into a constitutional crisis. In the event, the Westminster parliament refused to ratify the draft Withdrawal Agreement, and they also voted against leaving without an agreement, which effectively left the Article 50 process in 'deadlock' or 'stalemate'.

When parliament refused to ratify the Withdrawal Agreement, which provided for withdrawal with or without an agreement, and then voted to take 'no-deal' off the table, it left few alternatives. One alternative was to get an extension of the Article 50 deadline, to have more time to change the agreement and get it ratified by parliament, despite the EU having refused to revisit the agreement. Another alternative was to revoke Article 50 and remain a member of the EU, which would mean rejecting the result of the public referendum and ignoring the 'will of the people'.

Parliament had deliberately created a constitutional crisis by failing to ratify the Withdrawal Agreement, and then voting to take 'no-deal' off the table, effectively ignoring the Article 50 Withdrawal Agreement, which specifically provided for leaving 'with or without' an agreement or deal!

Incidentally, the leaders of the Labour Party appear to have had no experience of corporate negotiations, which require that any negotiators must have an option to 'walk away' without an agreement, otherwise their opponents would have no incentive to co-operate. They should have taken the advice of their trade union leader 'paymasters', who have experienced adversarial negotiations, and have often 'walked away' without an agreement, and then called an industrial strike, to force the hand of the employers, and these tactics often had the desired effect.

These are just some of the reasons why the author was compelled to write this book, to enlighten the 16,141,241 people who voted to 'remain', and to support the 17,410,742 people who voted to 'leave', as this project of the European political elite storms towards its 'clandestine' destination of a United States of Europe. The alternative, to leaving this project of the European political elite, is to accept that our country is a satellite state of a multi-national super-state, with Westminster subordinate to Brussels, and the people subjugated to European politicians and officials, whom they do not know and did not select or elect and cannot reject.

The main reason for writing this book, therefore, was to emphasise the importance of independent nation states and the concept of a 'people's democracy', rather than a 'parliamentary democracy', and the 'primacy of the people' over their elected representatives, those they select and elect to represent them in the 'corridors of power'. This is a serious battle between the 'will of the people' and the power of their parliamentarians.

However, things have turned nasty and the country is polarised between 'leavers' and 'remainers' and the future of our liberal democracy is in jeopardy. Whilst the Conservatives are determined to deliver on the 'will of the people', which is the essence of our liberal democracy, the leaders of the Liberal Democrats have pronounced that they will do whatever they can to 'Stop Brexit', which is profoundly illiberal and undemocratic and should they be successful our liberal democracy is virtually dead.

The author is not surprised at such undemocratic behaviour from the militant, socialist 'resistance movement', under the leadership of Jeremy Corbyn, the 'ultimate protestor', but for the Liberal Democrats to adopt such an 'illiberal' and 'undemocratic' approach to a public referendum, is a contradiction in terms. When the 'dust settles', those who opposed the result of the referendum and campaigned for a second referendum, a so-called 'People's Vote', must be held to account by the British people.

Incidentally, writing this book has been very much like 'painting the Forth Bridge', it's never ending but it has been a fascinating insight into our parliamentary democracy and the new power struggle between the 'will of the people' and the 'sovereignty of parliament' and the decision of so many elected representatives to ignore the instructions of the very people who elevated them to their 'exalted' positions in parliament.

These are just some of the reasons why the author was compelled to write this book, in support of our 'cherished' liberal western democracy and the decent people of our country, who ask for little but 'dare to dream'.

INTRODUCTION

The divisive events of the past few years, since the United Kingdom European Union membership referendum (2016) result, to leave the European Union, are deeply disturbing and prompted the author to defend the 17,410,742 people who voted to regain our independence.

Incidentally, no one could have forecast the dramatic reaction to the unexpected result of the Brexit referendum by the remain campaigns or the 'resistance movement', demanding a second referendum to overturn the result of the first referendum, and to remain in the European Union, which is deeply undemocratic and an attack on our liberal democracy.

One of the prominent 'cheerleaders' of the remain campaigns, wanting a second referendum on the terms of the Withdrawal Agreement, was the former New Labour Prime Minister, Tony Blair, who may have a vested interest in our continued membership of the European Union (EU).

His vested interest in the European Union project, was revealed in an article by Roy Greenslade of *The Guardian*, Friday 30th September 2016, under the heading 'The New European, Alastair Campbell's Stunning Revelation, Blair's secret plan to run Europe', which said: "Today's issue carries the first instalment, in which Alastair Campbell reveals that Tony Blair was sounding out the possibility of leaving No. 10 and becoming president of the European Commission, three years before he stood down as prime minister. It occurred during a period of tension with Gordon Brown in 2004. Blair got as far as asking Campbell, who had left his post as communications director in 2003, to consider a return to mastermind a campaign to secure the European job." After the Iraq War disaster, which destabilised the Middle East and displaced millions of people, this man would be the worst candidate for president of the European Union. Why would we want to entrust him with the power of a European army?

Incidentally, whilst this discredited former prime minister has 'crawled out of the woodwork' to lead a demand for a second referendum, which is profoundly undemocratic, there was a time when he didn't want to be a member of the European Economic Community or the Common Market, let alone the European Union. The following statement is extracted from his manifestos, when he sought election to parliament at Beaconsfield (1982) and Sedgefield (1983): "We'll negotiate withdrawal from the EEC, which has drained our natural resources and destroyed jobs."

It's also interesting to record that when Mr Blair arrived in Westminster in 1983, as an opponent of our membership of the Common Market, the author was a senior police advisor to government at the Home Office, and he had voted, in the 1975 referendum, to remain in the European Economic Community or the Common Market and would do so again, if there was no 'clandestine' plan to create a United States of Europe.

Incidentally, the Labour Party manifesto for the 1983 General Election, under 'Withdrawal from the Common Market' said: "The next Labour government (which) is committed to radical socialist policies for reviving the economy, is bound to find continued membership a most serious obstacle to the fulfilment of those policies. In particular, the rules of the Treaty of Rome are bound to conflict with our strategy for economic growth and full employment, our proposals on industrial policy and for increasing trade and... to regulate direct overseas investment. Moreover, by preventing us buying food from the best sources of world supply, they would run counter to our plans to control prices and inflation."

Furthermore, according to the book *A Nation Is a Nation, Is a Nation* by John Murray (1995), Neil Kinnock, leader of the Labour Party, told the *News of the World*, on 15th May 1983: "We want out of the Common Market" and the book said that despite his opposition to the economic community, he (later) became a Commissioner of the European Union and his wife became a Member of the European Parliament (MEP) and their son was employed by the organisation that his father described as the 'robber of the real sovereignty of the people'. Records show that Neil Kinnock became European

Commissioner for Transport (1995-1999) and Vice President of the European Commission (1999-2004), which appears to be breath-taking political hypocrisy on a grand scale.

Incidentally, Labour opposition to the European project went much further back than the 1980s. In 1960, the Labour Party abstained in a Commons vote that called for 'political and economic unity in Europe', then Labour opposed Britain's first application to join the Common Market in July 1961. In 1962, the party leader committed them to outright opposition to Europe. Labour had formed an 'Anti-Common Market Committee'. Their leader, Hugh Gaitskell, said that joining the EEC would mean the end of our control over the economy, agriculture, foreign policy and to link Britain with Europe would mean the end of Britain as an independent nation-state. In the event, President Charles de Gaulle of France closed the discussion by rejecting Britain's first bid to join the EEC in 1963 and Hugh Gaitskell died the same year.

However, his successor, Harold Wilson, applied to join the Common Market in 1967 but President de Gaulle again refused the application.

In the 1970s the Conservative Prime Minister, Edward Heath, wanted to take Britain into the European Economic Community (EEC) yet Labour's 'Special Conference on Europe' (1971) was consumed with Europhobia. Once Britain entered the EEC in 1973, Labour Eurosceptics refused to accept the decision of parliament and demanded a public referendum, which was held in 1975, and resulted in a clear majority to remain but 145 Labour Members of Parliament voted to leave. Furthermore, at a special Labour Party Congress in 1975, delegates voted two to one to leave the EEC. Even Michael Foot, who had been an advocate for a federal Europe (1945), wanted to withdraw from the Common Market.

The Labour Party manifesto for the 1979 General Election, under the heading 'European Community' said: "We aim to develop a Europe which is democratic and socialist... each country must be able to realize its own economic and social objectives, under the sovereignty of its own parliament and people... A Labour government will oppose any move towards turning the Community into a federation." In view of the fact that the European Economic Community did not turn into the European Union until the signing of the Maastricht Treaty (1992), the above manifesto statement suggests that the Labour Party knew of the intentions of Brussels, to turn the economic community into a political union.

Despite Labour's staunch opposition to our membership of the European Economic Community or the Common Market, it's interesting to note that their manifesto for the 1997 General Election, under the leadership of Tony Blair, included the following: "We will stand up for Britain's interests in Europe… but more than that, we will lead a campaign for reform in Europe. Europe isn't working in the way this country and Europe need but to lead means to be involved, to be constructive, to be capable of getting our own way." Well, New Labour won the General Election (1997) and the new Prime Minister, Tony Blair, declared that 'things could only get better', but there's no evidence to suggest that he achieved any significant reform or, to use his words, 'get his own way'.

So, what changed Tony Blair from a staunch Labour Eurosceptic (1983) to a campaigner for European reform (1997) and, without any significant reform having occurred, a prominent Europhile (2019), campaigning to overturn the referendum result (2016) and wanting a second referendum, which is profoundly undemocratic, coming from a former prime minister?

This man has a long track record of disregarding the 'will of the British people', when he ignored the millions of people who marched the streets of the United Kingdom in opposition of the Iraq War, which destroyed the country's infrastructure and killed and injured and displaced hundreds of thousands of innocent people and seriously destabilised the Middle East.

The author believes that we would not have needed a referendum on our membership of the EU, had it not been for the displacement of millions of people from the war-torn countries of the Middle East (and North Africa), which compounded some of the negative economic and social effects of the unmanaged and uncontrolled 'free movement of people' principle.

The author also urges the European political elite to reconsider their obsession with a multinational super-state, and return to the earlier construct of an economic community or a common market, which is what the British government joined in 1973 and the British people confirmed in a public referendum in 1975. The reality, however, is that it was never meant to remain as an economic community or a common market, it was always intended to be a 'staging post' on a 'clandestine' journey to a United States of Europe, but the political elite did not inform the people!

This book illuminates the many reasons to escape the stranglehold of the European political elite, and their 'clandestine' journey towards a United States of Europe, with a multitude of disparate member states, languages, cultures, traditions and religions, controlled by a remote parliament and commission, with as many as four presidents, a European Central Bank (ECB), a single currency (the euro), a single market and a customs union.

The European Union was managed (2019) by a President of the European Parliament, Antonio Tajani (Italy); a President of the European Council, Donald Tusk (Poland); a President of the Council of the European Union, Viorica Dăncilă (Romania) and a President of the European Commission, Jean-Claude Juncker (Luxembourg). The United Kingdom is, therefore, governed by these very powerful Italian, Polish, Romanian and Luxembourg politicians, who are a 'law unto themselves'.

Whilst we all know the 'strengths and weaknesses' of our own elected representatives (and there are many) and we can remove them from office at the next general election, few of us know much about the 'strengths and weaknesses' of Antonio Tajani or Donald Tusk or Viorica Dăncilă or Jean-Claude Juncker or their successors and we cannot remove them.

The book also discusses the many 'stealth-like' treaties, which have been introduced by the political elite, without the approval of the people, since the end of the last war, which have 'dragged' twenty-eight independent nation states towards 'ever-closer' union and the ultimate destination of a country called Europe or a United States of Europe, whilst keeping the unsuspecting people in the dark. In fact, the twenty-eight member states would have been thirty-one, had the United Kingdom been viewed as the individual countries of England, Scotland, Wales and Northern Ireland.

It also considers the principle of the 'free movement of people', across twenty-eight, member states, and the inordinate number of citizens who can move from the 'poorer' to the 'richer' member states, where they can gain immediate access to better funded public services, putting pressure on those services, which also support thousands of vulnerable refugees.

It also draws attention to the 'free movement of criminals' across open borders, and the 4,600 criminals from other EU countries, incarcerated in British prisons (2017), and the commensurate reduction in the prison population of many Eastern European countries, such as Poland (2,997), Romania (3,882) and Latvia (3,092), since joining the EU. What an indictment of the uncontrolled 'free movement of people' principle, when the so-called 'poorer' countries can join the 'club' and effectively export their criminals to the 'rich-pickings' of the so-called 'richer' countries.

It also debates our membership of the European Economic Community, which we joined in 1973 and confirmed in a referendum (1975), and the signing of the Maastricht Treaty (1992), which turned the EEC into the EU, without a referendum. This was the work of Prime Minister John Major, despite massive opposition from many of his senior parliamentary colleagues, who wanted to consult the people in a public referendum.

It also documents a brief history of the European project and the many transformative treaties, such as the treaties of Amsterdam (1997); Nice (2003); Lisbon (2009) and the European Enlargement programme, which turned an eminently sensible Western European trading bloc into a multi-national super-state, reaching into Eastern European countries, which were communist satellite states, under the former 'brutal' Soviet Union.

It also addresses the financial contributions of the twenty-eight member states and their toxic national debts and serious unemployment rates. It also considers the contributions of the so-called 'stronger' economies, which carry a large amount of national debt, to support the development of the so-called 'weaker' economies, which carry far less national debt.

It also debates the decision of the British people to leave the European Union, in the Brexit referendum of 23rd June 2016. The referendum on our membership of the European Union attracted 33,551,984 voters, with 16,141,241 voting to 'remain' (48.1%) and 17,410,742 voting to 'leave' (51.89%), with a significant majority of 1,269,501 votes.

It also suggests that the behaviour of those who voted to 'remain', and campaigned for a second referendum to change the inconvenient result of the first referendum, is profoundly undemocratic, as opposed to those who voted to 'leave', who would have accepted a majority to remain, and would not have formed a 'resistance movement' or marched the streets.

Many of those who voted to remain and demanded a second referendum, suggested that they lost by a 'slender margin'. Well a margin of 3.78%, based on 51.89% to leave and 48.1% to remain, may be diminished as a 'slender margin' by staunch remainers but a majority of 1,269,501 votes, based on 17,410,742 to leave and 16,141,241 to remain, simply cannot be construed as a 'narrow majority'. It's almost the number of people who live in the two northern cities of Leeds City, the third largest city in the UK, with a population of 794,250 (2016), and Bradford City, the sixth largest city in the UK with a population of 534,308 (2017).

To attempt to overturn the result of a democratic referendum involving 33,551,984 citizens, with a majority of 1,269,501 votes, through a second referendum, is an attack on the very foundations of democracy. If the vote was overturned by our elected representatives, those we elect to represent us in the 'corridors of power', and we were asked to vote again, to get the result they want, it would be a dark day for our liberal democracy.

Incidentally, no one challenged the result of the parliamentary elections (2017), when Stephen Gethins (MP) won Fife North East by two votes for the Scottish Nationalist Party (2017), which persistently campaigns for Scotland to leave the United Kingdom. Ironically, as a member of 'The People's Vote' campaign, which wants a 'people's vote' on the final deal, Stephen Gethins, who won his Scottish seat by two votes, had the audacity to challenge a majority of 1,269,501 votes to leave the European Union.

We live in a liberal democracy and it's imperative that we accept the 'will of the people', in any democratic elections, particularly when it's a public referendum, called by politicians to seek the view of the people.

The acceptance of the plebiscite is even more important when many of those who challenge the decision of the people, are former government ministers, who have been the beneficiaries of the 'first past the post' electoral system, which produces a winner with a minority of the votes cast in an election. More people vote against them, than vote for them.

When an elected government asks the people to vote in a referendum, the elected politicians must respect the 'will of the people', even with a small majority. However, with a majority of 1,269,501 votes, those politicians who have campaigned for a second referendum, to change the result of the first referendum, should be deselected by their constituency parties.

Sadly, this is what the Liberal Democrats feel about the result of the Brexit referendum. It's their policy to 'Stop Brexit' and remain in the European Union, despite 17,410,742 people voting to leave, preferably through another referendum, a so-called 'People's Vote'. This reckless policy to 'Stop Brexit', which is most undemocratic, was compounded by the actions of their MEPs, who wore yellow T-shirts on their first day back in the European Parliament (2nd July 2019), which had 'STOP BREXIT' on the front and 'BOLLOCKS TO BREXIT' on the back!

This juvenile behaviour was endorsed by their leader, Catherine Bearder (MEP), who said: "The real message was on the front, Stop Brexit."

Incidentally, the Conservative and Unionist Party, under the leadership of Prime Minister David Cameron, campaigned in the 2015 General Election with a manifesto commitment to give the people a referendum on our future relationship with the European Union, and a promise to accept the result. When the result of the Brexit referendum (2016) was announced, David Cameron, who had campaigned to remain, resigned and sparked a leadership contest, which was won by Theresa May. To her credit, the new prime minister, who had voted to remain, accepted the 'poisoned chalice', to release our country from the shackles of the EU, and said that "Brexit means Brexit". She could not, however, have foreseen the determination of the remain campaigns and the 'resistance movements', to undermine the withdrawal negotiations and demand a second referendum or a 'people's vote' on the complex legal terms of the Withdrawal Agreement, which would be very difficult for the people to understand. It needs to be emphasised that the Withdrawal Agreement is a legal document (legally binding when ratified), which extricates the United Kingdom from the European Union, and includes a draft Political Declaration (not legally binding), which is a 'framework' for our future relationship, including a trade deal, to be negotiated after withdrawal.

It is, of course, common knowledge that the European political elite have a track record of rejecting any treaty referendum which goes against them, and demanding a second referendum, to get the result they want, and they appear to have supported the formidable 'remain campaigns'.

However, the British people are made of 'stronger stuff' and may not be as compliant as those from other member states, who conceded under pressure from Brussels, but the process to leave the EU, under Article 50 of the Lisbon Treaty, has proven to be extremely challenging and may just have been written to deter member states from leaving the Union.

After the unexpected referendum result, parliament accepted the decision of the people and invoked Article 50 of the Lisbon Treaty (2009). The invocation of Article 50 started a two-year period for both parties to negotiate a Withdrawal Agreement and a 'framework' of our future relationship, including a trade deal, with a leaving date of 29th March 2019. Article 50 provided for the seceding country, the United Kingdom, to leave 'with or without' an agreement and there was no third option.

It's worth noting that the United Kingdom Parliament passed the European Union Referendum Act 2015 on 9th June 2015 by 544 to 53 votes, a large majority of 491 votes, and it was approved by the House of Lords on 14th December 2015. In other words, our elected representatives voted by a large majority to hold a public referendum, which meant that they wanted the people to decide on our future relationship with the EU.

Furthermore, having voted by a large majority to hold a referendum on our future relationship with the European Union, and having promised to accept the decision of the people, our political representatives had to vote to invoke Article 50 of the Lisbon Treaty 2009 or the Treaty on European Union (TEU), to start the lengthy Withdrawal Agreement process. They duly voted to invoke Article 50 on 7th December 2016, by 461 to 89 votes, a large majority of 372. The question is, however, why would 89 of our elected representatives vote against invoking Article 50, if it wasn't to wilfully obstruct the withdrawal process, against the 'will of the people'?

Those 89 elected representatives, who voted against invoking Article 50, after the British people had spoken in the plebiscite, included 51 Scottish Nationalists, 23 Labour and 5 Liberals, and they must be held to account, for disrespecting the 'will of the people', at the next general election.

The government triggered Article 50, to start the withdrawal process in March 2017 to end on 29th March 2019 (extended to 31st October 2019), when we would leave 'with or without' an agreement. It's, therefore, crucial that the people know that Article 50 concludes with the following unambiguous statement: "If negotiations do not result in a ratified agreement, the seceding country leaves without an agreement… without any substitute or transitional arrangements. As regards trade, the parties would likely follow World Trade Organisation (WTO) rules on tariffs."

We have listened to so many criticisms, suggesting that the Withdrawal Agreement was a 'bad deal', which often implied a bad trade deal, yet the Withdrawal Agreement only produced a 'framework' for our future relationship, including our future trading relationship. The Withdrawal Agreement was essentially a legal text, to extricate the United Kingdom from the rules and regulations and treaties of the European Union, and was never intended to develop a trade deal, during those negotiations.

We were also told that the Brussels negotiators would not start the discussions about the Withdrawal Agreement and the framework for our future relationship and future trade deal, until we accepted a divorce bill or settlement, which was agreed at £39 billion. How did they arrive at such a large settlement and what was the legal basis of that settlement?

Incidentally, there would appear to have been no discussions about the related subject of accrued assets. The UK had apparently invested circa £300 billion into the EEC or the Common Market and the EU budgets, since 1973, and have accrued no tangible assets whatsoever. That's no buildings, no machinery, no equipment, just an enormous debt, which includes current budget commitments and future pension liabilities.

What the British negotiators should have said at the outset of the talks, was that they would only accept a divorce settlement which was limited to current budget commitments and future pension liabilities, and that any divorce settlement payment would be dependent on a mutually beneficial trade deal. In other words, no trade deal, no divorce settlement payment.

However, on a more positive note, the draft Political Declaration, which accompanied the Withdrawal Agreement, included the following positive statement under 'Future Relationship': "This declaration establishes the parameters of an ambitious, broad, deep and flexible partnership across trade and economic co-operation, law enforcement and criminal justice, foreign policy, security and defence and wider areas of co-operation."

So far as trade is concerned, the draft Political Declaration includes the following statement under the heading 'Trade in Goods': "The Parties envisage having a trading relationship on goods that is as close as possible, with a view to facilitating the ease of legitimate trade."

So far as Customs is concerned, the draft Political Declaration includes the following statement under 'Customs': "The economic partnership should include no tariffs, fees, charges or quantitative restrictions across all sectors, with ambitious customs arrangements that… build and improve on the single customs territory provided for in the Agreement."

It's interesting to note that the European political elite have inextricably linked the single market and customs union with the European Union, which makes it virtually impossible to leave the European Union, without leaving the single market and customs union, which will destabilise any economy. This is a clever manoeuvre by the Europeans, to let the member states know of the 'dire' economic consequences of leaving their project.

Remember the statement which has been attributed to Jean Monnet that: "Europe's nations should be guided towards the superstate, without their people understanding what is happening. This can be accomplished by successive steps, each disguised as having an economic purpose, but which will eventually and irreversibly lead to (European) federation."

It's also interesting to note that Article 50 of the Lisbon Treaty (2009), which provides for the negotiation of a Withdrawal Agreement (legally binding when ratified), only provided for a 'framework' for a future relationship and a future trade deal (not legally binding), which means that had we ratified the agreement and become an independent country, we would have done so (knowingly) without any formal trade agreement.

This means that after two years of negotiations, to get a Withdrawal Agreement ratified, the leaving country arrives at the leaving date, when they are no longer members of the European Union or the single market or the customs union, without having negotiated their future relationship or a future trade deal. This is the policy of the Eurocrats, who drafted Article 50 of the Lisbon Treaty (2009), which means the leaving country will have to remain in the single market and the customs union during a lengthy transition period, to negotiate the future relationship and trade deal and continue to pay significant contributions to the EU budget.

In the event, parliament rejected the Withdrawal Agreement (deal) and the draft Political Declaration on our future relationship, including a future trading relationship, on 15th January 2019, by 202 votes for the deal and 432 votes against the deal, a large majority of 230 votes against the deal.

The reality is, however, regardless of the content of the draft Withdrawal Agreement and the draft Political Declaration, many parliamentarians voted against the deal on the basis that they didn't want to leave in the first place and they wanted a second referendum and had no intention of voting for any deal. This approach, by those who wanted to remain, is profoundly undemocratic, and when the 'dust settles', these, so-called elected representatives must be held to account by the British people.

The repeated rejection of the draft Withdrawal Agreement and the draft Political Declaration by the UK parliament threw our country into a serious constitutional crisis and the minority Conservative government, which was reliant on the support of the Democratic Unionist Party of Northern Ireland, had great difficulty attempting to sort out the mess.

Parliament had refused to accept the Withdrawal Agreement, with concerns over the wording of what was called the Northern Ireland

'Backstop' and had voted (indicative votes) to take the option of no-deal off the table, which effectively created parliamentary deadlock.

To make matters worse, the European Commission would not re-open the negotiations, having ratified the Withdrawal Agreement in the European Parliament, but agreed to extend the deadline to 31st October 2019, to give the British government more time to get the agreement ratified.

On Tuesday 29th January 2019, parliament considered some amendments to the government's draft Withdrawal Agreement and the following two amendments were successful: The first amendment by Sir Graham Brady allowed for the prime minister to return to Brussels to negotiate some alternative arrangements to the Northern Ireland 'backstop' text, to avoid a hard border in (the island of) Ireland. The 'Brady Amendment', which passed by 317 votes to 301 votes, called for 'alternative arrangements' to replace the 'backstop' and avoid a hard border on the island of Ireland.

It's important to note that the draft Withdrawal Agreement could have been ratified by parliament, if they had agreed alternative arrangements to the Northern Ireland 'backstop', which would have allowed them to move into the transitional period and negotiate our future relationship and a future trade deal and leave in an orderly manner. Incidentally, with 'goodwill' on both sides, the Northern Ireland 'backstop' text could have been removed from the draft Withdrawal Agreement and included in the discussions about our future relationship and a future trade deal, which would have removed the 'deadlock' and got the agreement ratified.

The second amendment, tabled by Dame Caroline Spelman, which passed by 318 to 310 votes, was an expression of parliamentarians to reject a no-deal Brexit, but that vote was not legally binding on the government.

It, perhaps, needs to be mentioned that no negotiator would consider taking no-deal off the table and this amendment, which passed with a small majority, was responsible for creating parliamentary 'deadlock'.

Parliament won't ratify the Withdrawal Agreement, which provides for leaving without a deal, and they won't approve leaving with no-deal, which leaves the option of a second referendum, which parliament 'crushed' in an indicative vote by 334 votes to 85 on 15th March 2019.

The immediate reaction from the leaders of the European Union, was to confirm that they would not revisit the Withdrawal Agreement, which had been ratified by the European Parliament. Donald Tusk, the President of the European Council, said: "The backstop is part of the withdrawal agreement, and the withdrawal agreement is not open for renegotiation."

Incidentally, the EU didn't want the UK to leave in the first place and the following are some of their unhelpful comments, following the rejection of the Withdrawal Agreement by parliament: Donald Tusk, President of the European Council, apparently tweeted the following: "If a deal is impossible, and no one wants no deal, then who will finally have the courage to say the only possible solution is?" Jean-Claude Juncker, the President of the European Commission, apparently warned that time was running out for the UK to strike a deal and said: "I urge the United Kingdom to clarify its intentions as soon as possible. Time is almost up. The risk of a disorderly withdrawal of the United Kingdom has increased with this evenings vote." Finally, President Macron of France said: "We will have to negotiate a transition period with them, because they cannot afford to no longer have planes taking off or landing at home."

The British negotiators should have said, at the outset, that they would be leaving on 29th March 2019, 'deal or no deal', and without a satisfactory free trade deal, they would trade under World Trade Organisation rules, which is not 'crashing out', as some have suggested. The respected *Times* columnist, Iain Martin, reported on 21st December 2018, that: "A no-deal Brexit would not be the end of the world and with the right spirit of compromise, we could make a success of leaving without an agreement."

Incidentally, the following information about World Trade Organisation global rules, provided by the Institute for Government, suggest that things may not be as bad as suggested by the remain campaigners: "The WTO sets the global rules of trade and has 164 members, which between them are responsible for 95% of world trade. It's a negotiating forum for its members to create international trade rules and an organisation to oversee how they put the rules into practice. The United Kingdom is already a WTO member but will need to extricate itself from the EU schedules. The UK is a member of the WTO, having co-founded the General Agreement on Tariffs and Trade (GATT), the predecessor to the WTO, with 22 other countries, in 1948. It does not have to re-apply to join the WTO when it leaves the EU. At present, the UK operates in the WTO under the EU's set of schedules – a list of commitments that sets the terms of the EU's tariffs, its quotas and its limits on subsidies. The UK will have to agree its own set of schedules at the WTO. The government has said that it plans to replicate their existing trade regime as far as possible in their new schedules. This is a sensible approach, which involves minimal disruption and reduces the scope for other members to object but could involve some three-way negotiations involving the EU."

A 'no-deal' Brexit may not be such a big deal and is probably being overplayed by the remain campaigners, who are determined to revoke Article 50 and remain in the European Union or have a second public referendum to overturn the result of the first referendum. Incidentally, Mark Wallace, the Executive Editor of *Conservative Home*, wrote in the *Independent* newspaper, on 18th January 2019, that the: "prospect of re-running a ballot until politicians are happy with the outcome, stinks".

Article 50 of the Lisbon Treaty was apparently written with the intention that it would never be used and provides for the two parties to negotiate a Withdrawal Agreement, which would end with or without an agreement. Should an agreement be ratified by both parliaments, it would include a 'framework' for their future relationship, including a future trade deal, which would then be open for negotiation and agreement. During that period of negotiation, the transition period, the leaver country would continue to be subject to the rules of the single market and customs union. However, if the leaver was unable to negotiate and ratify an agreement, they would leave without a deal or would 'crash out', which many from the remain campaign suggest would be 'catastrophic' for our country.

In the event, the British negotiators achieved a Withdrawal Agreement, which outlined the framework for our future relationship and trading arrangements, and an attempt to avoid a hard border between Eire and Ulster. It was no real surprise that the Withdrawal Agreement was not acceptable to those who had voted to remain and demanded a second referendum, with an option to remain. The undemocratic behaviour of the 'remain campaigners' suggests some contempt for the electoral system and included many former senior politicians, including two former prime ministers, John Major and Tony Blair, who should have known better.

The best example of political hypocrisy, on a grand scale, was when the former Prime Minister, John Major, who won the 1992 general election on the 'first past the post' electoral system, but lost the popular vote by a large margin, called the Brexit referendum result the 'tyranny of the majority'. Surely, he knew that he'd won the 1992 General Election on a minority vote, which could be construed as the 'tyranny of the minority'.

The Conservatives polled 14,093,007 votes in the 1992 General Election, producing 336 seats (41.9%). Labour polled 11,560,484 votes, producing 271 seats (34.4%) and the Liberals polled 5,999,606 votes, producing 20 seats (17.8%). This means that Labour and the Liberals together, polled 17,560,090 votes and the Conservatives polled 14,093,007 votes but the Conservatives won the election, which is a direct consequence of the 'first past the post' electoral system. This could be construed as the 'tyranny of the minority' by the losing majority. Labour and the Liberals polled 3,467,083 more votes than the Conservatives but lost the election, and that significant majority, was more than three times the number of people who live in Birmingham, with a population of circa 1,111,307 (2016).

The same applies to former Prime Minister, Tony Blair, who campaigned for a second referendum, to overturn the result of the first referendum, in which a massive 17,410,742 people voted to leave the European Union.

Thankfully, Prime Minister Theresa May, hit out at Tony Blair, accusing him of "insulting" the British people and the office of prime minister by "undermining" the talks, with calls in Brussels for a second referendum. She said: "For Tony Blair to go to Brussels and seek to undermine our negotiations by advocating a second referendum is an insult to the office he once held and the people he once served. We cannot, as he would, abdicate responsibility for this decision. Parliament has a democratic duty to deliver what the British people voted for. I remain determined to see that happen. I will not let the British people down."

In a series of high-profile interventions into the Brexit debate, Mr Blair insisted that a majority of MPs may decide a second referendum is the only way out of parliamentary 'gridlock' on withdrawal. Prime Minister Theresa May also said: "I am fighting for a good deal for Britain. I will continue to fight for a good deal for Britain. I have never lost sight of my duty and that is to deliver on the referendum result and to do so in a way that protects British jobs, keeps us safe and protects our precious Union. However, there are too many people, who want to subvert the process for their own political interests – rather than acting in the national interest."

Former Prime Minister Blair should be ashamed of his intervention into the Brexit debate and his arrogant attempt to undermine the negotiators and his disrespect for the 'will of the British people'. He has, of course, a track record of ignoring the 'will of the people', when their demands are contrary to his own political objectives, such as his disastrous military intervention into Iraq, which destroyed the country's infrastructure and killed and seriously injured and displaced millions of innocent people. Millions of people, worldwide, marched the streets in opposition to the Iraq War. Prime Minister Blair's response was to warn the protestors of the "bloody consequences" if Iraq was not confronted, and that he did not seek unpopularity as a 'badge of honour' but suggested that is the price of leadership and the cost of conviction! His intervention in Iraq did not find the alleged 'weapons of mass destruction' and the Middle East 'went up in flames'. If only he had shown real political leadership and listened to the British people, rather than embarking on a misguided mission, which ended in disaster for so many people, but not for him. His intervention into the Brexit debate is unforgiveable. He is now a seriously wealthy, property-owning, multi-millionaire, whilst many thousands of innocent war victims are either dead or seriously injured or suffering post-traumatic stress disorder, or are either homeless or stateless.

Whilst former Prime Minister Tony Blair has his own personal agenda, steeped in the virtues of 'globalism', whatever that means, and probably still harbours an obsession to become the first elected president of the European Union or the United States of Europe, the author believes in the virtues of independent nation states and limited government and localism and community. This is the difference between the ambitions of the political elite, in their 'ivory towers' and the 'view from the street' of ordinary people, whose political influence amounts to one single vote.

In this age of globalism, the liberal political elite have challenged the concepts of patriotism and nationalism, as being the province of the extreme right wing. This is what President Macron, of France, had to say about patriotism, nationalism and globalism, in a speech to mark the 100th anniversary of the First World War, when he 'criticised nationalism as a betrayal of patriotism'. He said that a "global order based on liberal values is worth defending against those who have sought to disrupt that system." He rejected the "selfishness of nations looking after their own interests because patriotism is the opposite of nationalism."

The author believes that 'charity begins at home' and patriotism and nationalism are non-negotiable. It's just human nature to have positive feelings about your community, your region and your country but that doesn't mean that you have negative feelings for those who come from elsewhere. Nationalism or patriotism and globalism or multi-nationalism are not mutually exclusive. We can have deep feelings for our families and friends and neighbours and still have positive feelings for strangers and foreigners. Being patriotic and nationalistic, should not be construed as being extreme, right wing, and certainly not racist or xenophobic.

So far as nationalism and multi-nationalism is concerned, the author supports more efficient and effective limited government and opposes remote national governance from the Westminster 'bubble', let alone distant governance from the Brussels and Strasbourg 'ivory towers'.

Consequently, he welcomes the opportunities presented by Brexit, to revive our distinctive identity and reshape our national governance and frame our own laws and control our own borders and live within our own means and balance our own nation's books and have the independence to negotiate free-trade deals with our business partners around the world.

National identity is based on shared culture, religion, history, language or ethnicity. These values are the foundation of nationalism and the reason ordinary people have a strong feeling of belonging to their nation state and are prepared to die for their nation, at times of war.

However, there's no escape, we are in an age of 'globalism' and 'multi-nationalism' and the concept of 'nationalism' is under attack. This is very disappointing to those people who have a deep-seated affection for their homeland and its history, culture and traditions but want their elected representatives to work with other nations to ensure economic and social security. These were probably the views of millions of people who voted to remain in the European Economic Community or the Common Market, but were not comfortable with the move to the European Union, through the Maastricht Treaty, without a referendum, driven by the European political elite, whom they did not know and had not elected.

It perhaps needs to be said that there's nothing extreme about wanting to select your own political representatives and there's nothing extreme about the benefits of local democracy and there's nothing extreme about being uncomfortable with remote control by the European political elite, from their comfortable Brussels-to-Strasbourg Express 'gravy train'.

Incidentally, talking about the Brussels-to-Strasbourg Express 'gravy train', this is what was reported on Euro News, Prime Edition, Raw Politics, on Thursday 13th September 2018: "The Strasbourg week is also known as 'The Travelling Circus'. Now this is a favourite target of Euro sceptics. Once a month, sometimes twice, the train from Brussels pulls into the (Strasbourg) station and with it, 751 MEPs and 3,500 support staff and 2,500 trunks, containing tens of thousands of documents. The cost is 180,000,000 euros a year, 19,000 tonnes of CO2 emissions and the 317 days a year that all these buildings stand empty, wasting energy."

Furthermore, for those concerned about a lack of transparency in the governance of the distant European Union, Euro News, Prime Edition, Raw Politics, reported on Wednesday 26th September 2018, that a ruling by the European Court of Justice (ECJ) meant that EU taxpayers are not entitled to know how their money is spent in relation to the expenses of the 751 MEPs. This ruling was made by the court in response to a legal challenge by a journalist, after the European Parliament had denied access to documents about the money MEPs receive on top of their salaries. Their monthly salaries are known to be 8,611 euros, that's 103,332 euros per year, which is then 'topped up' by expenses, such as general allowances, travel allowances and daily subsistence of 307 euros per day and funding for office staff. The court (ECJ) ruling said: "Institutions must refuse access to a document, where disclosure would undermine the protection of privacy and the integrity of the individual."

Moving to mass immigration, it's suggested that liberals should stop labelling those who oppose uncontrolled mass immigration, across Europe, as xenophobic or racist. It's not a fear or hatred of foreigners that's the problem, it's the fact that we've no control over the numbers.

It's also unfair to label white people, who oppose uncontrolled mass immigration, as being white supremacists, because many immigrants, from the Middle East and North and West Africa, are black or brown.

It's also unfair to label those who support independent nation states and oppose multi-national super-states, as extreme 'right-wing' nationalist zealots or even 'fascists' (i.e.: totalitarian, extreme nationalism). Such divisive language should have no place in our liberal western democracy.

The book also emphasises the need for independent nation states to negotiate mutually beneficial free-trade deals, and attempt to live within their means and balance their nations' books and eliminate their annual budget deficits and reduce their national debt and debt interest payments and embrace the interesting notion that 'when trade stops, wars start'!

Politicians would think long and hard before starting destructive wars with their trading partners, across the world, upon whom they depend for their commercial success, economic stability and national prosperity.

Furthermore, nationalism or patriotism must not be viewed as negative, as many smaller and weaker countries have for many years demanded their independence from bigger and stronger countries. How many of the satellite states of the former Union of Soviet Socialist Republics (USSR) wanted their independence from Soviet domination? Czechoslovakia and Hungary are just two examples. The Basques have wanted freedom from Spain for many years and are now virtually independent and Catalonia has recently joined the freedom queue. The patriotic Kurds have wanted an independent

Kurdistan for many years but are prevented from doing so by Iraq, Iran and Turkey. The Irish broke free from Great Britain in 1923 and, sadly, they would rather be part of a 'United States of Europe' than the United Kingdom, their immediate 'friends' and neighbours.

We are often told by the Scottish Nationalists (SNP) that the Scottish people want independence from the United Kingdom, but when they have an independence referendum, the majority vote for the security of a union with their island neighbour. We are a deeply integrated union of virtually independent nation states, and there are probably more Scottish-born people and their children and grandchildren living in England, Wales and Northern Ireland, than there are living in their beloved homeland.

Incidentally, the last Scottish independence referendum, which asked the question "Should Scotland be an independent country?" was held on 18th September 2014, with the following results: 2,001,926 voted No (55.3%) and 1,617,989 voted Yes (44.7%), a majority of 383,937 (10.6%), based on 3,619,915 (valid votes) from 4,283,392 registered voters.

The 2011 United Kingdom Census shows there were 708,872 people born in Scotland, resident in England, and 24,346 resident in Wales, and 15,455 resident in Northern Ireland. That means that there were 748,673 Scottish-born people living elsewhere in the United Kingdom (2011). It seems to be common sense for these 748,673 Scottish-born people to be consulted, should there be another independence referendum in Scotland.

Furthermore, there are probably millions of people of Scottish ancestry living elsewhere in the United Kingdom who may have a deep attachment to their ancestral homeland, the home of their forbears, and may want to have a vote in any plebiscite on the future of their ancestral homeland.

There has also been significant migration from Ireland (Eire) to the UK, over the generations, and the Irish people are deeply integrated into our diverse, multi-national, society. When we do escape the 'shackles' of the growing European Union super-state, and are free to trade with the rest of the world, our Irish neighbours may see the benefit of an economic union with their closest trading partners, rather than being a very small part of a remote, federal, European Union, super-state conglomerate.

However, in the unlikely event that the Irish would want an economic partnership with the UK rather than the EU, they would have difficulty extricating themselves from the European Union, particularly from their membership of the Eurozone or the European Monetary Union (EMU).

It is, however, worth considering the views of Ray Bassett, a senior fellow for European Union affairs, at the 'Policy Exchange' think-tank, and a former Irish ambassador, who recently said: "The huge choice facing Ireland is whether, given the circumstances, the country can live with the likely post-Brexit arrangements and stay a full member of the union (EU) or whether a radically different relationship with the union is required, including the possibility of an Irish departure from formal membership."

The 2001 British census was the first to allow citizens to express an Irish ethnicity. As many as six million people in Great Britain are thought to have at least one Irish grandparent, which entitles them to Irish (Eire) citizenship. However, the BBC News on 16th March 2001 reported that circa fourteen million Britons claimed to have Irish roots. Whatever the numbers, one thing is certain, millions of people in Great Britain were either born in Ireland or have Irish ancestry and may prefer that their ancestral homeland (Eire), had an economic union with their adopted homeland (United Kingdom), rather than with the European Union.

Whilst the UK should have left the EU on 29th March 2019, which was extended to 31st October 2019, it is suggested that the other twenty-seven member states should slow down this multinational 'juggernaut', as it thunders towards a country called Europe or a United States of Europe, and consider a return to the security of the eminently sensible European Economic Community (EEC) or the Common Market trading group.

Surely the Brussels political elite can see that a country called Europe, consisting of so many disparate nation states, with different economies, currencies, cultures, traditions, languages and religions, may not be for everyone. Many more citizens of the European Union may want to regain their independence and work with other trading nations in an economic community and not be a dependent state of a multinational super-state.

It's also common knowledge that many other member states, are not happy with the 'free movement of people', across 'open borders', which has led to mass immigration from 'poorer' Eastern European countries, to 'richer' Western European countries, together with immigrants from the war-torn Middle East and North and West Africa, putting pressure on essential public services. Brussels should have listened to the genuine concerns of the British people about the uncontrolled 'free movement of people', and we may not have needed the divisive Brexit referendum.

We must never let the obsession of the European political elite, to create a country called Europe, threaten any other member state wanting to leave, with a penal divorce settlement and a negative Withdrawal Agreement. Member states must be able to leave the European Union, when it's the 'will of the people', expressed through a 'people's vote', and a 'mutually beneficial' Withdrawal Agreement, including the future relationship and future trade deal, must be available, to ensure a smooth transition to independence without destabilising commercial restrictions.

Whilst the British negotiating team wanted the freedom to trade with the European Union and the rest of the world, the 'restrictive practices' of the European Union made it difficult to achieve. So far as trade is concerned, the European Union comprises of three elements; a Free Trade Area; a Customs Union and a Single Market. The Customs Union is an area with a common trade policy and common external tariffs against outsiders. The Single Market is a market in which non-tariff barriers to trade and regulations and standards are harmonised. To have access to the Free Trader Area, a country needs to be a member of the Union and that means compliance with the 'free movement of goods, services, capital and people'. We cannot leave the European Union and continue to be members of the Customs Union or the Single Market and to use the words of Michel Barnier, the European Commission Chief Negotiator, we 'can't cherry pick' and 'can't have our cake and eat it'.

Some say that we could negotiate a form of customs union with the EU, as Turkey has done, but to do so would prevent Britain from having an independent trade policy and we would not be able to negotiate trade deals with other countries. Some disadvantages of being in a customs union would include that we would be committed to the EU common trade policy, without any means of influencing decisions, and we would also have to accept any EU legislation regarding trade policy, and any legal decisions by the European Court, regarding a customs union.

An alternative approach could be to join the European Economic Area (EEA), of which Norway, Iceland and Liechtenstein are members. The members of the EEA are equal partners in the internal market on the same terms as member states. This includes having access to the internal market's four freedoms: the free movement of goods, persons, services and capital. It also covers co-operation in other important areas such as research and development, education, social policy, the environment, consumer protection, tourism and culture. It does not, however, cover the common agricultural and fisheries policies and the customs union, the common trade policy, the common foreign and security policy, justice and home affairs or the monetary union. They also participate in many EU programmes and agencies and are members of Schengen co-operation, which abolishes border controls between members and co-operates closely on foreign and security policy issues. Finally, Norway provides funding to fifteen (15) EU countries, in Central and Southern Europe, through the European Economic Area and Norway Grants, to reduce economic and social disparities and strengthen bilateral relations.

However, if the United Kingdom was to join the EEA, it would have to accept the 'free movement of goods, services, capital and people' and could not limit immigration from the EU and would be required to adopt EU legislation on employment policy, environmental policy, social policy and competition rules and would be required to contribute to the budget, which would be unacceptable to those who voted to leave the Union.

The most practical way forward for the British negotiators would have been to revert to World Trade Organisation rules, described in the book *Clean Brexit: Why leaving the EU still makes sense*, written by the respected economists Liam Halligan and Gerard Lyons, and published by Bite Back Publishing in 2017, which said: "Over half the UK's trade is with countries outside the EU – largely under WTO rules. The US and China conduct extensive trade with the EU under WTO rules – Britain can do the same. As part of the EU, the UK already trades under WTO rules with over 100 countries around the world, including the US, China, India, Brazil and Singapore. Access to the single market is not granted by the EU, but is available to all nations, provided regulatory standards are met and on payment of generally low tariffs. That is why countries across the world, that are not members of the single market, export successfully to the EU. The UK is well placed to trade with the EU on WTO terms – not least, as we start from a position of full regulatory compliance."

Having made the decision to leave the European Union, the British and Brussels negotiators produced a Withdrawal Agreement, which included the framework for a future relationship, including trading arrangements. This tortuous negotiation process appears to be designed by the remote Brussels political elite, to ensure that we 'can't have our cake and eat it' and to give notice to other member states not to make the same mistake!

We must look carefully at the movement of the European Union, towards a country called Europe, and consider the multiple reasons to leave this burgeoning, multi-national super-state, as it becomes Fortress Europe.

We'll look at the European Union project and come clean with the British people about the long-standing objectives of the European political elite to create a country called Europe or the United States of Europe. We'll discuss the stealth-like journey from the sensible Common Market or the European Economic Community, to the European Union and their ultimate destination of a multi-national super-state, with a federal government, an elected president, a single currency, a central bank, a standing army and a single market and customs union.

Incidentally, there's no doubt about the ulterior motive of the European political elite, who created the sensible European Economic Community, as the economic foundation for their long-term goal of a federal European super-state, without coming clean with the people.

This is what Stuart R. de la Mahotière said in his book *The Common Market* published by Hodder and Stoughton in 1961: "The Common Market is essentially the brain-child of the brilliant French economist Jean Monnet. But it would not have been born without such good Europeans as Dr Adenauer of Germany, Robert Schuman of France and Paul-Henri Spaak of Belgium. So, Jean Monnet, worked out a plan for the unification of Europe by stages. First there would be a modest beginning, by pooling Western Europe's iron, coal and steel resources, then, step by step, the whole of Europe's economic resources – and indeed working manpower – would be pooled in a Common Market. Lastly, but some way off, a United States of Europe would emerge."

The purpose of this book, therefore, is to consider the multitude of reasons to escape the 'clutches' of the Brussels political elite, as they travel 'business class' on the Brussels-to-Strasbourg Express 'gravy train', as it thunders towards a 'United States of Europe'. We must always remember the words of Prime Minister Theresa May (who voted to remain) that the government must respect the 'will of the people' in a public referendum or plebiscite and that 'Brexit means Brexit'.

It would also be helpful if the European political elite, in their Brussels and Strasbourg 'ivory towers', respected the 'will of the British people' as expressed through a referendum. However, their attitude throughout the Withdrawal Agreement negotiations suggests that they would prefer to disregard the result of the referendum and support those who wanted a second referendum or as it's often characterised: a 'People's Vote'.

As we watched these Withdrawal Agreement negotiations being played out in the full glare of the media headlights, one thing is certain, it has been an epic David and Goliath struggle. The European Commission, which represented the other twenty-seven member states, was always in the driving seat. Their adversarial approach seems to have been to make the leaving process so controversial and to create a toxic atmosphere of economic uncertainty and to encourage those who wanted to remain to campaign for a second referendum, to overturn the unexpected result of the first referendum, as they had done in every other EU referendum.

Incidentally, because of the inability of the government to get us out of the European Union by 29th March 2019, we had no choice but to take part in the European Parliamentary Elections on 23rd May 2019. The result was that 31% of the votes went to the newly formed Brexit Party, whose 'raison d'être' was to get us out of the European Union. However, the deep political divide was evident, between 'leavers' and 'remainers', as 20.3% of the votes went to the Liberal

Democrats, who wanted to 'Stop Brexit'. Furthermore, to show their contempt for the Labour opposition, opposing the withdrawal process at every turn, they got 14.1% of the votes. However, not surprisingly, the people kept their wrath for the Conservatives, who had failed to deliver on the referendum result, and got 9.1% of the votes. Again, the 'people had spoken', but the politicians were not listening, they were determined to scupper the whole process.

The failure of the government to get parliament to ratify the Withdrawal Agreement and the Political Declaration, resulted in the resignation of Prime Minister Theresa May, and her replacement, the Brexiteer, Boris Johnson, on 24th July 2019. Whilst Boris Johnson is a Marmite character, you either love him or hate him, he 'hit the ground running' and formed a government of Brexiteers, who were determined to get our country out of the European Union on 31st October 2019, come 'hell or highwater'.

The approach of the government, under the flamboyant Boris Johnson, was to accord with the parliamentary approval of Article 50 of the Lisbon Treaty, which decreed that we leave the European Union on 31st October 2019, 'with or without' an agreement. In view of the fact that the United Kingdom parliament had refused to ratify the Withdrawal Agreement and Political Declaration, and the European Union had refused to revisit or amend the agreement and declaration, which had been ratified by the European Parliament, the alternative for the British government was to leave on 31st October 2019 without an agreement, and make appropriate preparations to minimise any economic and commercial turbulence.

However, we may have had a government determined to deliver for the people, but we were still in a constitutional crisis and whilst most of the people were 'leavers', most of the politicians were 'remainers'. The politicians were determined to prevent our country leaving without an agreement, which they considered would be catastrophic, yet they were not prepared to ratify the agreement, creating parliamentary deadlock.

Even worse than that, the European political class refused to revisit the Withdrawal Agreement, which had been ratified by their parliament, which made it impossible to get the agreement through our parliament, when all they needed to do was remove the Northern Ireland 'backstop' text from the agreement, to be discussed during the negotiations on trade.

So, let's start this 'search for the truth' and this 'view from the street' by considering the Withdrawal Agreement process, under Article 50 of the Lisbon Treaty 2009, which seems to have been written with the intention that it would never be used. Under the Withdrawal Agreement process, the leaving date was scheduled for 29th March 2019 (extended to 31st October 2019) and had the Withdrawal Agreement been ratified by both parliaments, it included a transition period to December 2020, to allow for the negotiation of our future relationship and a future trade deal.

However, the reality of the Withdrawal Agreement process means that if the negotiated agreement is not ratified by both parliaments, there is no transition period and no opportunity to negotiate our future relationship or a future trade deal. This leaves the government with no option but to leave without an agreement, and parliament ready to vote against leaving without an agreement, which effectively creates deadlock and obstructive 'remainers' ready to revoke Article 50 or have another referendum!

1

THE WITHDRAWAL AGREEMENT

AND POLITICAL DECLARATION

Withdrawal from the European Union is the legal and political process whereby a member state ceases to be a member of the Union. They have the right to withdraw under Article 50 of the Lisbon Treaty 2009, which states: "Any Member State may decide to withdraw from the Union in accordance with its own constitutional requirements. A Member State which decides to withdraw shall notify the European Council of its intention... the Union shall negotiate and conclude an agreement with that State, setting out the arrangements for its withdrawal, taking account of the framework for its future relationship with the Union."

The Withdrawal Agreement also includes a Political Declaration, which sets out the 'framework' for the future relationship between the European Union and the United Kingdom and the future trading arrangements. It perhaps needs to be emphasised that this is not a negotiated agreement on our future relationship, including our future trading relationship, it's just a 'framework' for discussions, when we leave the European Union.

Whilst the politicians and the officials appear to be at 'each other's throats', particularly the obstructive attitude of the European political elite, the draft Withdrawal Agreement and draft Political Declaration documents appear to have been drafted in a very supportive manner and say all the right words to expect a positive outcome. For instance, paragraph 16 of the Political Declaration, under the heading 'Economic Partnership: Objectives and Principles' states: "The parties recognise they have a particularly important trading and investment relationship, reflecting more than 45 years of economic integration, during the United Kingdom's membership of the Union, the size of the economies and their geographic proximity, which have led to complex and integrated supply chains." Furthermore, paragraph 17 of the Political Declaration states: "Against this backdrop, the parties agree to develop an ambitious, wide-ranging and balanced economic partnership which will be comprehensive and encompass a free trade area as well as wider sectoral co-operation, where it is in the mutual interests of both parties."

Incidentally, we have not been members of the European Union for forty-five (45) years, as suggested above. We joined the Common Market or the European Economic Community (EEC) in 1973, which changed to the European Union (EU), when the Conservative government signed the Maastricht Treaty (1992). We were, therefore, a member of the Common Market or the European Economic Community (EEC) from 1973 to 1992 and a member of the European Union (EU) from 1992 to 2019 (27 years).

Whilst the United Kingdom has been a net-contributor to the European Economic Community (EEC) and the European Union (EU) budgets for decades, our European Union (EU) partners have made the Withdrawal Agreement process, particularly the uncertainty concerning our future trading relationship, so difficult, that they are prepared to damage the economy of one of their biggest benefactors and biggest trading partners.

However, the public must be informed that the Withdrawal Agreement was never intended to include a trade deal, it was only intended to agree a 'framework' for our future relationship, including our future trading relationship, and provided for an implementation period to the end of 2020 to ensure a smooth transition, particularly in relation to trade.

The draft Withdrawal Agreement document (legally binding when ratified) was accompanied by a draft Political Declaration (not legally binding) which sets out the framework for the future relationship between the two parties. It provided instructions to deliver a future relationship by the end of 2020, which covered an economic partnership, a security partnership and agreement on many other areas of shared interest.

It, perhaps, needs to be emphasised, that the Withdrawal Agreement, which has been criticised by many politicians as a 'bad deal', does not include a trade deal, that's for negotiations after withdrawal. In other words, under the terms of Article 50, it was never intended to negotiate a trade deal during the Withdrawal Agreement negotiations, it was always intended to negotiate a future trade deal, when the member state had left the Union, which appears to be designed to create economic uncertainty.

For any country leaving the European Union, to arrive at the leaving date with just a 'framework' of a future trade deal, is bound to create economic uncertainty. Why could a future trade deal not be negotiated at the same time as the Withdrawal Agreement talks, to give business owners the confidence to plan their imports and exports to the European Union?

The negotiation of the Withdrawal Agreement would always be a complex legal process, but the European Union, being the dominant partner, held most of the cards, and should have approached the complex negotiations in a spirit of mutual respect, good faith and goodwill, rather than creating a negative atmosphere, which started with them pronouncing: "We can't have our cake and eat it," and, "We can't cherry pick."

This obstructive approach to the Withdrawal Agreement and our future relationship by the dominant partner, was bound to create commercial uncertainty. Why would the European political elite want to damage the economies of some of their own member states and a former member state, one of their biggest trading partners, just because they didn't want them to leave the club? The toxic attitude of the EU leaders towards the UK was illustrated by the following strange comments made by Donald Tusk, President of the European Council, on Thursday 7th February 2019: "By the way, I've been wondering, what the special place in hell looks like, for those who promoted Brexit, without even a sketch of a plan, how to carry it out safely." These ridiculous comments were particularly unhelpful and beneath the office of President of the European Council.

Incidentally, the only reason the United Kingdom hasn't a "sketch of a plan", as mentioned by Donald Tusk, is because they are conforming to the EU rules and regulations, which are designed for a leaving country, to arrive at the leaving date, without having negotiated a future trading relationship. This situation is not accidental, it's written into Article 50 of the Lisbon Treaty or the Treaty on European Union (TEU) as follows: "(2) A Member State which decides to withdraw shall notify the European Council of its intention... the Union shall negotiate and conclude an agreement with that State, setting out the arrangements for withdrawal, taking account of the framework for its future relationship with the Union. That agreement shall be negotiated in accordance with Article 218 (3) of the Treaty on the Functioning of the European Union."

This corporate reluctance to let member states leave the European Union and their negative approach to the Withdrawal Agreement negotiations, is undemocratic and smacks of corporate retribution. Do they really want to disrupt our smooth trading relationship, creating economic uncertainty, which would damage both economies and the well-being of the people?

Such a negative attitude by the leaders of one of the largest economies in the world, demanding a divorce settlement before any negotiations, and stating that we can't have our cake and eat it and we can't cherry pick, is bound to cause economic uncertainty and damage future trade relations. This obstructive attitude, towards a leaving member state, may be a sensible negotiating strategy, but it's contrary to the spirit of the Political Declaration, setting out the framework for future relationships, which makes such positive statements, as follows: "We are determined to work together to safeguard the high standards of free and fair trade..." and, "In that spirit, this declaration establishes the parameters of an ambitious, broad, deep and flexible partnership across trade and economic co-operation... This relationship will be rooted in the values and interests that (we) share. These arise from their geography, history and ideals, anchored in (a) common European heritage. (We) agree that prosperity and security are enhanced by embracing free and fair trade."

In view of the behaviour of the Brussels negotiators towards a member state wanting to leave, it's interesting to compare their behaviour (which could destabilise both economies) with the Kremlin, which ran the Soviet Union with a 'rod of iron' but later, as the Russian Federation, created a Commonwealth of Independent States (CIS) and did not challenge their national independence and does not punish those who want to leave.

The CIS was founded by Russia, Belarus and Ukraine (1991) and they were later joined by Kazakhstan, Kyrgyzstan, Tajikistan, Turkmenistan and Uzbekistan and then Armenia, Azerbaijan, Georgia and Moldova. Although Ukraine is one of the three founder members, it's legally not a member, as it never ratified the CIS Charter (1993) and Turkmenistan is now an 'associate member', having withdrawn from full membership in 2005, presumably without any retribution. It's also instructive to observe that in 2008, Georgia notified the CIS executive of its decision to leave the Commonwealth and according to the charter (Section 1, Article 9) the decision came into effect twelve months later, without retribution.

It's an indictment on the leadership of the European Union, that they don't have a withdrawal treaty process which allows member states to leave, without vindictive divorce settlements and negative trade deals. The wording of Article 50 is positive, regarding withdrawal negotiations, using the words 'good faith', 'mutual respect' and 'goodwill', yet the words of the European negotiators are positively negative, saying such things as: 'We can't have our cake and eat it' and 'We can't cherry pick'.

Incidentally, the rules state that if the withdrawal negotiations do not result in an agreement, ratified by both parties, the leaving member state would then leave without an agreement and… without any transitional arrangements being put in place. So far as trade is concerned the leaving country would have to follow the World Trade Organisation (WTO) rules, which would cause some short-term disruption to commercial enterprise.

However, having been a member of the European Union and the single market and customs union for decades, any negotiations need an element of 'goodwill' from the stronger partner (EU), to allow the much weaker partner (UK) to continue to trade with the remaining member states. To start with a threat from the dominant partner, that you 'can't have your cake and eat it' and you 'can't cherry pick', is not a good start!

It is, however, refreshing to note that Article 4a of the 'Draft Agreement on the Withdrawal of the United Kingdom from the

European Union', under the heading 'Good Faith', says: "The Parties shall, in full mutual respect and good faith, assist each other in carrying out tasks, which flow from this agreement. They shall take all appropriate measures, whether general or particular, to ensure fulfilment of the obligations arising from this agreement and shall refrain from any measures which could jeopardise the attainment of the objectives of this agreement… particularly the principle of sincere co-operation."

It's probably worth repeating, that Article 4a clearly states that both parties must work together with 'mutual respect' and 'good faith' and 'sincere co-operation', to negotiate a future trade deal. However, that depends on reaching a Withdrawal Agreement and a 'framework' for a future relationship and a transition period, in the first place.

If the Brussels negotiators do not act with 'mutual respect' and 'good faith' and 'sincere co-operation' during the Withdrawal Agreement negotiations, they may not be able to achieve an acceptable Withdrawal Agreement and framework for a future relationship, including trade, in which case Article 4a (which mentions 'mutual respect' and 'good faith' in tasks which flow from the agreement) will not come into play.

It perhaps needs to be emphasised that the United Kingdom are leaving the European Union and not their European trading partners. However, whilst British businesses want to continue trading within the single market and the customs union, the EU rules state that you can't be a member of either, when not a member of the Union. Consequently, the British negotiators should have been able to strike a trade deal with the EU, to allow trade to continue without disruption after 29th March 2019 or the extended date of 31st October 2019, which is Independence Day.

However, is this not exactly what they did? If the British parliament had ratified the 'Withdrawal Agreement', things would have stayed as they were, during a transition period to negotiate our future relationship and a future trade deal. Instead of suggesting that the Withdrawal Agreement was a bad deal, parliament should have made it absolutely clear that they would ratify the agreement if the Northern Ireland 'Backstop' text, which was of major concern, was removed from the agreement and renegotiated as part of the discussions on our future relationship and our future trade arrangements, during the transition period. Alternatively, both parties to the agreement could have shown 'good will' and 'mutual respect' and set up an independent commission to produce a text on the 'Backstop', acceptable to both sides. It was, however, in the interests of the remain campaigners to allow the 'Backstop' text to derail the ratification of the agreement, in the hope that 'deadlock' would prevail, as the European Parliament would not amend the ratified agreement and the pro-remain British parliament would not ratify the agreement unless it was amended.

Surely, the simple transfer of the Northern Ireland 'Backstop' from the Withdrawal Agreement text, to the Political Declaration, to be resolved during the trade deal negotiations, would have given the agreement a good chance of ratification by the British parliament. This would have enabled them to move to the transition period negotiations and avoid leaving without an agreement, the 'no-deal' scenario, which is the major concern of the parliamentarians determined to obstruct the agreement.

As the European political elite were not prepared to make such a simple change to the Withdrawal Agreement, which may have ensured a smooth transition to withdrawal, this suggests that they wanted to make it as difficult as possible for any member state to leave their grand project, and send a stern warning to any other member state that leaving would be very difficult and not recommended.

Naturally, British businesses want to continue to trade with their European business partners, and the rest of the world, as they always have done, and because they were in compliance with the rules of the single market and customs union, it should not have been too difficult to continue trading across Europe. What the United Kingdom needed was a free-trade deal with the European Union, which conformed with the rules of the single market and the customs union, without being members of the European Union, but the Brussels negotiators said that we 'can't have our cake and eat it', which is like 'cutting off their nose, to spite their face', as they export more goods to Britain, than Britain does to them.

The political controversy surrounding the Withdrawal Agreement has been distressing to watch and our parliamentarians need to behave in a more mature manner. The Withdrawal Agreement included a punitive 'divorce settlement' payment of £39 billion and a 'framework' for our future relationship but did not include a free-trade deal. It did, however, include a transition period, after 29th March 2019, during which we could have negotiated a trade deal, which gave British businesses access to the single market and the customs union and the success of those trade deal talks should have been linked to the 'divorce settlement' payments. No free-trade deal, no punitive divorce settlement. To do otherwise was not in the national interest. Why would the British government negotiators agree to give the European Union a massive £39 billion, if they are not prepared to 'pave the way' for a 'mutually beneficial' free-trade deal?

If the Withdrawal Agreement (in its original form) is not ratified by the UK parliament, then the UK will have to leave the EU on 29th March 2019 (extended to 31st October 2019) without an agreement and then revert to World Trade Organisation (WTO) rules, to trade with our European business partners, which apparently creates commercial uncertainty and logistical transport problems and delays commercial decisions on financial investment, which will hinder commercial growth. However, whilst this may be the legal position, the British parliament have voted to stop the British government leaving the Union without a deal!

Many of the politicians who oppose the draft Withdrawal Agreement, oppose it because they want a second referendum and don't want to leave the European Union and the single market and the customs union. This is an undemocratic approach to the Withdrawal Agreement, and they must 'search their consciences' and accept the decision of the British people and consider the Withdrawal Agreement document in the public interest.

It needs to be clear that the Withdrawal Agreement, negotiated by the British government, agrees a time-limited implementation period, that provides a bridge to a future relationship, allowing businesses to trade, as they do now, until the end of 2020. It also provides a free-trade area and deep co-operation on goods, with zero tariffs and quotas, and gives the right to strike trade deals around the world, in the national interest.

We perhaps need to repeat that the Withdrawal Agreement, just includes a 'framework' for our future relationship, and a future trade deal. The politicians and the media are exercised about the nature of the 'deal', which many consider to be a 'bad deal' and refuse to approve the 'deal' in parliament. The reality is, however, that the Withdrawal Agreement is a legal document, designed to release a leaving member state from the rules and regulations and treaties of the European Union, and does not include a 'trade deal'. The Withdrawal Agreement document provides a 'framework' for our future relationship and the 'framework' of a future trade deal, and a transition period, in which to negotiate our future relationship and a future trade deal in the interests of both parties.

On 15th January 2019, parliament rejected the Withdrawal Agreement and the Political Declaration on our future relationship and future trade deal, by a large majority. There were 202 votes for and 432 votes against the agreement, a majority against of 230 votes. However, many of those who voted against the agreement, did so because they don't want to leave the EU, and some wanted a second referendum. They did this, despite the fact that parliament had previously voted to invoke Article 50 by a very large majority, which implies that they had accepted the result of the Brexit referendum and approved the Withdrawal Agreement negotiations.

Incidentally, following the parliamentary vote, President of the European Council, Donald Tusk, tweeted the following unhelpful words: "If a deal is impossible, and no-one wants no deal, then who will finally have the courage to say what the only positive solution is" (presumably remain!)

The President of the European Commission, Jean-Claude Juncker, warned that time was running out for the UK to strike a deal and he said: "I urge the United Kingdom to clarify its intentions as soon as possible. Time is almost up. The risk of a disorderly withdrawal of the UK has increased with this evenings vote."

The chief negotiator for the EU Commission, Michel Barnier, said: "It's now up to the British government to say what the next stage is. The EU will remain united and determined to find a deal." Even the German Finance Minister, Olaf Scholz, said that Tuesday was a bitter day for Europe and "We are well prepared, but a hard Brexit would be the least attractive choice for the EU and the UK."

Annegret Kramp-Karrenbauer, the leader of the German ruling Christian Democratic Union Party said: "A hard Brexit will be the worst of all options." The French President, Emmanuel Macron, warned that a transition period was essential, because a no-deal would be damaging, and said: "We will have to negotiate a transition period with them, because the British cannot afford to no longer have planes taking off or landing at home."

This parliamentary 'deadlock' has been created by those dissident politicians, who disrespect the decision of the British people, in a 'fair and free' plebiscite, to decide whether to stay or leave the European Union, as it moves towards a United States of Europe. This behaviour is unacceptable on the basis that parliament approved the referendum by a large majority, which means that they wanted the people to decide on our future relationship with the European Union. Then, having accepted the result of the referendum, parliament approved by a very large majority to invoke Article 50 of the Lisbon Treaty 2009, which implies that they had read and understood the terms of Article 50. If that was the case, Article 50 makes it clear that we'll leave on 29th March 2019 (extended to 31st October 2019) 'with or without' an agreement. So why has it been so difficult to get parliament to ratify the agreement, which paves the way for a transition period to discuss our future relationship and a trade deal and understand that not ratifying the agreement, means we have to leave without an agreement, under existing legislation approved by them?

It appears that the dissident politicians, who want to stay in the EU and want a second referendum, to change the result of the first referendum, are behaving like 'saboteurs' wanting to overturn the legislation already approved by them, to invoke Article 50 to start the withdrawal process.

Consequently, parliament should approve the Withdrawal Agreement and let the negotiators get on with the trade negotiations and strike a trade deal with our EU partners, to avoid damage to our economies or accept the fact that we will have to leave the security of the single market and the customs union without a deal, which could be disruptive. However, the 'saboteurs' in parliament, who do not want to leave, were determined to obstruct any smooth transition from the Withdrawal Agreement to the negotiations about our future relationship and a future trade deal.

Sadly, it's not the European Commission that's created

parliamentary 'deadlock', it's many elected representatives of the British parliament, who don't want to leave the European Union and want to force a second referendum on the 'final deal' or agreement, in an attempt to change the people's minds, probably out of sheer frustration with the politicians. We are, however, told that most people, regardless of how they voted, just want the politicians to get on with it and get us out of the EU and put the Brexit nightmare behind us! This episode has deeply divided our nation.

However, the government put the Withdrawal Agreement to parliament on 15th January 2019 (the first 'meaningful vote') and the government was defeated by 432 to 202 votes. The margin of defeat (230 votes) was the worst defeat for any government in modern parliamentary history.

The government put the Withdrawal Agreement before parliament for a second time on 12th March 2019 (the second 'meaningful vote') and was rejected by 391 votes to 242 (margin of 149), with one MP unable to vote.

On the same day (12th March 2019) parliament voted to reject leaving the European Union without an agreement or a deal by 321 votes to 278 with 35 abstentions. This vote was not legally binding on the government but warned of the staunch parliamentary resistance to a 'no-deal' scenario.

This vote, to block leaving without a deal, meant that the government could not get parliament to approve the agreement (or deal) and they know that they won't approve leaving without an agreement (no-deal), which is the legal position, under Article 50, should parliament not ratify the agreement (or deal), which amounted to parliamentary 'deadlock'.

As leaving the European Union without an agreement or deal was rejected by parliament, the government was then required to bring a motion before parliament on 14th March, to extend the leaving date, under Article 50, beyond the 29th March 2019. The motion stated, that if the Withdrawal Agreement had not been ratified by parliament by 20th March 2019, they would seek an extension to 30th June, the last day that Brexit could take place without requiring British participation in the May (2019) European Elections. The motion was approved by 412 to 202.

In the event the European Parliament approved an extension of the leaving date, under Article 50, to 31st October 2019, to give the British more time to get parliament to approve the Withdrawal Agreement and the British had no option but to participate in the European Elections in May 2019. Not surprisingly, the newly formed Brexit Party, under the leadership of Nigel Farage (MEP) did very well, which showed that the people were frustrated with the delay in leaving the European Union.

Furthermore, an amendment was tabled by Sir Oliver Letwin MP on 25th March 2019, requiring parliament to hold a series of 'indicative votes' to indicate parliament's preferred Brexit options, to be held on 27th March 2019, and the amendment passed by 329 to 302 votes. However, all eight 'indicative votes' failed to agree on any parliamentary preferred options.

The Speaker of the House of Commons, John Bercow, would not allow the government to seek a third 'meaningful vote' on the Withdrawal Agreement if it was 'the same proposition or substantially the same proposition'. Not to be thwarted, the government removed the Political Declaration from the Withdrawal Agreement and brought it forward for a third 'meaningful vote' on 29th March 2019, but it was voted down.

Just to add to the parliamentary obfuscation, there was a second round of 'indicative votes' on 1st April 2019, but all four failed to get parliamentary approval. It's interesting, however, to note that one of the 'indicative votes' sought approval for a 'confirmatory public vote' on any deal and it failed by 292 to 280 with 62 abstentions. Another interesting 'indicative vote' was to seek approval for the revocation of Article 50 to avoid a 'no-deal' and it failed by 292 to 191 with 151 abstentions. These were two of the most controversial matters in the whole debate. Attempting to hold a second referendum on any agreement or deal is profoundly undemocratic and attempting to revoke Article 50 to avoid a 'no-deal' goes against the terms of Article 50, which was previously approved by parliament and provides for leaving with no deal if an agreement cannot be ratified.

If we are not very careful, our respected liberal democracy and electoral process will be decided on the 'best of three', which is nonsense.

The people are right to be frustrated with the political obfuscation of their elected representatives, those that they elect to represent them in the 'corridors of power'. Some of them were attempting to 'sabotage' the withdrawal process, by seeking a second referendum, to overturn the result of the first referendum, or to revoke the Article 50 withdrawal process and remain in the European Union, or to stop the government leaving without a deal, when that is the legal 'fall-back' position of Article 50, should parliament not approve a Withdrawal Agreement.

Incidentally, our elected representatives perhaps need to be reminded that a significant 17,410,742 people voted to leave the European Union 'with or without' a deal. So far as our parliamentary constituencies are concerned, 406 voted to leave and 242 to remain. So far as our political parties are concerned, 148 Labour constituencies voted to leave and 84 to remain and 247 Conservative constituencies voted to leave and 80 to remain. However, whilst the people voted by a majority of 1,269,501 to leave, the politicians voted the other way (486 of them voted to remain and 160 voted to leave). There appears to be a massive divide between the views of the elected representatives and the views of the people.

So far as the Labour Party is concerned, there were at least 72 Labour constituencies where support for 'leave' was estimated to be more than 55% – such as the 69.3% in Normanton, Pontefract and Castleford, where Yvette Cooper, who campaigned for 'remain', is an MP. It has been noted that some of her constituents have protested on the streets against their elected representative voting and campaigning for remain, which is directly opposed to the views of most of her constituents.

This is the crux of the parliamentary obfuscation, around the ratification of a Withdrawal Agreement. The people voted by a large majority to leave and their elected representatives, those they elect to represent them in parliament, voted by a large majority to remain! How have we got such a political divide between the people and their elected representatives?

Regardless of the constant political obfuscation towards the Withdrawal Agreement, particularly the problems around the Northern Ireland 'Backstop', the government must conform with the 'will of the people' and get us out of the European Union, in accordance with the result of the Brexit referendum (2016), and negotiate a sensible trade deal with the European Commission on behalf of our 'anxious' business-people.

Surely, with some 'goodwill' on both sides, they could have reached an amicable agreement to change the Northern Ireland 'Backstop' text, in the Withdrawal Agreement, to be acceptable to parliamentarians and released the parliamentary 'log-jam'. Conversely, they could just remove the Northern Ireland 'Backstop' text from the Withdrawal Agreement document and put it into the Political Declaration. It would then be discussed, during the lengthy transition period negotiations on our future relationship and future trade deal, as it is very much about trade and customs, and both sides need a mutually beneficial free-trade deal.

Whether or not the new British government attempts to resurrect the Withdrawal Agreement or attempts to change the Northern Ireland 'Backstop' arrangements, they do intend to leave, in accordance with Article 50, on 31st October 2019, with or without a deal. However, surely it is not beyond the capacity of Westminster and Brussels to produce an outline of a mutually beneficial free-trade deal and approach the divorce in a spirit of co-operation and goodwill, to suppress the public anxiety.

2

A MUTUALLY BENEFICIAL FREE-

TRADE DEAL

After decades as a member of the European Economic Community (EEC) or the Common Market and its successor the European Union, the United Kingdom business regulations are fully harmonised with the European Union, which means that Brussels could negotiate a free-trade deal with Westminster and continue to apply those rules in exchange for access to the single market, similar to Norway, but that would involve the 'free movement of people' and continued contributions to the EU budget.

So far as trade is concerned, the UK's main trading partners, between January and November 2016, according to HM Revenue and Customs 'Overseas Trade Statistics' included our European partners, as follows:

Imports: Germany £58.91 billion; the Netherlands £31.37 billion; France £22.47 billion; Belgium £21.19 billion; Italy £15.64 billion; Spain £14.87 billion; and the Irish Republic £12.03 billion.

Exports: Germany £29.68 billion; Netherlands £17.55 billion; France £17.48 billion; Belgium £10.81 billion; Italy £8.91 billion; Spain £8.55 billion and the Irish Republic £15.39 billion.

Based on these trade figures, particularly the imports, why would Germany, the Netherlands, France, Belgium, Italy, Spain and Eire, not insist that the EU negotiates a mutually beneficial free-trade deal with the UK, which does not include the 'free movement of people' or the need to pay into the EU budget? The total import value from Germany, the Netherlands, France, Belgium, Italy, Spain and Ireland, between January and November 2016, was £176.48 billion, against exports to them of £108.37 billion, which is a trade deficit of £68.11 billion, which means that a 'bad deal' or 'no deal' would hurt our European trading partners more than it would hurt the British, except that in their case the pain would be spread across seven nations!

Any trade deal, between the European Union and the United Kingdom, will have to be approved by the other twenty-seven member states but surely the views of our seven biggest EU trading partners – Germany, the Netherlands, France, Belgium, Italy, Spain and Ireland – must be given more weight, than the other twenty member states. Should the two main players, Germany and France, instruct the Brussels negotiating team to produce a special free trade deal with the British, then it would probably happen immediately, to avoid destabilising commercial uncertainty.

In 2016 the gross domestic product (GDP) of the European Union (EU) was circa 14,800 billion euros and over half was generated by the three member states, Germany, France and the United Kingdom. Furthermore, according to Eurostat, Germany, with a gross domestic product (GDP) of 3,100 billion euros in 2016, was the leading EU economy, accounting for over one fifth (21.1%) of the GDP of the EU, followed by the United Kingdom (16%), France (15%), Italy (11.3%), Spain (7.5%) and the Netherlands (4.7%). At the other end of the scale, eleven member states provided less than one percent of the EU GDP, as follows: Hungary (0.8%); Slovakia (0.5%); Luxembourg (0.4%); Bulgaria (0.3%); Croatia (0.3%); Slovenia (0.3%); Lithuania (0.3%); Latvia (0.2%); Estonia (0.1%); Cyprus (0.1%) and Malta (0.1%). The other member states (those in the middle) provided the following percentage of the EU, GDP, as follows: Sweden (3.1%); Poland (2.9%); Belgium (2.8%); Austria (2.4%); Denmark (1.9%); Ireland (1.8%); Finland (1.4%); Portugal (1.2%); Greece (1.2%); the Czech Republic (1.2%) and Romania (1.1%).

Incidentally, the UK, with a 16% contribution to the GDP of the EU, contributed more than the bottom nineteen (19) member states combined; that's Austria (2.4%); Denmark (1.9%); Ireland (1.8%); Finland (1.4%); Portugal (1.2%); Greece (1.2%); the Czech Republic (1.2%); Romania (1.1%); Hungary (0.8%); Slovakia (0.5%); Luxembourg (0.4%); Bulgaria (0.3%); Croatia (0.3%); Slovenia (0.3%); Lithuania (0.3%); Latvia (0.2%); Estonia (0.1%); Cyprus (0.1%) and Malta (0.1%).

Wouldn't it be appropriate for the leaders of the bottom nineteen member states, mentioned above, to have thanked the United Kingdom for their contributions to their well-being and instructed the EU negotiators to agree a mutually beneficial free-trade deal with the United Kingdom?

Furthermore, wouldn't it have been appropriate for the leaders of our seven biggest trading partners in the European Union, that's Germany, the Netherlands, France, Belgium, Italy, Spain and Ireland, to instruct the European negotiators to strike a mutually beneficial free-trade deal with the United Kingdom, to allow trade to continue unhindered, or is the future of the European Union project more important than free trade?

Incidentally, the Withdrawal Agreement could not be approved by the British parliament because of concerns about the imposition of a hard border between Northern Ireland and the Irish Republic, when we leave the single market and the customs union. However, imports from the Irish Republic (2016) were £12.03 billion and exports to the Irish Republic were £15.39 billion; the Irish have a trade deficit with the British of £3.36 billion, so any damage to cross-border trade would damage the Irish economy more than the British economy. Sadly, the Northern Ireland 'Backstop' arrangements, which are designed to stop a 'hard border' on the island of Ireland, have become the reason for leaving without a deal.

Furthermore, there was some public concern at the increasing cost of our membership of the European Union, which has almost doubled in recent times. The UK net contribution to the EU budget, which was born out of our membership of the European Economic Community or the Common Market, was £4.6 billion in 2007; £3.3bn in 2008; £4.3bn in 2009; £7.4bn in 2010; £8.1bn in 2011; £8.5bn in 2012 and £8.6bn in 2013 and so on.

Information from the Office for National Statistics (ONS), released on 31st October 2017, said that our gross contribution to the

EU was £18.9 billion but this amount was never actually transferred to the EU. We apparently made a £13.5 billion contribution, after a rebate of £5 billion. However, the UK made a £9.4 billion net contribution, with £4.4 billion public and private sector credits (which includes £359 million through the Regional Development Fund and £2.4 billion through the Agricultural Guarantee Fund) and a £5 billion rebate. What a bureaucratic nonsense!

How can any ordinary citizen make any sense of these complex numbers?

The reality is, however, that the United Kingdom is a net-contributor to the European Union budget and a benevolent benefactor to the recipient nations, which should be supportive of a respectful withdrawal process.

Wouldn't it have been appropriate for the leaders of the bottom nineteen member states, which have benefitted from the benevolent British budget contributions, to have supported the British negotiators, during these divisive negotiations, which have seen the British 'hung out to dry'?

Apparently at the eleventh hour, the EU chief negotiator, Michel Barnier, said that the £39 billion divorce settlement could guarantee a UK-EU trade deal. If the expected payment of £39 billion does not persuade Brussels to amend the Withdrawal Agreement and move on to a mutually beneficial trade deal with the United Kingdom, then nothing will, as 'he who pays the piper' should always 'call the tune' but we shall see.

Incidentally, the obstinate Michel Barnier has previously insisted that the payment of the divorce settlement, a central part of the Withdrawal Agreement, could not be made conditional on a UK-EU trade deal. He then argued that the payment would only settle existing debts and that any future trade deal must be a separate agreement, which is ridiculous. The agreement to pay such a punitive divorce settlement, and the need to agree a mutually beneficial free-trade deal should be inextricably linked.

Until the eleventh hour, the Brussels negotiating team were prepared to make the leaving process so damaging to the British economy, with loose media talk of 'crashing out' without a deal, that the other member states would be afraid to want to leave, particularly those member states in the single-currency, such as Greece. Having suffered this negative process, under Article 50 of the Lisbon Treaty, it's clear that members of the Eurozone would risk bankruptcy, should they attempt to leave the European Union and the European Monetary Union at the same time.

Ironically, the pro-EU resistance movement, which warns of an economic disaster should we 'crash out' without a trade deal or agreement and want another referendum, a so-called 'People's Vote', on any deal or no deal, have weakened the hand of the British and strengthened the hand of Brussels and made a bad deal or no deal more likely. No negotiators can expect a good deal, when their every move is argued in parliament and dramatized in the media. The British have tried to negotiate a Withdrawal Agreement, from a position of weakness, with their opponents wanting them to stay. Naturally, getting a bad deal or no deal, which would cause economic instability and uncertainty, is attractive to the remainers, who want another vote on the final deal, with an option to remain in the EU.

No negotiations team can expect a positive outcome to any negotiations, when they are being undermined by people who should be on their side.

When the British people voted by a significant majority of 1,269,501 votes to leave the European Union, in a 'free and fair' referendum, the country should then have rallied behind their government to achieve a positive outcome to the Withdrawal Agreement and a future trade deal.

The challenge of the British 'resistance movement', to the unexpected result of a democratic referendum to leave the European Union, as it moves inexorably towards a United States of Europe, plays into the hands of the European Union (Brussels) regime, who like the former Soviet Union (Kremlin) regime, cannot tolerate opposition to their movement.

It is, therefore, appropriate to compare the behaviour of the European Union (Brussels), as they 'thunder' towards a United States of Europe, with the behaviour of the Soviet Union (Kremlin), as it sustained the Union of Soviet Socialist Republics (USSR), which demonstrates that both structures were prepared to 'stamp out' dissent, one with brutal military intervention and the other with commercial uncertainty and instability.

This comparison may be frivolous to some, but if the alleged statement by Mikhail Gorbachev, the former leader of the Soviet Union (USSR), is to be believed, then the comparison may have some relevance: "The most puzzling development in politics during the last decade, is the apparent determination of Western European leaders to recreate the Soviet Union in Western Europe." So, let's compare the 'obstructive' behaviour of the European Union (Brussels), towards a long-standing, net-contributor member state, the United Kingdom, wanting to leave their grand project, with the behaviour of the former brutal Soviet Union (Kremlin), when faced with dissent from one of their subordinate and compliant states.

3

THE EUROPEAN UNION AND THE

FORMER SOVIET UNION

Multi-national political constructs, such as the European Union and the former Soviet Union, were created by the political class and are little to do with the 'will of the people'. The people of the other twenty-seven member states of the European Union, should be concerned about the threat to their independence, caused by the creation of a federal country called Europe or the ultimate destination of a United States of Europe.

The question is, of course, do the people of the other twenty-seven member states know that the ultimate destination of the European Union is a federal country called Europe or the United States of Europe, under the control of the Brussels political elite, from their secure 'ivory tower'?

However, whilst the European Union has morphed from the sensible European Economic Community (EEC) or the Common Market, towards a country called Europe or a United States of Europe, with member states gradually losing their independence, the Kremlin (Russian Federation) created a Commonwealth of Independent States (CIS), which is an alliance of independent countries, with mutually beneficial agreements, including economic co-operation, but retaining their independence.

It's worth repeating that the Commonwealth of Independent States (CIS) was founded by Russia, Belarus and Ukraine (1991) and they were later joined by Kazakhstan, Kyrgyzstan, Tajikistan, Turkmenistan and Uzbekistan and then Armenia, Azerbaijan, Georgia and Moldova. Although Ukraine is one of the three founder members, it's legally not a member, as it never ratified the CIS Charter (1993) and Turkmenistan is now an 'associate member', having withdrawn from full membership in 2005, presumably without retribution. It's also instructive to note that in 2008, Georgia notified the CIS executive of its decision to leave the Commonwealth and according to the Charter (Section 1, Article 9) the decision came into effect twelve months later, without retribution.

The question is, therefore, has the Commonwealth of Independent States (CIS), founded by Russia, Belarus and Ukraine, adopted a more liberal commercial trading bloc than the supposed democratic European Union?

It's, therefore, interesting to compare the negative behaviour of the European Union negotiators towards the British negotiators, and the economic uncertainty and commercial instability they were prepared to inflict on the British people, with the aggressive military behaviour of the Soviet Union towards Hungary (1956), which wanted to escape Soviet domination, and Czechoslovakia (1968), which wanted some limited reform, but the Soviet Union (Kremlin) sent in the troops and the tanks.

The Hungarian uprising was a nationwide revolt against their own government and its Soviet-Union-imposed policies, which lasted from the 23rd October to the 10th November 1956, when the Soviet Union tanks and troops rolled into Budapest and crushed the uprising, killing 2,500 people and causing 200,000 people to leave the country, as refugees.

The Soviet Union invasion of Czechoslovakia on 20th August 1968, which involved 200,000 troops and 5,000 tanks, killing 100 people, was a crackdown on reformist trends in Prague by a Conservative government, under the leadership of Prime Minister Alexander Dubcek, who was quickly removed from office and replaced by a more compliant leader.

Like the people of Czechoslovakia, who wanted some limited reform from the Soviet Union, the British people wanted some limited reform from the European Union, particularly to the uncontrolled 'free movement of people' across 'open borders', but their concerns were ignored by the Brussels political elite. It was so embarrassing, to watch Prime Minister David Cameron 'scuttling' around the 'corridors of power' in Brussels, in a vain attempt to negotiate some limited reform and being isolated and ignored by some of the arrogant leaders of the European Union.

Whilst the Hungarian people revolted against Soviet-Union-imposed policies, and the Kremlin sent in the tanks, the British people voted to leave the European Union and Brussels sent in the 'awkward squad' to reverse the democratic decision, as they had done many times before.

The tragedy of the British revolt against the European Union political project, is that the Brussels Eurocrats have been supported by a British 'resistance movement', including former senior politicians, which the Soviet Union, through the Kremlin, would call 'saboteurs', which means people who are prepared to 'destroy', 'disrupt', 'subvert' or 'wreck'.

Incidentally, why would the leaders of the East European member states, particularly Hungary, Slovakia, and the Czech Republic, want to escape the brutal Soviet Union regime in Moscow, to regain their independence, then join the dominant European Union regime in Brussels, and be part of a discrete political project designed to reduce their independence? Why would they want to 'jump out of the frying pan and into the fire'? Why would they want to be part of an intolerant European Union, which has disregarded and disrespected the views of the British people, who voted to leave their grand project, and watch their negotiators playing 'hard-ball' and watch the parliamentary turmoil in Westminster?

Having escaped the 'shackles' of the Soviet Union, the East European countries should ensure that the European Union is an association of independent nation states, like the Commonwealth of Independent States (CIS), run by the Russian Federation (Kremlin), and not a multi-national super-state, where independent member states gradually surrender their independence, or they have just 'jumped from the frying pan into the fire'.

The perpetual motion of the Brussels-to-Strasbourg Express towards a monumental country called the United States of Europe, needs to slow down before it hits the buffers. The remote European political elite must reconsider their flawed project and resurrect the

European Economic Community or the Common Market, with a small central authority or commission in Brussels. This return to an economic community or common market would be very similar to the Commonwealth of Independent States (CIS), based in Minsk, Belarus, which has an Assembly of Member Nations and an Executive Director.

The Commonwealth of Independent States is an alliance of independent countries, which have signed agreements for economic and foreign policy and defence co-operation and other matters. It is, however, interesting to note that all these countries retained their own national currencies and remarkably, they managed to trade with each other, without the need for a common currency, which would inevitably have led to a domineering federal government, a central bank and one powerful finance minister.

Had the objective of the architects of the European Union (EU) been to create an economic union or alliance of independent nation states (which seemed to be the case with the European Economic Community (EEC) or the Common Market), like the Commonwealth of Independent States (CIS), the British people would not have wanted (or needed) to escape.

Looking back, it all started with the European Coal and Steel Community (ECSC, 1952) and the European Atomic Energy Community (EAEC or Euratom) and the European Economic Community (EEC, 1957), which was known as the Common Market. The UK first applied to join the Common Market or EEC in 1961 but the application was vetoed by the French. A later application was made, and the UK joined in 1973, which was confirmed in a public referendum in 1975 with 67.2% approval.

Had it stayed as an economic community or a common market, there would have been no problem, and the British people would not have been confronted with the gradual movement towards a multi-national super-state, and the erosion of their independence and the 'free movement of people' across 'open borders' putting pressure on public services.

The European political elite should have emulated the Commonwealth of Independent States (CIS) and formed an assembly of member nations and a relatively small executive, which would have looked very much like the early construct of the European Economic

Community or the Common Market but that was not the objective of the architects of the European Union (EU) or more accurately, the United States of Europe.

Whilst the expansion of the European project has had many treaties, the first nail in the coffin of the European Economic Community (EEC) was the Maastricht Treaty (1992), which turned the economic community into the European Union (EU), without reference to the people, which is an illustration of the unhealthy power of the European political elite.

To illustrate the determination of the European Union political elite to dictate to their member states or make them conform to their rules and regulations, the European Court of Justice (ECJ) has recently dismissed complaints by Hungary and Slovakia (supported by Poland) about the EU migration policy, to impose migration quotas on member states. This is an important victory for the European political elite, which intends to relocate 120,000 asylum seekers, from Greece and Italy, around other member states, with or without their approval. Budapest condemned the court's ruling as "appalling and irresponsible". The Hungarian Foreign Minister, Péter Szijjártó, said: "This decision jeopardises the security and future of Europe. Politics has raped European law and values."

The EU leaders agreed the emergency plan in September 2015, at the height of the migration crisis, as thousands of people arrived, many of whom were dependent refugees from Syria, Iraq and Eritrea. Along with Hungary and Slovakia, Romania and the Czech Republic voted against the quota scheme and Poland threw its weight behind the legal case after the Conservative Law and Justice Party came to power in late 2015. The migration of so many dependent refugees, is a social problem that could cause division between Brussels and their compliant member states. It's not dissimilar to the 'free movement of people' principle, across open borders, adopted by the European political elite, which allows citizens to move from the 'poorer' to the 'richer' member states, to take advantage of their public services, regardless of their ability to sustain themselves.

Whilst it could be considered preposterous to compare the behaviour of the brutal Soviet Union (Kremlin) towards its compliant satellite states, with the more liberal European Union (Brussels) as it thunders towards a federal super-state, destroying anything in its path, such as a member state wanting to leave, it may not be as ridiculous as it seems.

However, whilst the brutal Soviet Union (Kremlin) adopted a military response to dissent from their subordinate satellite states, the dominant European Union (Brussels), which operates like a multi-national 'welfare state', with the 'poorer' member states subordinated by handouts from the 'richer' member states, approaches dissent with the threat of serious damage to the economies of those misguided member states, with the temerity or audacity to threaten their grand project.

When comparing the corporate behaviour of the former Soviet Union with the European Union, it's instructive to consider an article in *The Times*, on Thursday 14th February 2019, by Oliver Moody, which said that George Soros (the Hungarian billionaire) had warned that the EU is "sleep-walking into oblivion" and risks collapsing like the Soviet Union.

In an article for Project Syndicate, a Prague-based website, he said: "One can still make a case for preserving the EU in order radically to reinvent it. But that would require a change of heart in the EU. The current leadership is reminiscent of the politburo when the Soviet Union collapsed, continuing to issue (edicts) as if they were still relevant."

It's not, therefore, so preposterous, to consider the comments attributed to President Mikhail Gorbachev (USSR), General Secretary of the Communist Party, when he said: "The most puzzling development in politics, during the last decade, is the apparent determination of Western European leaders, to create a Soviet Union in Western Europe."

So, whether or not the European political elite are driving their project towards a dominant centralised structure, similar to the former Soviet Union, with 'subjugated' satellite states, or whether they are creating a more liberal structure, with 'compliant' member states, let's look at the wealth redistribution of this multi-national 'welfare state', which is bound together by 'poorer' countries, dependent on 'richer' countries.

4

A MULTI-NATIONAL

'WELFARE STATE'

Whilst most reasonable people would not compare the behaviour of the brutal Soviet Union or the Union of Soviet Socialist Republics (USSR) towards their dependent satellite states, with the more liberal European Union, the development of a dominant, federal, European, multi-national super-state, with dependent or compliant member states, is very similar.

The creation of a multi-national super-state, with some very powerful benefactor states such as Germany and France and many more weaker recipient states, dependent on donations from the Brussels machine, is a recipe for discontent amongst recipient nations, as they gradually lose their independence, as inevitably 'he who pays the piper calls the tune'.

When the British people were concerned about the movement of the Brussels super-tanker from the safe haven of the European Economic Community or the Common Market, towards the European Union and a United States of Europe, which behaves like a benevolent, multi-national welfare state (where the British are a significant net-contributor), their genuine concerns were met with apathy by the Brussels political elite.

It's clear that the Brussels political elite had no respect for the 'will of the British people', expressed through a public referendum, and they made it clear that they would prefer a change of heart (through a second referendum), which they had done many times before. Naturally, they wanted the UK to remain in the European Union, as they were a net-contributor to the budget, which is effectively funding a multi-national welfare state, which is illustrated by the disparity in contributions to the EU budget and the redistribution of funds to the 'poorer' member states.

This disparity in contributions to the EU budget is illustrated by the fact that Germany contributed 21.1% of the gross domestic product (GDP) of the EU (2016), followed by the United Kingdom with 16% and France with 15% and Italy with 11.3% and Spain with 7.5%, which is a total contribution of 70.9 % by just five of the twenty-eight member states.

However, according to Statista, the following is the share of the total contributions of member states to the EU Budget (2016); Germany 19%; France 16.63%; the United Kingdom 13.45%; Italy 12.49%; Spain 8.55%; Belgium 4.47%; the Netherlands 3.71%; Poland 3.26%; Sweden 2.45%; Austria 2.36%; Denmark 1.83%; Ireland 1.61%; Finland 1.56%; Portugal 1.35%; the Czech Republic 1.3%; Greece 1.29%; Romania 1.15%; Hungary 0.82%; Slovakia 0.58%; Bulgaria 0.34%; Croatia 0.33%; Slovenia 0.32%; Lithuania 0.31%; Luxembourg 0.25%; Latvia 0.19%; Estonia 0.16%; Cyprus 0.14% and Malta 0.07%.

This means that the United Kingdom contributed a similar amount to the EU budget (2016) as the collective contributions from the following eighteen (18) member states: Denmark, Ireland, Finland, Portugal, the Czech Republic, Greece, Romania, Hungary, Slovakia, Bulgaria, Croatia, Slovenia, Lithuania, Luxembourg, Latvia, Estonia, Cyprus and Malta.

The British people need to know that their country has a huge national debt burden of 85.8% of their gross domestic product (first quarter of 2018), whilst, according to Statista, provided 13.45% of the contributions to the EU budget (2016). The benevolent contributions are meant to raise the living standards of member states with 'weaker' economies, yet those benevolent member states with so-called 'stronger' economies, still get so many economic migrants from the 'poorer' member states, including serious criminals, under the 'free movement of people' principle.

Incidentally, it's very concerning that there were 4,600 criminals from other EU countries incarcerated in British jails (2017) and to 'add insult to injury' there has, apparently, been a commensurate reduction in the prison population of many Eastern European countries, such as Poland, with a reduction of 2,997 and Romania, with a reduction of 3,882, and Latvia, with a reduction of 3,092, since joining the EU. What an awful indictment on the uncontrolled 'free movement of people' principle, when the so-called 'poorer' countries, can join the European 'club' and export their criminals to the 'rich pickings' of the so-called 'richer' countries.

If there was ever a reason for the British people to vote to leave the European Union, the importing of East European criminals, who have increased the population of our already overcrowded prisons, whilst their own prisons experienced a significant reduction, is reason enough!

Whilst this information is dated, it's instructive to compare the financial contributions of member states to the EU annual budget (2011) and the total spending on those member states, including agricultural spending (which incorporates rural development and a small amount on fisheries), published by the Guardian Data blog website www.theguardian.com.

At one end of the scale, the net-contributors to the EU budget, such as Germany, contributed 19,671.10 million euros to the budget and received 12,132.98 million euros from the budget. France contributed 18,050.84 million euros and received 13,162.33 million euros. Italy contributed 14,366.22 million euros and received 9,585.87 million euros. The United Kingdom contributed 11,273.41 million euros and received 6,570.05 euros. The Netherlands contributed 3,933.27 million euros and received 2,064.32 million euros. Sweden contributed 2,866.65 million euros and received 1,757.02 million euros. Austria contributed 2,499.17 million euros and received 1,875.81 million euros. Denmark contributed 2,120.73 million euros and received 1,473.07 million euros and Finland contributed 1,802.80 million euros and received 1,293.00 million euros.

At the other end of the scale, the beneficiaries from the EU budget were Spain, which contributed 9,876.14 million euros and received 13,599.01 million euros. Greece contributed 1,762.03 million euros and received 6,536.93 million euros. Romania contributed

1,116.05 million euros and received 2,659.47 million euros. Portugal contributed 1,599.40 million euros and received 4,715.26 million euros. Poland contributed 3,227.80 million euros and received 14,440.60 million euros. Belgium contributed 3,345.49 million euros and received 6,796.71 million euros. The Czech Republic contributed 1,461.95 million euros and received 3,029.07 million euros. Ireland (Eire) contributed 1,138.96 million euros and received 1,639.45 million euros. Hungary contributed 836.43 million euros and received 5,330.92 million euros. Bulgaria contributed 346.07 million euros and received 1,107.11 million euros. Slovakia contributed 576.31 million euros and received 1,785.12 million euros. Slovenia contributed 326.94 million euros and received 846.98 million euros. Cyprus contributed 160.15 million euros and received 183.57 million euros. Latvia contributed 159.75 million euros and received 910.98 million euros. Estonia contributed 136.67 million euros and received 504.69 million euros. Luxembourg contributed 278.83 million euros and received 1,548.52 million euros. Lithuania contributed 257.44 million euros and received 1,652.80 million euros. Malta contributed 56.32 million euros and received 135.24 million euros and Croatia made no contribution but received 113.17 million euros.

The European Union agricultural spending (2011) of 43.8 billion euros, was the biggest item of spending in the EU budget, which incorporated rural development and a small amount on fisheries.

Incidentally, why would France, a net-contributor to the EU budget, send a contribution of 18,050.84 million euros to Brussels, for them to return 13,162.33 million euros, which included an agricultural subsidy of 8,679.88 million euros? Surely, the French could have decided on the extent of subsidies for their own farming and fisheries communities?

Why would Germany, a net-contributor to the EU budget, send a contribution of 19,671.10 million euros to Brussels, for them to return 12,132.98 million euros, including an agricultural subsidy of 5,498.09 million euros? Surely the Germans could have decided on the extent of subsidies for their own farming and fisheries communities?

Why would the United Kingdom, a significant net-contributor to the EU budget, send a contribution of 11,273.41 million euros to Brussels, for them to return 6,570.05 million euros, including an agricultural subsidy of 3,315.46 million euros? Surely the British could have decided on the extent of subsidies for their own farming and fisheries communities?

The other beneficiaries of the European Union agricultural subsidies were Denmark with 964.20 million euros; Ireland with 873.05 million euros; the Netherlands with 860.16 million euros; Romania with 795.70 million euros; Portugal with 760.95 million euros; Austria with 739.85 million euros; Sweden with 697.77 million euros; the Czech Republic with 667.95 million euros; Belgium with 556.89 million euros; Finland with 496.41 million euros; Bulgaria with 315.07 million euros; Slovakia with 296.91 million euros; Lithuania with 279.91 million euros; Latvia with 109.17 million euros; Slovenia with 108.68 million euros; Estonia with 74.79 million euros; Cyprus with 42 million euros; Luxembourg with 38.86 million euros and Malta with 4.39 million euros.

The above subsidies suggest that the EU is a multi-national welfare state, which takes from the 'richer' member states and donates to the 'poorer' member states, to stimulate industrial and commercial growth and increase employment opportunities and provide essential funding for infrastructure projects and payment of agricultural subsidies. The Baltic states of Latvia, Estonia and Lithuania, must have been very keen to join the Union, with these significant 'pots of gold' at the end of the rainbow. Latvia is a country of circa 1,949,670 citizens (2017), which according to the above, contributed 159.75 million euros and received 910.98 million euros (including an agricultural subsidy), a balance of 751.23 million euros (2011). Estonia is a country of circa 1,309,632 citizens (2017), which contributed 136.67 million euros and received 1,652.80 million euros, a balance of 1,516.13 million euros. Lithuania is a country of circa 2,890,297 citizens (2017), which contributed 257.44 million euros and received 1,652.80 million euros, a balance of 1,395.36 million euros.

There's no wonder that the many receiving countries of the European Union project, such as Latvia, Estonia and Lithuania, don't want the net-contributor or 'donor' countries, such as the United Kingdom, to leave the Union and withdraw their contributions and leave a black hole in the finances, which could mean a reduction in their generous subsidies.

Incidentally, the 'richer' countries, such as Germany, France and the United Kingdom, are all 'debtor nations' and they don't really have the spare capacity to provide financial support to the 'poorer' countries, which don't carry as much debt. According to EU standards, the national debt of member states should not exceed 60% of their gross domestic product (GDP), yet many member states far exceed that standard.

The national debt in member states, as a percentage of gross domestic product (GDP), in the first quarter of 2018, starting with those that exceed the 60% standard, was as follows: Greece 180.4%; Italy 133.4%; Portugal 126.4%; Belgium 106.3%; Spain 98.8%; France 97.7%; Cyprus 94.7%; United Kingdom 85.8%; Austria 77.2%; Croatia 76.2%; Slovenia 75.1%; Hungary 73.9%; Ireland 69.3% and Germany 62.9%.

The following member states, many of which are beneficiaries of the benevolent Brussels redistribution process, have the following levels of national debt, as a percentage of GDP, which do not exceed the EU standard of 60%: Finland 59.8%; Netherlands 55.2%; Poland 51.2%; Slovakia 50.8%; Malta 50.4%; Sweden 37.9%; Lithuania 36.3%; Denmark 36.2%; Latvia 35.8%; the Czech Republic 35.8%; Romania 34.4%; Bulgaria 24.1%; Luxembourg 22.2% and Estonia 8.7%.

It's instructive to note that member states, such as Latvia, Estonia and Lithuania, are significant beneficiaries of the Brussels largesse, yet they carry very little national debt, as follows: Latvia received a balance of 751,230,000 euros, yet they have a small national debt of 35.8% of GDP. Estonia received a balance of 1,516,130,000 euros, yet they have a very small national debt of 8.7% of GDP. Lithuania received a balance of 1,395,360,000, yet they have a small national debt of 36.3% of GDP.

Clearly, these so-called 'poorer' member states, appear to be in a stronger financial position, than their 'net-contributor' member states, which are borrowing to finance their membership contributions.

One of the biggest beneficiaries of the Brussels largesse, is Poland, which contributed 3,227,800,000 euros and received 14,440,600,000 euros, a positive boost to their economy of 11,212,800,000 euros, yet they have a relatively small national debt burden of 51.2% of their GDP. It's no wonder that their former prime minister, Donald Tusk, President of the European Council, was so abusive about the withdrawal of the UK from the EU, and the loss of their contribution! Another beneficiary of the EU largesse is Romania, which contributed 1,116,050,000 euros and received 2,659,470,000 euros, a boost to their economy of 1,543,420,000 euros, yet they have a small national debt burden of 34.4% of GDP. Bulgaria is another beneficiary, which contributed 346,070,000 euros and received 1,107,110,000 euros, a boost to their economy of 761,040,000 euros and a small national debt burden of 24.1% of GDP.

The UK was a major net-contributor to the EU budget, with a significant national debt burden, yet it supports countries such as Poland, Romania, Bulgaria, Latvia, Estonia and Lithuania, with much less national debt, and simultaneously gets thousands of economic immigrants from those countries, under the uncontrolled 'free movement of people' principle.

Incidentally, the Labour Party, under the dubious leadership of Jeremy Corbyn and his Marxist cohorts, gave a solemn pledge in its manifesto, prior to the 2017 General Election, that 'Labour accepts the result of the referendum' and that the 'freedom of movement will end', yet they are now campaigning as a remain party! This volte-face should be treated with serious contempt by the British people at the next general election.

This is a party which constantly complains about Conservative austerity measures, to deal with the serious 'overspending' of the New Labour government, who when leaving office (2010), left a hand-written note to the new Conservative government, apologising for running out of money!

So far as immigration is concerned, Lord Andrew Green of Migration Watch recently said: "Southern European youth unemployment was astronomical and that's why they come here for employment and so far as Eastern Europe is concerned, particularly Romania and Bulgaria, he suggested that they come here because their standard of living is about a quarter of ours." Furthermore, Oxford University's 'Migration Observatory', based on an analysis of the official 'Labour Force Survey' reported that more than 250,000 Romanians and Bulgarian nationals live in the United Kingdom, a figure that rose by almost 50,000 in recent times. The following number of immigrants who registered for National Insurance numbers in the year to June 2014 included 103,000 Romanians, which is up 468% on the previous year and 31,000 Bulgarians, which is up 205% and 98,000 Poles, which is down 7%.

The whole point of the European Union project, which redistributes wealth from the 'richer' countries, to the 'poorer' countries, a form of multi-national welfare state, is to help to raise the living standards of those 'poorer' countries. Consequently, their people should stay in their countries to help with the redevelopment process, not 'jump ship' to take advantage of the higher living standards in the 'richer' countries.

Many of these so-called 'richer' member states carry a serious national debt burden, and can't really afford to finance the redevelopment of the 'poorer' countries, which don't carry such a serious national debt. The 'richer' member states are effectively borrowing the money, and creating national debt, to finance their largesse to the 'poorer' member states, and then they are required to receive thousands of their economic migrants.

So, this leads us onto the flawed 'free movement of people' across 'open borders' principle of the European Union political elite, which could eventually bring down this fragile project of the European political class.

This was one of the main reasons why the British people voted to leave the European Union (2016). However, had their reasonable concerns about the 'free movement of people' been properly addressed by the obdurate European political class, the people may have voted to remain.

5

THE 'FREE MOVEMENT OF PEOPLE'

According to Eurostat 'Migration and migrant population statistics' (March 2018), Germany reported the largest number of immigrants (arrivals) in 2016 (1,029,900), followed by the United Kingdom (589,000), Spain (414,700), France (378,100) and Italy (300,800).

Germany also reported the highest number of emigrants (leavers) in 2016 (533,800), followed by the United Kingdom (340,400), Spain (327,300), France (309,800), Poland (236,400) and Romania (207,600). A total of twenty-one EU member states reported more immigration (arrivals) than emigration (leavers) in 2016, however, in Bulgaria, Croatia, Latvia, Lithuania, Poland, Portugal and Romania the number of emigrants (leavers) outnumbered immigrants (arrivals), which is not surprising.

Furthermore, it's not xenophobic (a hatred of foreigners) for the British people to question the logic of subsidising 'weaker' European economies, such as Bulgaria and Romania, through the EU budget, whilst receiving a significant number of economic migrants from those same countries.

Uncontrolled immigration from the 'poorer' to the 'richer' member states, under the 'free movement of people' principle, and the provision of financial support to grow their economy, is a 'double whammy' for the donor states. Consequently, the Eurocrats must ensure that recipient countries can either have financial support to stimulate their economies and raise their living standards or allow an exodus of their citizens to donor states, but they can't have both. In other words, they 'can't have their cake and eat it'. It is, of course, not unusual for the citizens of 'poorer' countries to emigrate to 'richer' countries, to improve their living standards, but Brussels must modify the 'free movement of people' principle, to ensure that the 'richer' donor states are not abused.

To understand the public concern about immigration from the European Union, under the 'free movement of people' principle and refugees from elsewhere in the world, Lord Andrew Green of Migration Watch recently suggested that before New Labour came to power (1997), net migration was circa 50,000 per year, and during their term of office (1997-2010) it peaked at circa 320,000 per year, which put an enormous strain on our public services. Lord Green said that we needed temporary relief from the 'free movement of people', which is a basic principle of membership of the European Union. He also said that Southern European youth unemployment was 'astronomical' and that's why they come here for jobs. However, so far as Eastern Europe is concerned, particularly Romania and Bulgaria, he suggested that they come here because their standard of living is about a quarter of ours. When asked what would be an acceptable level of net immigration (per year), he said 70,000, which means that we could welcome 120,000 immigrants to our country, on the understanding that 50,000 people would probably leave.

We were recently informed by Oxford University's respected Migration Observatory, based on an analysis of the official 'Labour Force Survey', that more than 250,000 Romanian and Bulgarian nationals live in the United Kingdom, a figure that rose by almost 50,000 in recent times. The number of immigrants from Romania and Bulgaria currently living in the United Kingdom (2018), are approaching the number of people who live in the conurbation of Wolverhampton, with 255,945 citizens (2016).

When we wonder why so many East Europeans come to our country, often for low-paid work, the following wage comparisons from 'Open Europe' shows that a low-paid Polish worker, with no children, would get a minimum wage of £114 per week in Poland and £290 per week in the UK, consisting of the minimum wage and working tax credits. After taking away working tax credits, the worker would get £197 per week.

The following are the number of immigrants, from the European Union, who registered for National Insurance numbers, in the year to

June 2014: Romanians 103,000, which is up 468% on the previous year; Bulgarians 31,000, which is up 205%; Polish 98,000, which is down 7%; Spanish 46,000, which is down 9%; and Italians 45,000, which is up 16%.

So far as employment is concerned the Office of National Statistics (ONS) reported that in the year to June 2014, there were 2.9 million non-UK nationals employed, which was an increase of 9% on the previous year. They also reported that 1.7 million EU nationals were employed in the UK, which is an increase of 16% on the previous year. However, to keep things in perspective, the Department of Work and Pensions (DWP) announced (2015) that 11.7% of those on 'job-seekers allowance' and 5.8% of those claiming 'incapacity benefits' were non-UK nationals and of the 5.3 million who claimed 'working age benefits' 395,000 were non-UK nationals. It's concerning that 5.8% of those claiming 'incapacity benefits' are not British citizens, which suggests that we are importing foreign nationals to claim incapacity benefits, rather than employment.

More recently, the Department of Work and Pensions (DWP) released official figures of the allocation of National Insurance numbers for foreign nationals, during a period when the employment rate was at a record high of 75.6%. They allocated 826,000 National Insurance numbers to adult overseas nationals in 2015/16 of which 630,000 (76%) were from the EU and 195,000 from elsewhere. The allocation of a National Insurance number is to authorise work or claim benefits or tax credits. They also issued 683,000 National Insurance numbers to adult overseas nationals in the year to December 2017, of which 497,000 (73%) were from the EU. The top five nationalities from the EU were Romanian (154,000); Poland (62,000); Italy (51,000); Bulgaria (39,000); and Spain (36,000). Incidentally, of the 185,000 non-EU immigrants, 32,000 were from India; 12,000 were from Pakistan; 11,000 were from Australia; 11,000 were from China; and 10,000 were from the USA. Nationalities with the largest increase in registrations in the year to December 2017 were 4,000 from Iran (up 27%); 4,000 from Turkey (up 24%); and 2,000 from Iraq (up 35%).

The EU bureaucrats should have recognised these economic and social challenges on the so-called 'richer' member states, which often have a serious national debt and are often living well beyond their means. Consequently, they should have listened to the concerns of the British people and introduced some restrictions on the 'free movement of people' from the 'poorer' to the 'richer' member states, in accordance with their capacity to absorb them, in addition to many refugees from elsewhere.

This 'free movement of people' across 'open borders' principle, is clearly necessary, when the ultimate 'clandestine' destination of the EU is a country called Europe or the United States of Europe. However, there should still be some restrictions on the free movement of people, because of the economic disparities between the member states and the pressure from the global refugee crisis, where there are so many military conflicts and human rights abuses and so many displaced people seeking refuge.

Incidentally, according to government figures, there were 9,066 foreign criminals in British jails (2018) and just 1,583 foreign criminals have been removed from the UK in the past four years, despite having agreements with about 70 countries to send them home. The Prime Minister, Theresa May, said the following, in response to a question from a parliamentary select committee: "Foreign nationals who commit crimes here, should be in no doubt of our determination to deport them."

Furthermore, the Government admitted last year (2017) that they had lost track of almost 500 foreign criminals who were facing deportation after serving prison sentences during the previous two years. We are told that 494 foreign criminals absconded while they were subject to deportation orders from 2014 to the end of March 2016. The figures also reveal a steep rise in the number of Albanian criminals in our jails with 742 criminals compared to 492 the previous year. Poland remains top of the list with 822 prisoners, down from 965 in 2016. Ireland is third on the list with 720 prisoners, down from 762 (2016) and Romania is fourth with 644 prisoners. Under current laws, offenders from outside the EU, jailed for more than twelve months, are referred for automatic deportation, and those from the EU can also be deported after two years or one year if the conviction is for a sex attack. However, not surprisingly, these foreign criminals can appeal against deportation and in many cases disappear while awaiting deportation. The Ministry of Justice advised that it had removed 6,000 foreign offenders last year (2017) and more than 44,000 since 2010, which illustrates the problem of processing foreign criminals who should not be in the country and offenders from elsewhere in the EU who are allowed to move freely across twenty-eight different countries under the EU 'free movement of people' principle.

Do the political class, who manage the European Union, have any idea of the challenges of law enforcement, when terrorists and other dangerous criminals can move freely across open borders of member states? Do they understand the challenges of law enforcement, when police officers are confronted with so many foreign criminals who do not or will not speak their language? Do they understand the challenges of the criminal justice system, when serious criminals are bailed to court or deportation proceedings, and disappear across the open borders of the European Union, without any satisfactory means of monitoring their movements?

The numbers of foreign criminals in United Kingdom prisons (2018), according to the Home Office figures are as follows; Poland 822; Albania 742; Ireland 720; Romania 644; Jamaica 483; Lithuania 382; Pakistan 333; Somalia 293; Portugal 253; India 244; Nigeria 239; Iraq 199; Netherlands 167; Iran 165; Zimbabwe 158; Bangladesh 142; Vietnam 140; Latvia 125; Afghanistan 124 and Slovakia 108.

Whilst the 'free movement of people' across 'open borders' principle is essential for the development of a country called Europe or the 'United States of Europe', it does nothing for the internal security of the member states, when unknown criminals are 'free to roam' and 'free to abscond', across the wide-open national borders of member states. How can the authorities keep track of these mobile criminals, who are a threat to their people, and can come and go as they please, without the authorities being able to record their nefarious movements and without them having easy access to their criminal or vehicle records, in their country of origin?

Opponents of the 'free movement of people' principle are often labelled as xenophobic, which means a fear or hatred of strangers or foreigners. This is disrespectful to ordinary citizens who consider it important to control mass immigration and its economic and social consequences. Surely, no reasonable person welcomes the uncontrolled free movement of dangerous criminals across so many member states. Surely, no one can welcome the complexity of dealing with so many foreign criminals on the streets or the challenge of so many foreign criminals in our prisons.

Incidentally, the socialist New Labour Government (1997-2010) had the opportunity to restrict the influx of economic migrants from the expanded European Union in 2004 but chose to lift controls on Eastern European migrants, one of the very few countries in the EU to do so. They estimated, or probably 'guessed', that less than 13,000 migrants would come to the United Kingdom each year, but the numbers were nearer 130,000 per year, which is a conservative estimate. The former New Labour Cabinet Minister, Jack Straw, later admitted that it was a 'spectacular mistake' for the New Labour Government to throw open its borders in this way, when most EU countries retained controls for a further seven years.

It is suggested that had the New Labour Government not taken the country into the Iraq War, which displaced millions of people, and not allowed immediate access to the new East European migrants, which compounded the arrival of thousands of refugees from elsewhere in the world, the people would not have been so concerned about immigration and there would have been no need for a referendum to leave the Union.

Whilst managed immigration can produce significant economic benefits, uncontrolled immigration of those who don't or won't speak English, can put an intolerable strain onto public services of the receiving country and can lead to feelings of xenophobia from the indigenous population. New Labour probably saw the East European economic migrants as a form of social engineering, which would benefit their socialist cause, as most East Europeans have been unfamiliar with liberalism or conservatism. New Labour's decision to remove the sensible restrictions on East European migrants, was not as innocent as a 'spectacular mistake'.

What the British government joined in 1973, and was confirmed in a referendum in 1975, was a Western European free-trade bloc, called the European Economic Community (EEC) or the Common Market, which through a series of treaties, morphed into the European Union (EU). This was a project of the European political elite, without the approval of the people, where member states gradually lose their independence, as they move 'ever closer' towards a country called Europe. This multi-national super-state project will have an elected European president, a European Central Bank (ECB), a single currency (Euro) and the free movement of its citizens, which are the basic requirements of any country.

Incidentally, supporters of the EU say that the existence of the European Union has created peace and stability throughout Europe over the past sixty years, since the Second World War. However, they make no mention of the damage to peace and stability in the Middle East and North Africa, with wars involving European armies, often in support of the USA. The western military interventions in Afghanistan and Iraq and the conflicts in Yemen, Somalia, Eritrea, Egypt, Libya and Morocco, have destabilised the two regions and displaced millions of innocent people, many of whom have sought refuge in western and northern Europe.

The massive displacement of 'Muslims' from the above conflicts, to northern European 'Christian' countries, has probably created the circumstances for a 'clash of civilisations' rather than the evolutionary assimilation and integration of diverse cultures, traditions and religions.

Whilst the humanitarian instincts of civilised northern European liberal western democracies, is to accept thousands of vulnerable refugees from devastated war zones, the uncivilised, radical, Islamic terrorist group, known as ISIS (Islamic State of Iraq and Syria), made it clear that they intended to infiltrate the refugee population and wreak 'death and destruction' onto nonbelievers in those benevolent receiving countries. The ISIS threats of death and destruction did materialise in France, Belgium, Germany, Sweden and Great Britain and elsewhere, causing mistrust between the indigenous and immigrant populations.

Whilst managed immigration can produce economic and social benefits, in countries which encourage integration and assimilation, unmanaged immigration and the 'free movement of people' across 'open borders' in the European Union, can cause serious economic and social damage.

The recent referendum decision of the United Kingdom voters to leave the European Union, was, to a certain extent, instigated by the social problems caused by the 'free movement of people' across the 'open borders' of the European Union and made much worse by the exodus of vulnerable refugees from the war-torn countries of the Middle East and North Africa, mainly to the 'wealthy' industrial countries of western and northern Europe, such as Germany, France, Italy and Great Britain.

There are not many refugees and asylum seekers heading for the 'poorer' Eastern European countries of the European Union, such as Romania, Bulgaria, Slovakia, Hungary, Estonia, Latvia or Lithuania, which is quite understandable. In fact, at least one of these East European countries, Hungary, has resisted refugee redistribution quotas prepared by the European Commission, saying that they are not an immigrant country.

Whilst the EU Commissioners knew that the benevolent British people were concerned about the adverse social effects of the 'free movement of people' within the European Union, which is compounded by vulnerable refugees from the Middle East and North Africa, they were not prepared to reform the principle, which was linked to the free movement of goods and services, in the free-trade area. In other words, to be part of the 'single market', member states must accept the principle of the 'free movement of goods, services and people'. Their refusal to moderate the adverse social effects of the 'free movement of people' across the 'open borders', from the 'poorer' to the 'richer' countries, together with the perpetual motion towards 'ever-closer' union, contributed to more than seventeen million (17,410,742) British people voting to leave the Union.

No one should have any concerns about the free movement of labour, when there are jobs and housing available for the workers. However, the free movement of dependent families, from the 'poorer' to the 'richer' European countries, when there are few jobs and few houses available, results in a strain on the essential public services, such as education, health, welfare and housing, in countries which have no spare capacity.

Something that we should be concerned about is the 'free movement of people' or economic migrants, from the European Union or elsewhere, who were not able to find employment and they find themselves homeless and on the mean streets (in a foreign country) and get involved in crime.

The tragedy is that any citizen who is genuinely concerned about the negative consequences of uncontrolled immigration is labelled racist and xenophobic by the liberal media and many of those who voted to remain. It's not individual immigrants who are the problem, regardless of their ethnicity or religion, it's the sheer numbers of dependent immigrants.

There are more than one million Poles living in Britain and there are now more Romanians living in Britain than Irish, which is remarkable. The foreign-born population of Britain is approaching ten million. In Boston, in Lincolnshire, foreign-born nationals make up 29% of the local population. It's no wonder that the Boston residents voted overwhelmingly to leave the Union. Yet the dysfunctional Labour Party have suggested that they would throw open the doors even wider, but they will say whatever they've got to say or 'sit on the fence', to attract votes!

It's understandable that the people are concerned about the enormous numbers of immigrants arriving in our country, when we had about 333,000 (net) in one year (2015). We would have had to build a town, bigger than Wolverhampton, with a population of 255,945 (2016), every year to accommodate so many immigrants and we haven't done so.

If we had been aware of the numbers of immigrants wanting to come to our country, we should have planned to build thousands of private and public houses and for the availability of planners and architects and builders and tradesmen. We should have planned to build new schools, colleges and universities and for the availability of teachers and lecturers and support services. We should have planned to build new doctors' surgeries, medical centres and hospitals and for the availability of doctors and nurses and support staff. We should have planned to build new police stations and for the availability of police officers and support staff and we should have planned for the building of shops, restaurants, offices, factories and warehouses, for the workers from the immigrant communities, and the harsh reality is that we have not done so.

This lack of forward planning means that thousands of immigrants are distributed around the country, to reduce the social impact, but the sheer numbers of immigrants put pressure onto already overstretched public services. We cannot accept thousands of 'dependent' immigrants who need housing, when we have a shortage of housing and many of our own people are homeless and are often begging on the streets. We cannot accept thousands of immigrants who need jobs, when so many of our own people are unemployed and exist on welfare. We cannot accept thousands of young immigrants, who need school places, when they can't speak the language, which places a severe burden on the teachers and support staff and reduces the time spent with our own children. We cannot accept thousands of immigrants who need medical treatment when our doctors and nurses and support staff are working under so much pressure.

The Brexit vote should mean that when we leave the European Union, we will not have to conform to the 'free movement of people' principle, to the extent that we will not have to provide EU citizens with essential public services (other than where we have reciprocal arrangements) and we must ensure that immigrants seeking jobs can maintain themselves. This is just straight-forward common sense, as our social welfare budget is oversubscribed, and we have funded a National Health Service (NHS), not an International Health Service, and we carry a large national debt.

The uncontrolled 'free movement of people' across 'open borders' and the movement towards 'ever-closer' union and a federal country called Europe, were the main reasons why the British people voted to leave the European Union, and their unexpected decision must be respected by the Westminster and Brussels political elite. Those we elect to represent us in the 'corridors of power' must respect the 'will of the British people'.

6

IT'S THE 'WILL OF THE BRITISH

PEOPLE'

In our increasingly fragile democracy, our elected representatives must be constantly reminded of the words of Thomas Jefferson, President of the USA (1801-1809), that: "The will of the people is the only legitimate foundation of any government and to protect its free expression should be our first objective." We should also remind our politicians of the saying that 'democracy grows from the bottom up and dies from the top down'.

There is no point in our political representatives asking the people to make a decision on one of the most important constitutional matters of our day and then rejecting their inconvenient answer, which was the case with many parliamentarians, who rejected the result of the referendum and campaigned for a second referendum. Their unacceptable behaviour was a 'slap in the face' to the concept of a 'people's democracy', yet they campaigned for a second referendum, which they call a 'people's vote'. What exactly was the first referendum, if it wasn't a 'people's vote'?

It was also interesting to note the views of the well-respected philosopher, A. C. Grayling, in his recent book *Democracy and its Crisis* published by Oneworld Publications in 2017, in which he said: "The Brexit referendum on 23rd June 2016 is an example of how the constitutional and political order of the UK is in a highly questionable state … it is arguable that the EU referendum itself and the governments subsequent actions resemble something like a coup … the EU membership referendum franchise excluded … sixteen and seventeen year olds, expatriate British citizens who had lived abroad for more than a certain number of years and EU citizens resident in the UK and paying their taxes there. It would seem obvious that all these groups should have been included, as having the most material interest in the outcome of the vote … it is in the public domain that seventeen million voted for Brexit, sixteen million opposed it and thirty-two million did not vote. Proponents of Brexit constantly iterate the 'will of the people' claim … the basis of their claim is only 37% of the electorate which represents 26% of the people … the population of the UK."

On the contrary, this was the largest number of British people to vote for anything in the history of our elections and referendums, yet A. C. Grayling disparages the result by alleging it was 'something like a coup' and that sixteen- and seventeen-year-olds were excluded, when they are not of legal voting age. He also refers to expatriate British citizens who had lived abroad for a certain number of years, not being able to vote, but there was no criticism of the last Scottish independence referendum, which excluded circa 800,000 Scottish-born citizens, who lived elsewhere in the United Kingdom, who were not able to vote on the future of their beloved homeland. He also suggests that the 'government's subsequent actions resembled something like a coup'. An alternative view would be to congratulate the government for accepting the 'will of the people' and attempting to extricate our country from the European Union, against the resistance from our parliamentarians.

Incidentally, parliament voted by a large majority to give the people their say, on this crucial constitutional matter, and accepted the decision of the British people, when they voted, by a large majority, to invoke Article 50, to start the withdrawal process. He also 'waters down' the 51.8% of those who voted, who voted to leave the EU, to be just 37% of the total electorate (including those who did not vote) and to be just 26% of the total population (including those who are not eligible to vote). This is an attack on our respected electoral system, which in the eyes of the dogmatic remainers, did not produce the desired result of remaining as a satellite state of the distant European Union.

It is suggested that had the result of the Brexit referendum been to remain in the EU, the 'status quo', the 'leavers', now known as the 'Brexiteers', would have accepted the result and got on with the rest of their lives. As democrats, they would have reluctantly accepted the 'will of the people'.

However, the staunch 'remainers' have rejected the result of the Brexit referendum and have vociferously campaigned for a second referendum, to overturn the result of the first referendum, which begs the question, should they win a second referendum, would the leavers then demand a third referendum, which would create the farce of the 'best of three'? It is, however, suggested, that another vote would produce a similar result, as it would be very difficult to change the minds of 1,269,501 people from 'leave' to 'remain', unless they would be happy with a smaller majority!

Incidentally, there appears to be no doubt that the vociferous 'remain campaigners' were being supported by the Brussels political elite, who did not want the net-contributor United Kingdom to leave the European Union, as it could have a 'domino effect' with other member states who want constitutional reform and are not supporters of a federal Europe.

It should, of course, be noted that the European political elite have a long track record of reversing the 'will of the people' in those member states which had the temerity to challenge their grand project. On numerous occasions, the Brussels machine has forced member states to call a second referendum, because they did not agree with the inconvenient result of the first referendum, which affected their grand project, and that's not respecting the 'will of the people' and that's not democracy.

In 1992 the people of Denmark voted not to ratify the Maastricht Treaty, which set out terms for greater European integration, but the people were forced to vote again to achieve a yes vote. The first Danish referendum was held on 2nd June 1992 and 50.7% voted against, on a turnout of 83.1%. The second referendum was held on 18th May 1993 and 56.7% voted in favour, on a turnout of 86.5%, having received concessions.

The French government held a referendum on the Maastricht Treaty on 20th September 1992 and 51% voted in favour of the Treaty and 49% against the Treaty, and there was, of course, no need for a re-run!

In 2001 the people of Ireland rejected the Treaty of Nice, with 53.9% against, on a turnout of 34.8%, which suggests a high degree of 'voter apathy'. They were required to vote again on 19th October 2002, having received concessions, and 62.9% voted in favour, on a turnout of 49.5%.

In 2008 the Irish voters rejected the Lisbon Treaty, which created the framework for a country called Europe, but they were persuaded to change their minds. The first referendum was held on 12th June 2008 and 53.2% voted against, on a turnout of 53.1%. The second referendum was held on 2nd October 2009 and 67.1% voted in favour on a turnout of 59%, having received certain guarantees from the European political elite.

Since the British electorate voted to remain in the European Economic Community (EEC) in 1975, there have been many treaties which moved the community towards 'ever-closer' union and a country called Europe, but the political elite have not been straight with the British people.

Was Prime Minister Edward Heath aware of the following comments of the French economist Jean Monnet and the French Foreign Minister Robert Schuman, who are known as the founding fathers of the European Union, when he took us into the European Economic Community (EEC) or the Common Market in 1973, without consulting the people? Was he aware of the Schuman declaration of 9th May 1950, which is believed to be the founding text of European integration? The declaration included the following: "Europe will not be made all at once, or according to a single plan. It will be built through concrete achievements, which first create a de facto solidarity. The coming together of the nations of Europe requires the elimination of the opposition of France and Germany... The pooling of coal and steel production should immediately provide for the setting-up of common foundations for economic development, as a first step in the federation of Europe." Was he aware of the following quote attributed to Jean Monnet, on 30th April 1952? "Europe's nations should be guided towards the super state, without their people understanding what is happening. This can be accomplished by successive steps, each disguised as having an economic purpose, but which will eventually and irreversibly lead to federation." If Edward Heath was aware that the ultimate destination of the Common Market was a federal European Union super-state, then he should have informed the unsuspecting British people, and given them a referendum, to decide whether they wanted to lose their 'hard-won' status as an independent nation state.

Furthermore, was Prime Minister Harold Wilson aware of the ultimate destination of this political project, according to the founding fathers, when he gave the British people a referendum (1975) to confirm our membership of the European Economic Community or Common Market?

We must also ask whether Prime Ministers John Major (Conservative) and Gordon Brown (New Labour) were aware of the ultimate destination of this ambitious project of the European political elite, according to the founding fathers Jean Monnet and Robert Schuman, as they signed the Maastricht Treaty (1992) and the Lisbon Treaty (2009), without reference to the people. Prime Minister John Major refused to hold a referendum on the Maastricht Treaty, despite a great deal of clamour for him to do so, and Prime Minister Gordon Brown denied the people a referendum on the Lisbon Treaty, despite a party manifesto commitment to do so.

It was, however, the emergence of the United Kingdom Independence Party (UKIP), under the leadership of Nigel Farage, a Member of the European Parliament (MEP), which brought the matter to the surface.

Without the popularity of the United Kingdom Independence Party, Prime Minister David Cameron would not have given the British people a referendum on our continued membership of the European Union (2016).

It's important, therefore, to look at the history of the European project, from the aftermath of the Second World War, when the allies created a joint plan for a liberated and united Europe or a United States of Europe.

7

A BRIEF HISTORY OF THE

EUROPEAN PROJECT

This is a brief reminder of how the European Union (EU) grand project emerged, after the devastating events of the Second World War, and the consensus of the allies that future generations must be spared the scourge of war and that (extreme) nationalism (or fascism) must be suppressed.

In February 1945, in the aftermath of the Second World War, Franklin D. Roosevelt, the President of the United States of America (USA), Winston Churchill, Prime Minister of Great Britain, and Joseph Stalin, the Soviet Union Premier, marked out a joint plan for a liberated Europe. This initiative was the beginning of a grand narrative of a unified Western European bloc, which would be a bulwark against Soviet aggression.

The first stage in the long process towards a United States of Europe was the 'Marshal Plan' (1948), which was known as the 'European Recovery Programme', which distributed $13 billion of USA aid across ravished Western Europe, which had at its heart, the aim of a united Europe, which the USA, under President Harry Truman and Secretary of State George Marshal, thought would attract some eastern satellite (communist) states away from the Russians (USSR) and, remarkably, they were right.

In May 1950, two years after the 'Marshal Plan', France's Foreign Minister, Robert Schuman, laid bare the vision of European unity when he said: "Europe will not be made all at once or according to a single plan. It will be built through concrete achievements, which first create a de facto solidarity." The Robert Schuman declaration had been drafted by French diplomat Jean Monnet, paving the way for the Treaty of Paris in 1951, which brought together France, West Germany, Italy, Belgium, Luxembourg and the Netherlands, to establish the 'European Coal and Steel Community' under the presidency of Jean Monnet.

In 1955 Jean Monnet set up the 'Action Committee for the United States of Europe', aiming for nothing less than a European super-state, which was supported by the United States of America, pushing the Europeans down the federalist road, to mirror the most powerful nation on earth.

In 1957 the Treaty of Rome transformed the six nations of the European Coal and Steel Community into the European Economic Community (EEC) or the Common Market. It's suggested, that this multi-national super-state project was not widely understood by the British people, who would later vote to remain in the European Economic Community or the Common Market, in a referendum (1975), thinking that they were part of a secure Western European trading bloc, not being aware of the wider political and economic objectives to create a United States of Europe.

We should, therefore, revisit Article 2 of the Treaty of Rome (1957) which established the European Economic Community (EEC) and said: "The Community shall have as its task, by establishing a Common Market and progressively approximating the economic policies of member states, to promote throughout the Community, a harmonious development of economic activities, a continuous and balanced expansion, an increase in stability and accelerated raising of standards of living and closer relations between the (member) states." The key words of Article 2 are 'closer relations between the states' which is very similar to the more recent use of the words 'ever-closer' union by the EU political elite.

The British people were taken into the European Economic Community (EEC), or the Common Market, without reference to the people. They were led to believe that they were joining an economic community of Western European nations, with no knowledge of the ambitions of the European political elite to create a European Union super-state.

The 'United Kingdom European Communities' membership referendum, also known as the 'European Economic Community' (EEC) membership referendum, and the 'Common Market' membership referendum, took place on 5th June 1975, to gauge support for our continued membership of the European Communities (EC) or the 'Common Market', which we joined on 1st January 1973 (without a referendum) under the leadership of the Conservative Prime Minister, Edward Heath. The result was that a significant 17,378,581 (67.23%) citizens voted to remain in the Common Market or the European Economic Community (EEC) and 8,470,073 (32.77%) voted to leave, with a turnout of 64.62% or 25,903,194 citizens.

It's, perhaps, relevant to note that the author voted to remain in the European Economic Community (EEC) or the Common Market, in the 1975 referendum, without any knowledge of the wider political ambitions of the European political elite, and would do so again, but only if it was to remain as a European economic community. It's only in recent times that the author has become aware of the 'clandestine' motivation of the European political elite, to create a federal country called Europe.

It's interesting to note that the 1975 referendum was called by the Labour Government, under Prime Minister Harold Wilson, and the voters were asked the question: "Do you think that the United Kingdom should stay in the European Community (the Common Market)? Labour also produced a public information pamphlet, which said: "Now the time has come for you to decide. The government will accept your decision, whatever way it goes." The Labour Party had pledged, in its general election manifesto (1974), to renegotiate the terms of our accession to the Common Market or European Community (EC) or European Economic Community (EEC) and to consult (referendum) the public on whether we should stay in the community on the new terms, if they were acceptable to the government.

They did not, however, inform the unsuspecting people of the intentions of the European political elite, to create a federal United States of Europe.

It's interesting to compare the statement of the old Labour

government (1975), that they would accept the decision of the public, whatever way it went, and their negative resistance to the unexpected result of the British referendum on our continued membership of the European Union (2016), including the lack of clarity of the current Labour 'resistance movement'.

It's also very interesting to note that the Scottish National Party (SNP), together with Plaid Cymru, the Ulster Unionists, the National Front and the Communist Party, voted to leave the European Community (EC) or the European Economic Community (EEC) or Common Market (1975), yet their current leader, Nicola Sturgeon, has been so bellicose about the unexpected referendum vote to leave the European Union (EU) (2016).

Why would the Scottish National Party (SNP) be so keen to leave the eminently sensible Common Market or European Economic Community (EEC), an economic community of twelve Western European trading nations, that's Germany, France, Italy, Spain, Belgium, the Netherlands, Denmark, Ireland, Greece, Portugal, Luxembourg and the United Kingdom, yet they are now so keen to remain in the European Union, consisting of twenty-eight Western, Southern and Eastern European nations, moving inexorably towards a United States of Europe?

To illustrate the level of hypocrisy of the Scottish National Party (SNP), one of the most ardent supporters of the European Union super-state project, is the SNP MP for North East Fife, Stephen Gethins, who is a member of the 'People's Vote' campaign group, calling for a public vote on the final Brexit deal. Stephen Gethins has the cheek to challenge the Brexit majority of 1,269,501 votes, when he won his parliamentary seat by just two votes! In the 2017 General Election, he got 13,743 votes, as the SNP candidate, with 13,741 votes for the Liberals and 10,088 for the Conservatives. To put it another way, 13,743 citizens of North East Fife voted for the SNP candidate, who won the seat, yet 28,079 citizens voted for another candidate! The reality is that the electorate voted against him by a majority of 14,336 votes, yet he won the election and is now the member for North East Fife. The irony is that having won the election by just two votes and having lost the 'popular vote' by 14,336 votes, he has the temerity to oppose the 'will of the British people', who voted to leave the European Union project by a large majority of 1,269,501 votes!

Another fundamental move towards the European Union, was the 1992 Maastricht Treaty (The Treaty of the European Union), which brought the European Union into existence and set a timetable for economic and monetary union and the introduction of the single currency (Euro) and established EU citizenship, which allowed EU citizens to move freely between member states. Whilst the treaty was mainly about the single currency, the overall treaty was leading towards a political entity in Europe, with a European government and a European state. It was not widely known by the people of the European Economic Community (EEC) that the Maastricht Treaty created a state-like bureaucracy in Brussels, under the dubious leadership of the unelected European political elite.

As well as paving the way for a common currency, the treaty made the twelve member states share economic, social and security policies. The political and economic strings of the European Union were being pulled by the unelected officials in Brussels. The gap between governance and the governed was getting even greater. Suddenly we had all these rules we had to follow and standards we had to meet. In 1999 when the euro was launched, it energised 'nationalist' parties to oppose the project and they were labelled 'right-wing' extremists by the Brussels political elite.

It is, however, important to note that the Maastricht Treaty (1992), was one of the final 'nails in the coffin' of the European Economic Community (EEC) or the Common Market, and was approved by the United Kingdom parliament, under a Conservative Government and Prime Minister John Major, without reference to the British people.

It is, therefore, necessary to revisit the circumstances surrounding the approval of the Maastricht Treaty (1992) by the European political elite and our own Conservative Government, under the leadership of Prime Minister John Major, who was responsible for the transfer of significant powers to the European Union, without reference to the British people, and despite a major 'resistance movement' wanting a public referendum.

8

THE MAASTRICHT TREATY (1992)

The Maastricht Treaty was signed by the twelve member states on 7th February 1992, and came into force on 1st November 1993, and changed the European Economic Community (EEC) or the Common Market, into the European Union (EU) under Article 2, which said: "This treaty marks a new stage in the process of creating an ever-closer union among the peoples of Europe…" This was a dramatic change from an economic community to a political union, mainly without reference to the people.

Surely the British people should have been given a referendum on such an important treaty, which was changing the community from a sensible European Economic Community (EEC) or Common Market, through 'ever-closer' union, to the European Union (EU), with the ultimate 'clandestine' destination of a federal United States of Europe.

It's interesting to note that twenty-two Conservative MPs rebelled against their own government for refusing to grant a referendum on the Maastricht Treaty, which was another huge transfer of power to Brussels. These twenty-two rebels were called 'bastards' by the then Conservative Prime Minister, John Major, who years later referred to the result of the Brexit 'democratic' public referendum as the 'tyranny of the majority'.

It's also interesting to note that Norris McWhirter and Rodney Atkinson wrote the book *Treason at Maastricht, The Destruction of the Nation State*, published by Compuprint Publishing (1994), which said: "The entire British legal system has been subordinated to the

European Court, a fact so frustratingly evident to our judges. The British people have had their passports taken away and been turned into European citizens, with obligations and duties towards the European Union... The British parliament may discuss policies and pass motions but in virtually any area of economic, social, industrial relations, environment, energy, fishing, agriculture, trade, pensions and employment policy, it must defer to Europe. The laws of the United Kingdom are now made in the form of directives and regulations from Brussels, without having ever been proposed in the election manifesto of a British political party and for the most part not even debated by the Westminster parliament. UK laws can (now) be suspended by the European Court – a court which, by its own admission, is dedicated to promoting European Integration. The court creates new laws... and the British people are powerless to resist."

The biggest culprit in this dubious political saga, taking our citizens from the pragmatic European Economic Community (EEC) or the Common Market, to the European Union super-state, with a federal government, a central bank (ECB), a single currency (euro), and the 'free movement of people' across 'open borders', and the final destination of a United States of Europe, is former Prime Minister John Major, who refused to give the people a referendum on the crucial Maastricht Treaty (1992).

Incidentally, the Danes were given a referendum on the Maastricht Treaty on 2nd June 1992 and they rejected the treaty by 50.7%, on a turnout of 83.1%. The Danish rejection was thought to be a blow to the process of European integration. However, the Danes were required to have a second referendum, which was held on 18th May 1993 and, having been granted four exceptions to the treaty, they approved the treaty by 56.7% on a turnout of 86.5%. That's 1,930,391 people in favour of the treaty and 1,471,914 against the treaty, which is a majority of 458,477.

The Irish were also given a referendum on the Maastricht Treaty on 18th June 1992 and they approved the treaty by 69.05%, on a turnout of 57.31%, which suggests a degree of voter apathy: 42.69% of the Irish electorate didn't bother to turnout. 1,001,076 citizens voted in favour of the treaty (69.05%) and 448,655 voted against the treaty (30.95%).

The French also had a referendum on the Maastricht Treaty in

September 1992, and they narrowly ratified the treaty, with 50.8% in favour and 49.2% against! It's interesting to note that there was no controversy from the European political elite towards the result of the French referendum, which ratified the treaty by a slender margin of 1.6%, yet there has been so much organised resistance to the result of the Brexit referendum (2016), to leave the European Union, by a larger margin of 3.78% or to put it into something we can understand, a majority of 1,269,501 votes.

Incidentally, it's interesting to consider the results of research, conducted in Denmark and Ireland by Ece Özlem Atikcan, on 'why voters change their minds in second referendums on EU treaties'? The research concluded as follows: "Yes campaigners in both Denmark and Ireland learned from previous referendums and developed an approach that reframed the issue by emphasising (the) concessions gained from the EU and the risks of rejecting a treaty for a second time." In addition to the arguments on the guarantees or concessions given by the EU, the 'Yes' campaign emphasised the (serious) consequences of a second 'No' vote, such as potential exclusion from the EU and economic costs. This shift was also visible in the choice of slogans. In Denmark, the Liberal Party went from 'Vote Yes' to 'Go for the safe choice, you will not get another chance'. In Ireland too, abstract 'Yes' slogans, such as 'Europe: Let's be at the heart of it' were replaced with more dramatic messages, such as, 'Ruin versus Recovery'. In other words the sceptical voters were exposed to 'project fear' and warned of the serious economic costs of opposing this European federal 'super-state' project of the European political elite.

The Maastricht Treaty was such an important stage in the evolution of the European project, from the European Economic Community (EEC) or the Common Market, towards a country called Europe, where England, Scotland, Wales and Northern Ireland, would effectively become states of a United States of Europe, that British people should have been given a public referendum on, as the French, Danish and Irish people were in 1992.

Whilst the Maastricht rebels, in the Conservative Party, were defeated by their own government under Prime Minister John Major, the infighting continued, and they were heavily defeated at the next general election in May 1997. This should have served as a warning to the Conservative Party and government, which has 'wrestled' with the Brexit negotiations.

However, one thing is certain, the Maastricht Treaty rebels were right to demand a referendum on such an important treaty, which changed an economic community into a political (and economic) union, without reference to the unsuspecting people. The following is a 'roll of honour' of those Conservative Members of Parliament who stood up to their own government and demanded that the British people should be consulted.

The rebels who had the whip withdrawn were Michael Carttiss (Great Yarmouth); Nicholas Budgen (Wolverhampton South West); Tony Marlow (Northampton North); John Wilkinson (Ruislip Northwood); Richard Shepherd (Aldridge-Brownhills); Teresa Gorman (Billericay); Christopher Gill (Ludlow); Sir Teddy Taylor (Southend East); Sir Richard Body (Holland and Boston) and later Rupert Allason (Torbay).

The rebels who also voted against their own government were Bill Cash (Stafford); Nicholas Winterton (Macclesfield); Ann Winterton (Congleton); James Cran (Beverley); Michael Lord (Central Suffolk); John Biffen (North Shropshire); Bill Walker (North Tayside); Michael Spicer (South Worcestershire); George Gardiner (Reigate); Roger Knapman (Stroud); Peter Tapsell (East Lindsey); Walter Sweeney (Vale of Glamorgan); Sir Trevor Skeet (Bedfordshire North); Sir Ivan Lawrence (Burton); Toby Jessel (Twickenham); Andrew Hunter (Basingstoke); Warren Hawksley (Halesowen and Stourbridge) and John Carlisle (Luton North). The rebels who abstained were Iain Duncan Smith (Chingford); Nicholas Fairbairn (Perth and Kinross); Rhodes Boyson (Brent North); Bernard Jenkin (Colchester North); Kenneth Baker (Mole Valley); Vivian Bendall (Ilford North); Sir Nicholas Bonsor (Upminster); John Butcher (Coventry South West); Sir Peter Fry (Wellingborough); Sir Michael Grylls (North West Surrey); Sir Roger Moate (Faversham); Barry Legg (Milton Keynes South West); David Porter (Waveney); John Townend (Bridlington); George Walden (Buckingham) and John Whittingdale (Colchester South and Malden). Finally, other rebels were Liam Fox (Woodspring); Alan Duncan (Rutland and Melton) and David Willetts (Havant).

Incidentally, the following may be the reason why Prime Minister John Major failed to give the people a referendum on such an important treaty, when the French, the Danes and the Irish people were consulted.

The reason is probably embedded in the Exchange Rate Mechanism (ERM) fiasco of 1992, under Prime Minister John Major, a former Chancellor of the Exchequer under Prime Minister Margaret Thatcher.

The Exchange Rate mechanism (ERM), which was created in 1979, was the foundation for the Economic and Monetary Union (EMU). The United Kingdom government joined the Exchange Rate Mechanism (ERM) in 1990 and crashed out in 1992 but then obtained an opt-out from joining the Economic and Monetary Union (EMU), in return for agreeing to the next major treaty amendment, which was the Maastricht Treaty (1992).

Had the British people been consulted over the Maastricht Treaty or the Treaty on European Union (TEU), as the Irish, the French and the Danes were, which changed the European Economic Community (EEC) or the Common Market, into the European Union (EU), then the sceptical British may have decided to leave the European project much earlier.

Furthermore, had the Conservative Government consulted the sceptical British people over our entry into the Exchange Rate Mechanism (ERM), the precursor of the Economic and Monetary Union (EMU) which would have led to the adoption of the euro and the loss of the pound sterling, they may have refused to join the ERM and avoided the embarrassment of 'crashing out', on what was known as 'Black Friday', when interest rates went 'through the roof'. It may also have cautioned the government about the dangers of accepting the Maastricht Treaty, without reference to the people, and would have avoided internal strife and the need for the 'final showdown', with the controversial Brexit referendum on 23rd June 2016.

When the French people were consulted over the Maastricht Treaty or the Treaty on European Union (TEU), which changed the economic community into a political and economic entity, which they approved by a slender margin, surely the British people should have been consulted, particularly as there was such a 'hue and cry' for a public referendum by so many elected representatives in the governing Conservative Party.

This autocratic behaviour by a British prime minister makes a mockery of his outrageous statement, that the result of the 'Brexit' referendum was the "tyranny of the majority". His behaviour was dictatorial. He didn't think it necessary to consult the ordinary people, those who voted them into power, despite a mini revolution in his own party and government.

We, the people, have very little power. We only have one electoral vote. We elect others to represent us in the 'corridors of power' and we trust their judgement. Should they fail to behave in accordance with the 'will of the people', we can vote them out of power. However, to their credit, many of our elected representatives revolted against their own party in government, under the leadership of an obstinate prime minister, but they were swept aside. This crucial stage in the grand project of the European political elite was apparently much too important to risk on a 'people's vote', as they may have had a different view, had they been consulted.

This behaviour, by a prime minister, strikes at the heart of the democratic process and disregards the primacy of the people, according to Thomas Jefferson, President of the United States of America (1801-1809) who said: "The will of the people is the only legitimate foundation of any government and to protect its free expression, should be our first objective." Prime Minister John Major should reflect on his attitude towards the Maastricht Treaty or the Treaty on European Union, in the light of his later views on Brexit. On the one hand, he refused to allow a referendum on the Maastricht Treaty or the Treaty on European Union, then on the other, he characterised the majority vote to leave the Union as the 'tyranny of the majority' and encouraged a second referendum, despite a large majority of 1,269,501 votes, which is almost as many people as live in the two northern conurbations of Leeds and Bradford.

There's no question that the Maastricht Treaty was the most influential treaty on the tortuous journey from the Common Market or the European Economic Community (EEC), towards a federal country called Europe or the United States of Europe, as envisaged by Jean Monnet and Robert Schuman, the founding fathers of the European Union, and the people were not told the truth about the ultimate destination of this project.

The burning question, however, is why would a prime minister of the United Kingdom, the birthplace of liberal western democracy, reject the genuine concerns of a large number of his parliamentary colleagues, and effectively lend support to the European political elite as they thunder towards a federal country called Europe, which will inevitably diminish our independence and sovereignty, without reference to the people?

The next challenge to our national independence and sovereignty was the Treaty of Amsterdam (1997), which again was not exposed to the people.

9

THE TREATY OF AMSTERDAM (1997)

How many people had ever heard of the Treaty of Amsterdam (1997), which was signed on 2nd October 1997 and came into force on 1st May 1999 and made substantial changes to the Treaty of Maastricht (1992)? Under the Treaty of Amsterdam (1997), member states agreed to devolve certain powers from national governments to the European Parliament, across such areas as immigration, civil and criminal laws and enacting foreign and security policy, as well as implementing institutional changes for expansion, as new member nations joined the European Union.

The EU became responsible for legislating on immigration, civil law or civil procedure, in so far as this was necessary for the 'free movement of people' within the EU. Furthermore, inter-governmental co-operation was intensified in the areas of policing and criminal justice to enable member states to co-ordinate their activities more effectively. The EU aimed to establish an area of freedom, security and justice for its citizens.

The treaty laid down new principles and responsibilities in the areas of a common foreign and security policy, with an emphasis on protecting the values and interests of the European Union to the outside world.

The treaty also introduced a 'High Representative of the European Union for Foreign Affairs and Security Policy' who together with the Presidents of the European Council and the European Commission would put a name and a face on European Union policy to the outside world.

Surely, member states should have consulted their people on such an important treaty, which devolved powers from national governments to the European Parliament, across such areas as immigration, civil and criminal laws and enacting foreign and security policy, as well as implementing institutional changes for expansion and the introduction of a High Representative for Foreign Affairs and Security Policy?

The question that should have been asked by the British people, of their elected representatives, was whether they knew that the treaty was another stage on the journey to a European super-state, particularly the plans for (eastward) expansion and the appointment of a 'Foreign Secretary' and did they not consider that the people should be informed and consulted?

The Danish people were given a referendum on the Amsterdam Treaty (1998) which was held on 28th May 1998 and was approved by 55.1% of voters, with a turnout of 76.2%. So far as the numbers are concerned, 1,647,692 Danish people voted in favour of the treaty and 1,342,595 voted against the treaty, which is a majority of 305,097.

Similarly, the Irish were given a referendum on the Amsterdam Treaty (1998) which was held on 22nd May 1998 and was approved by 61.74% of voters, with a turnout of 56.2%. So far as the numbers are concerned, 932,632 Irish people voted in favour of the treaty and 578,070 voted against the treaty, which is a majority of 354,562 votes. It is, however, interesting to record that the referendum on the Amsterdam Treaty (1998) was held on the same date (22/5/98) as the referendum on the Nineteenth Amendment, which related to the controversial Good Friday Agreement.

It begs the question, whether the debate about the Amsterdam Treaty was 'masked' by the controversial debate about the Good Friday Agreement.

It also begs the question, did the Irish government deliberately hold the referendum on the Amsterdam Treaty on the same day as the referendum on the controversial Good Friday Agreement, to reduce the chances of the Irish people voting against a treaty, as they had done before?

Sadly, the British people were denied a referendum on the Amsterdam Treaty, which was another stage in this project of the

European political elite, as it moved inexorably towards a federal European super-state.

The next stage in the journey towards a federal European super-state, which again was not exposed to the British people, was the Treaty of Nice (2003), which was the foundation for eastward expansion, into the former Eastern European countries, former satellite states of the Soviet Union.

10

THE TREATY OF NICE (2003)

How many citizens had ever heard of the Treaty of Nice, which was signed on 26th February 2001 and came into force on 1st February 2003, which reformed the institutional structure of the Union to withstand eastward expansion? This was such an important treaty, designed to enable expansion into the former Soviet-dominated communist countries of Eastern Europe. Surely, the member states should have consulted their people on such an important treaty, which reformed the institutional structure of the Union, to withstand eastward expansion into the former communist states, associated with the former Soviet Union or Union of Soviet Socialist Republics (USSR), many of which were unfamiliar with the democratic process and free-market, capitalist economies.

It's thought that the Brussels political elite wanted to accept the many former communist countries of Eastern Europe, to avoid them returning to the communist fold, under the auspices of the Russian Federation.

However, this was such a momentous decision by the Brussels political elite, which attracted so many former communist countries, with active communist parties, politicians, activists and supporters, which would change the political landscape of the European Union for ever.

The British people should have been consulted in a referendum on such an important treaty, which would change the face of the European Union forever, particularly the expansion into the Eastern European, former communist countries, previously associated with the Soviet Union, and the commitment by Brussels to lay the groundwork for a European Army.

European Union leaders faced a political crisis (9th June 2001) when the Irish people rejected the Treaty of Nice, which reformed institutional structures to withstand eastward expansion into the former Soviet-dominated communist countries of Eastern Europe. Only Ireland held a referendum on the Treaty of Nice proposals, which were designed to pave the way for expansion into Eastern Europe and give more voting power to the larger EU member states and something that should really concern the other member states, laying the groundwork for a European Army.

Romano Prodi, the President of the European Commission, expressed "profound disappointment" at the Irish people's referendum result. In France, the leader of the UDF party, Francois Bayrou, said: "I hope the Irish vote means that this treaty is dead... President Chirac should have the courage and the political honesty to call a referendum in France."

Other opponents of the treaty believed it gave too much voting power to the larger member states, particularly Germany. As in Ireland, the Spanish people feared that the expansion into Eastern Europe would lead to the transfer of regional subsidies from the poorer Western European member states to the poorer Eastern European member states.

The Irish people voted against the Treaty of Nice on 7th June 2001, with 53.9% against the treaty on a derisory turnout of 34.8%. As usual the Irish government was given some concessions and they were required to vote again on 19th October 2002, when 62.9% voted in favour of the treaty, on an improved turnout of 49.5% or 1.4 million people.

Over the next two years Cyprus, the Czech Republic, Estonia, Latvia, Lithuania, Hungary, Malta, Slovakia, Slovenia and Poland waited to join the European Union, with Romania and Bulgaria waiting patiently in the wings. In 2004, the enlargement process involved the above ten candidate states, eight from Central and Eastern Europe, and the Mediterranean islands of Malta and Cyprus. In 2003, public referendums on joining the European Union were held in all these states, except Cyprus.

If the British people had been consulted on the Treaty of Nice proposals, which paved the way for expansion into the former communist countries of Central and Eastern Europe and the controversial proposal to have a European Army, they may have rejected the treaty proposals and they would not have been intimidated by the call for a second referendum.

If that referendum had taken place and had been rejected by the British people, the Brussels political elite would have had to reconsider their ambitions to expand into Eastern Europe and to create a European Army and debate the future of the United Kingdom in the European Union.

That would have been the appropriate time to discuss the future of the European project and come clean with the people about the ambitions of the political elite to create a federal European super-state, and seriously consider an option to return to a European Economic Community (EEC) or a Common Market, consisting of independent, sovereign nation states.

The next treaty to come out of Brussels was the Treaty of Lisbon (2009), which made important changes on the journey towards a European super-state, and despite being promised a referendum by the New Labour government, the treaty was signed by them without public consultation.

11

THE TREATY OF LISBON (2009)

Many citizens may remember the Treaty of Lisbon (initially known as the Reform Treaty), which was signed by the member states on 13th December 2007 and came into force on 1st December 2009, and made amendments to the Maastricht Treaty (1993), now known as the Treaty on European Union (2007), and to the Treaty of Rome (1957), now known as the Treaty on the Functioning of the European Union (2007).

The Treaty of Lisbon made many changes, including the creation of a long-term President of the European Council and a High Representative for Foreign Affairs and Security Policy, and gave member states the explicit legal right to leave the Union and the procedures to do so.

The main purpose of the treaty was to complete the process started by the Treaty of Amsterdam (1997) and the Treaty of Nice (2001) to enhance the efficiency and democratic legitimacy of the European Union. However, opponents of the treaty, such as former Danish Member of the European Parliament (MEP) Jens-Peter Bonde, argued that it would centralise the European Union and weaken democracy by transferring power from national electorates and parliaments. Jens-Peter Bonde was elected to the European Parliament, with the Danish 'People's Movement Against the European Union' in 1979, and he resigned in May 2008.

It's interesting to note that negotiations to modify the European Union institutions started in 2001, which resulted in the Treaty Establishing a Constitution for Europe, which would have repealed existing European treaties and replaced them with a 'constitution'. Although the treaty was ratified by most member states, it was abandoned after being rejected by 54.67% of French voters on 29th May 2005 and 61.54% of Danish voters on 1st June 2005. After a period of reflection, the member states agreed to retain and amend the existing treaties and salvage some reforms, which were envisaged in the constitution. An amending 'reform' treaty was produced and signed in Lisbon in 2007. It was intended to be ratified by the end of 2008, but Irish voters rejected the treaty in June 2008, which was reversed in a second referendum in October 2009, after they had secured some concessions from the European Union bureaucrats.

The Irish people voted against the Treaty of Lisbon (2009) on 12th June 2008, with 53.2% against the treaty, on a turnout of 53.1%. However, having been given certain guarantees, the Irish people were required to vote again and 67.1% voted in favour of the treaty on a turnout of 59%.

The concerns of the French and Danish voters, according to a House of Commons research paper (05/45, 13 June 2005 – The Future of the European Constitution), were believed to include fears about national identity and sovereignty, the increase in EU legislation, the pace of EU enlargement and the single currency (euro) but neither were allowed to express their concerns in a referendum on the Lisbon Treaty (2009).

So far as the United Kingdom is concerned, the New Labour manifesto pledges (2005) included the following: "We will put the EU constitutional Treaty to the British people in a referendum and campaign whole-heartedly for a 'Yes' vote to keep Britain a leading nation in Europe."

The New Labour manifesto pledge, referred to the 'Treaty establishing a Constitution for Europe', which was signed in October 2004, but was abandoned when it was rejected by the French and Danish electorate.

A Reform Treaty, also known as the Lisbon Treaty, was created instead and unelected Prime Minister, Gordon Brown, signed it in 2007, through the back door, without reference to the British people. The question is, therefore, did the New Labour government break their manifesto pledge to put the constitutional treaty to the British people, when it had been rejected and replaced with the Reform

Treaty or the Lisbon Treaty?

The answer can be found in a House of Commons research paper, which stated: "The content of the treaty, though not its structure, is similar in a great many respects to the EU constitution." Incidentally, Open Europe, a think-tank that calls for radical reform of the EU, calculated that the original treaty and the Lisbon Treaty were 90% the same.

It can be concluded, therefore, that the New Labour government, under the unelected Prime Minister, Gordon Brown, approved and signed the Lisbon Treaty in December 2007 without reference to the British people, when their manifesto pledge (2005) was to put the constitutional treaty to the people in a referendum, and they did not keep their promise.

A report by Brian Denny of the 'Campaign against Euro-federalism' under the banner 'Let the People Decide', revealed that 248 Members of Parliament voted for a referendum amendment on the Lisbon Treaty and 311 voted against. Twenty-nine New Labour Members of Parliament defied their government whips to keep the promise they had made to the electorate (2005) to back a call for a referendum. Thankfully, twenty-nine New Labour members had the decency to defy their whips. Even Tony Benn's last-minute plea to members, pointing out that: "The Lisbon Treaty transfers important powers, which belong to us, to others we do not elect and cannot remove", failed to have much effect. The report went on to say that the Europe minister Jim Murphy's main argument for opposing a referendum, was that the Tories had rammed through EU treaties, from the Single European Act to the Maastricht Treaty, with similar contempt for democracy and so would New Labour!

Since the Treaty of Lisbon (2009), Article 15 of the Treaty on European Union states that the European Council should appoint a full-time president for a two-and-a-half-year term. On 19th November 2009, the European Council agreed that its first president under the Lisbon Treaty would be Herman Van Rompuy of the European People's Party, Belgium.

Herman Van Rompuy took office when the Lisbon Treaty came into force on 1st December 2009, with a term stretching until 31st May 2012, which was extended to 30th November 2014. He was succeeded by the former Polish Prime Minister, Donald Tusk, with a term from 1ˢᵗ December 2014 to 31ˢᵗ May 2017, which was extended for a second term on 9ᵗʰ March 2017.

Surely the member states should have given their citizens a referendum on such an important treaty, which created a full-time president of the European Council, effectively President of the European Union, with significant powers over member states. Incidentally, did anyone know President Herman Van Rompuy (Belgian) or Donald Tusk (Polish), before they were appointed as President of the European Council?

Furthermore, the High Representative for Foreign Affairs and Security Policy, since 1ˢᵗ November 2014 is an Italian politician, Federica Maria Mogherini, who was Italy's Minister for Foreign Affairs in the centre-left Renzi Cabinet. At the beginning of her political career she was a member of the Italian Communist Youth Federation (1988) and became a member of the National Council of the Democrats of the Left (2001). Did anyone in the member states, other than Italy, know this woman and did anyone have any influence over her appointment to such an important position?

There's no doubt that the political elite have not been straight with the British people, since they voted to remain in the European Community (EC) or the European Economic Community (EEC) or the Common Market (1975), and through a plethora of covert EU treaties and the principle of 'ever-closer' union, created the European Union (EU), with the ultimate ambition to create a federal United States of Europe.

It was, therefore, essential that the British people came together to deliver our escape from this political construct, and 'ever-closer union', and recover our national independence and celebrate our unique identity and navigate our own future, as an independent nation state, trading with the world, and that's what they did in the 2016 Brexit referendum.

The best outcome for the European Union super-liner, cruising towards a federal country called Europe, would be to slow it down and turn it around and return it to a safe haven of a European economic community or a common market of independent, sovereign, European nation states.

Furthermore, what was the point of the Treaty of Lisbon (2009) giving member states the explicit right to leave the European Union and the procedure to do so, when, at the first hurdle, with the British, they made it so difficult to leave? They immediately demanded a punitive 'divorce settlement', to include our share of current budgetary commitments and future pension liabilities and refused to discuss our future relationship or future trade deals, until a settlement was reached. Their initial approach to a future trade deal, was that we can't expect access to the single market and the customs union, when we are not members of the European Union, and that 'we can't have our cake and eat it'. They also said that it was the British who decided to leave and there will be consequences.

Incidentally, for those member states who decide to leave the Union and invoke Article 50 of the Treaty of Lisbon, and are subjected to resistance from the autocratic European Commission, they need to know that Article 8 of the Treaty directs the following: "The EU must develop a special relationship with neighbouring countries, aiming to establish an area of prosperity and good neighbourliness, founded on values of the Union and characterised by close and peaceful relations, based on co-operation."

The European Commission negotiators, under the leadership of Michelle Barnier, ignored the spirit of Article 8 of the Treaty of Lisbon, when they said that the United Kingdom cannot be given a free trade deal, as it "can't have its cake and eat it." Clearly, a bad deal or a no-deal would damage the economies of both the EU and the UK and, therefore, would not conform to the principles of Article 8 of the treaty, which direct that they develop a 'special relationship' and establish an area of 'prosperity' and 'good-neighbourliness', founded on their values and characterised by 'close and peaceful' relations, based on 'co-operation'. Warm words!

The European Parliament and the European Council and the Council of Ministers, appear to have ceded too much power to the unelected officials of the European Commission, such as Michelle Barnier, a former French politician, and many will remember the obstructive attitude of the French President, Charles De Gaul, towards Great Britain, when they applied to join the European Economic Community (EEC) or the Common Market.

If the unelected Prime Minister, Gordon Brown, had given the people a referendum on the Lisbon Treaty, as New Labour had promised in their manifesto, we may not have had the Brexit referendum and the tortuous negotiations to extricate ourselves from the obdurate Brussels machine.

When the leaders of the European Union project are appointing a full-time President of the European Council and a High Representative for Foreign Affairs and Security Policy and expanding into Eastern Europe and transferring powers from national governments, they are creating a federal country called Europe or a European super-state, or a United States of Europe, despite the denials of the European political elite. So, let's consider a brief history of the continuous enlargement programme, which forges ahead, with or without reference to the European people.

12

THE EU ENLARGEMENT

PROGRAMME

In 1972, four countries held referendums on the 1973 enlargement of the European Communities. Before allowing the four new candidate member states to join the European Communities, France, one of the founding members, held a referendum to approve the enlargement. The French European Communities enlargement referendum was held on 23rd April 1972 and the enlargement was approved by 68.3% of the electorate on a turnout of 60.5%. Following the French approval, three of the four candidate member states, Ireland, Denmark and Norway, then held referendums on whether to join the European Communities, which was essentially a European trading group. The United Kingdom government did not ask the British people for approval before joining the European Communities or as it was known, the European Economic Community (EEC) or the Common Market in 1973. The Irish referendum to approve the Third Amendment of the Constitution of Ireland, was held on 10th May 1972 and was approved by 83.1% of the electorate on a turnout of 70.9%. The Danish European Communities membership referendum was held on 2nd October 1972 and was approved by 63.3% of the electorate on a turnout of 90.1%. Finally, the Norwegian European Communities membership referendum was held on 25th September 1972 and was rejected by 53.5% of the electorate on a turnout of 79%.

The United Kingdom, Labour government, held a referendum on our continued membership of the European Communities (the European Economic Community or the Common Market) on 5th June 1975, which was approved by 67.23% of the electorate on a turnout of 64.62%. It needs to be emphasised that the British people were asked by their government if they wanted to remain in the Common Market, which was an economic community of Western European nations (trading partners), and no mention of the ultimate objective to create the European Union (EU) or a United States of Europe, run by the European political elite and their unelected scribes in the Brussels and Strasbourg 'ivory towers'.

In 1994 four countries held referendums on membership of the European Union, resulting in the 1995 enlargement. The Austrian European Union membership referendum was held on 12th June 1994 and 66.6% voted in favour of membership, with a turnout of 82.3%. The Finnish European Union membership referendum was held on 16th October 1994 and 56.9% voted in favour of membership, with a turnout of 70.8%. The Swedish European Union membership referendum was held on 13th November 1994 and 52.3% voted in favour of membership, with a turnout of 83.3%. Finally, the Norwegian European Union membership referendum was held on 28th November 1994 and 52.2% voted against membership, with a turnout of 89% and this was the second time that the Norwegian voters had rejected their government's proposal to join the European Union. Consequently, Norway did not become a member, but Austria, Finland and Sweden were admitted as members on 1st January 1995.

The 2004 enlargement of the European Union involved ten candidate states, eight from central and Eastern Europe and the Mediterranean islands of Malta and Cyprus. In 2003, referendums were held in all these countries except Cyprus. A referendum was held in Malta on 8th March 2003 and 53.6% voted in favour of membership, with a turnout of 90.9%. A referendum was held in Slovenia on 23rd March 2003 and 89.6% voted in favour of membership, with a turnout of 60.2%. A referendum was held in Hungary on 12th April 2003 and 83.8% voted in favour of membership, with a low turnout of 45.6%. Lithuania held a referendum on 10th-11th May 2003 and 91.9% voted in favour of membership, with a turnout of 63.4%. Slovakia held a referendum on

16th-17th May 2003 and 93.7% voted in favour of membership, with a turnout of 52.1%. Poland held a referendum on 7th-8th June 2003 and 77.5% voted in favour of membership, with a turnout of 58.9%. The Czech Republic held a referendum on 13th-14th June 2003 and 77.3% voted in favour of membership, with a turnout of 55.2%. Estonia held a referendum on 14th September 2003 and 66.8% voted in favour of membership, with a turnout of 64.1%. Finally, Latvia held a referendum on 20th September 2003 and 67.5% voted in favour of membership, with a turnout of 71.5%. All ten candidate countries were admitted as members of the European Union on 1st May 2004.

Incidentally, the voters in these former communist countries, previously associated with the former Soviet Union or the Union of Socialist Soviet Republics (USSR), were obviously very keen to join the more liberal and democratic European Union but did they know that the final destination was a federal super-state, to be called the United States of Europe?

In 2004 the European political elite had embarked on a most ambitious enlargement programme, when they took in ten countries, including eight from Central and Eastern Europe, and the 'free movement of people' and 'open borders' principles adopted by the Union would be the catalyst for another European diaspora, with thousands of people moving from the 'poorer' former communist countries of Central and Eastern Europe to the 'richer' western and Northern European countries. Mass immigration across Europe was again under the spotlight. Further enlargement of the European Union, saw Bulgaria and Romania join, on 1st January 2007.

This dubious political project, leading towards a country called Europe, or the United States of Europe, was achieved with a series of stealth-like treaties, created by the Brussels political elite and signed by the leaders of the member states, who ceded their national independence to the European Union project, without properly consulting their electorate, which was bound, eventually, to produce a backlash from the people.

The ordinary people had been misled by their political representatives, whom they had elected to public office, to think that the European project was a 'commercial enterprise' of Western European trading nations, referred to as the Common Market, when their 'clandestine' destination was a federal European super-state, run from Brussels and Strasbourg. This 'cloak and dagger' deception by the remote European political elite, could not be kept from the people forever, as member states continued to cede their independence and sovereignty from their national parliaments to the European Parliament and the unelected European Commission.

So far as future enlargement of the European Union is concerned, there are five candidates as follows: Turkey applied on 14th April 1987 but talks with the EU are at a standstill. Macedonia applied on 22nd March 2004, Montenegro applied in 2008, Albania applied in 2009 and Serbia applied in 2009. Apparently, all except Albania and Macedonia have started accession negotiations. Kosovo (whose independence is not recognised by five member states) and Bosnia and Herzegovina are recognised as potential candidates for future membership.

According to an Eastern Partnership strategy, the European Union is unlikely to invite any more of its post-Soviet neighbours to join before 2020 but in 2014 they did sign 'association agreements' with Georgia, Moldova and Ukraine. However, in 2005, the European Commission had apparently suggested in a strategy paper, that the enlargement agenda could potentially block the possibility of a future accession of Armenia, Azerbaijan, Belarus, Georgia, Moldova and Ukraine. Interestingly, in 2003, the European Council decreed that integration of the Western Balkans was an expansion priority, in order to stabilise the region in the wake of the civil wars in Yugoslavia during the 1990s, which led to the break-up of Yugoslavia. Slovenia was the first former Yugoslav country to obtain independence and joined in 2004, followed by Croatia in 2013. Albania, Serbia, Macedonia and Montenegro are all candidate states. Apparently, Serbia and Montenegro are expected to join by 2025 and Macedonia and Albania are expected to start talks by the end of 2019 and could also join by 2025. Turkey's candidacy to join the European Union has been a matter of controversy since it was granted in 1999 and since the European Council announced that membership negotiations were opened on 3rd October 2005. However, relations have deteriorated in recent times due to concerns over autocratic rule and human rights and the rule of law and accession talks are effectively at a standstill.

There appears to be no limit to the potential growth of this

European super-state, as it heads towards a United States of Europe. What does the Russian Federation think of these enlargement proposals, spreading into countries such as Armenia, Azerbaijan, Belarus, Georgia and Ukraine?

So far as enlargement of the European Union is concerned, the following are the (radical) views of Dominique Strauss-Khan, the former French Foreign Minister, in the book *Why Europe Will Run the 21st Century* by Mark Leonard and published by Fourth Estate in 2005: "After opening to the East, Europe must now turn to the South. We will have to think about how to make it possible for countries from the ex-Soviet Union and the Mediterranean Basin, such as those of the Maghreb (Algeria, Libya, Mauritania, Morocco and Tunisia), to join our political area. It might be too early to start preparing for a European Union, that stretches from the icebergs of the Arctic North to the sand dunes of the Sahara, with the Mediterranean in their midst. But it would be criminal to rule it out."

The book revealed that the Italian politician, Silvio Berlusconi, had held out the prospect of membership to Russia on a recent visit and that there had been discussions with Israeli political circles in 2001-2!

Is there any limit to the expansion ambitions of the European political elite? Is there any wonder that the British people were concerned about the growth of the European Union, from the sensible Western European trading group, known as the European Economic Community (EEC), into the numerous countries of Eastern Europe, previously associated with the Soviet Union, and the continuous loss of sovereignty and independence?

Surely, the European political elite (and the British government) should have realised that their obsession with expansion, particularly into the former communist states of the former Soviet Union, and the consequent increase in economic migration from those states, may not meet with the approval of the people and they may be faced with a 'backlash'.

The 'backlash' occurred in the United Kingdom on 23rd June 2016, when the people (not the politicians) were asked whether they wanted to leave or remain in the expanding European Union and the unexpected result was that they voted to leave. So, let's look at the result of the referendum.

13

THE BREXIT REFERENDUM (2016)

The democratic 'backlash' occurred on 23rd June 2016, when the British people were asked in a referendum or a 'people's vote': "Should the United Kingdom remain as a member of the European Union or leave the European Union"? The shock result was that 16,141,241 (48.11%) citizens voted to remain and 17,410,742 (51.89%) voted to leave. The number eligible to vote was 46,500,001 and there was a large turnout of 33,573,000 or 72.2%. Whilst those who voted to remain complained of the narrowness of the margin at 3.78%, which translates into 1,269,501 votes, this was the largest number of citizens to vote for anything in the history of British elections, and 1,269,501 votes is not a narrow majority.

A majority of 1,269,501 voters, is almost the number of people who lived in the cities of Leeds (818,662) and Bradford (534,362) in 2019! This is not a small majority, as the remain campaigners have suggested. It's a very significant majority vote, which would take a revolution to overturn.

Incidentally, those who wanted a second referendum or a 'confirmatory referendum' or a 'people's vote', when the terms of the Withdrawal Agreement were known, must realise that, based on a turnout of 33,573,000 (2016), they would have to retain their 16,141,241 'remain' voters and change the minds of 634,751 'leave' voters, to win by just one solitary vote! Do they realise that changing the minds of 634,751 voters is more than the number of people who lived in Newcastle (312,476) and Sunderland (290,000) in 2019 and that would be an enormous task?

Furthermore, the remain voters who complained about the 'narrow margin' of 3.78% to leave (a significant majority of 1,269,501 votes) would need to retain their 16,141,241 'remain' voters and attempt to convert 1,269,501 leave voters, to win a second referendum by the same 'narrow margin'. Had the 'remain' campaign won a second referendum, a 'people's vote', and had they won that referendum, leave voters would then demand a third referendum, particularly if the majority was less than 1,269,501! The question is, of course, should British elections now be decided on the 'best of three', which would be a complete nonsense?

It's also interesting to compare the European Union referendum (2016), with the European Community (EC) or European Economic Community (EEC) or Common Market, referendum (1975), when the electorate were asked the simple question: "Do you think that the UK should stay in the European Community (the Common Market)." A comparison shows that 17,378,581 voters (1975), were happy to be part of a Western European trading group, but 17,410,742 voters (2016) were not happy to be part of the European Union, with the political objective of 'ever-closer union' and an ultimate 'discrete' objective of a federal United States of Europe.

It's also suggested that had the remain voters won the referendum by a 'narrow margin' of 3.78% or a majority of 1,269,501 votes, the leave voters would have accepted the result without question, and we would have remained a member of the European Union and helplessly watched the Brussels-to-Strasbourg Express 'thunder' towards a country called Europe or a multi-national conglomerate, the United States of Europe.

Before we discuss the Westminster and Brussels 'resistance movements', which have undermined the legitimacy of the 2016 referendum result and campaigned for a second referendum or a 'people's vote', because, they suggest, the 'leave' voters 'had been misled' and they 'didn't know what they were voting for', let's look at the result of the subsequent European Elections (2019) to get some idea of the determined mood of the people.

Having voted to leave the European Union in the Brexit Referendum (2016), according to Article 50 of the Lisbon Treaty (2009), we should have negotiated a 'Withdrawal Agreement' and 'Political Declaration' and become an independent country on 29th

March 2019, with or without an agreement. However, the Westminster and Brussels 'resistance movements' and the British 'remain' campaigns had undermined the leaving process and the leaving date was extended to 31st October 2019. That meant that the United Kingdom, which was still a reluctant member of the European Union, had to participate in the European Parliamentary Elections (23rd May 2019) and the following 'national share of votes and seats' gives some indication of the mood of the British people towards their political leaders, who failed to deliver on the 'will of the people'.

The National Share of votes and seats in the European Parliamentary Elections was dominated by the success of the Brexit Party (which had only recently been formed) which won 31.6% of the votes and 29 seats. This was the reaction of many people who had voted to leave the Union.

On the other hand, there was a resurgence in the popularity of the Liberal Democrats, who were a 'remain' party, and won 20.3% of the votes and 16 seats (+15). They were, however, let down by some of their new MEPs, who were seen on television in the European Parliament wearing bright yellow T-shirts, bearing the message 'Bollocks to Brexit'!

The socialist Labour Party, under its dubious Marxist leadership and militant 'grass-roots' supporters, known as Momentum, which had been 'sitting on the fence', obstructing the withdrawal process, got a well-deserved drubbing. They won 14.1% of the vote and 10 seats (-10).

Finally, the Conservative Party and the party of government, which had failed to get us out of the European Union, despite the valiant efforts of the Prime Minister, Theresa May, also got a drubbing by the electorate. They won 9.1% (-14.8%) and 4 seats (-15), resulting in the resignation of the prime minister, which sparked a leadership election, the winner of which would become the next prime minister, charged with getting us out of the European Union in accordance with the 'will of the people', as expressed through the Brexit referendum (2016) and the success of the new Brexit Party, in the European Parliamentary Elections (23rd May 2019).

So far as the regions are concerned, the newly formed Brexit Party won the European Parliamentary Elections in every part of the United Kingdom, except Scotland, Northern Ireland and London.

The Brexit Party won 32.5% of the vote in Wales; 31.2% of the votes in the North West; 38.7% in the North East: 36.5% in Yorkshire and Humberside; 38.2% in the East Midlands; 37.7% in the West Midlands; 37.8% in the East of England; 36.7% in the South West and 36.1% in the South East. So far as London was concerned, the Europhile Liberal Democrats won 27.2%, Labour 24% and the Brexit Party 17.9%. So far as Scotland was concerned the Europhile Scottish Nationalist Party (SNP) won 37.8% and the Brexit Party 14.8%. So far as Northern Ireland was concerned the votes went to Sinn Fein 22.2%; the Democratic Unionist Party (DUP) 21.8% and the Alliance Party (APNI) 18.5%.

The resounding message from the European Parliamentary Elections (23rd June 2019), almost three years after the Brexit Referendum (23rd May 2019), was that the people, particularly England (except London) and Wales, came out in force for the newly formed Brexit Party, which exists to get the United Kingdom out of the European Union.

However, we have had the Brexit Referendum (2016) and the European Parliamentary Elections (2019), which both demonstrated the urgent desire of the majority of the British electorate to leave the European Union, as it moves inexorably towards a United States of Europe, but the government has failed to get the Withdrawal Agreement through parliament. They have been obstructed at every turn by the Westminster and Brussels 'resistance movement' and the many 'remain' campaigns, which are determined to thwart the 'will of the British people' and impose the sovereignty of parliament and remain in the European Union. This is a battle between the 'will of the people' or the 'power of the people' and the sovereignty of a parliamentary democracy. To be frank, this is now a battle between the people, those who have just one vote, and those they elect to the 'corridors of power' to represent their views and they must be 'brought to heel' by the people. They must now be 'delegates', sent to parliament to represent the views of the people and not be their political masters, making decisions on behalf of the people, without consultation.

The reality is, however, that the behaviour of the Westminster 'resistance movement', suggests that many of our political representatives do not agree with the reasonable views of their constituents and have taken it upon themselves to evoke the sovereignty of parliament and ignore the instructions of the electorate. This is a constitutional crisis, created by those we've elected to represent us in the 'corridors of power', and when the 'dust settles', they must be held to account for their actions and that should mean them being deselected before the next general election.

In the meantime, let's look at the Westminster 'resistance movement' and the Brussels 'resistance movement' and the many 'remain campaigns', just to give the reader some understanding of what we are up against, in our attempt to recover our independence and leave the European Union.

14

THE WESTMINSTER 'RESISTANCE

MOVEMENT'

So far as the result of the EU Referendum is concerned, unlike any other election, there is a stubborn 'resistance movement' which includes many well-known former senior politicians wanting to change the result, which is undemocratic. Nick Clegg, the former leader of the Liberal Democrats and former Deputy Prime Minister, wrote a book entitled *How to Stop Brexit*, when his political career had been based on the 'first past the post' electoral system, where a simple majority is enough for victory. So how does he justify his resistance to the 17,410,742 citizens who voted to 'leave' the European Union, with a majority of 1,269,501 votes?

The book entitled *How to Stop Brexit (And Make Britain Great Again)*, published by The Bodley Head, in 2017, said: "There's nothing remotely inevitable about Brexit, except it will be deeply damaging, if it happens. Extricating Britain (UK) from Europe will be the greatest challenge this country has faced since the Second World War. And as the negotiations expose the promises of the Brexit campaign to have been hollow, even some Brexit voters (may) now wish to exercise their democratic right to change their mind, seeing that the most pragmatic option is to stop. It would certainly be the best thing for Britain. But how can it be done? Haven't the people spoken? No."

He categorically debunks the various myths that have been used to force Brexit on Britain, not by 'the people' but by a small, extremely rich, self-serving elite, and explains precisely how this 'historic mistake' can be reversed – and what you (the reader) can do to make sure that it is (reversed). Incidentally, where are the practical examples of the electorate's democratic right to change their minds? The losers in any general election depend upon the opposition to hold the winners to account until the next general election. We don't get a second election, because we didn't like the result of the first election. We all know that's not how liberal western parliamentary democracies work.

Incidentally, when Nick Clegg lost his Sheffield Hallam seat, on 8th June 2017, to the uninspiring Jared O'Mara, Labour, a seat which had been in Liberal control since 1997, he said: "In politics, you live by the sword and die by the sword." In the 'first past the post' electoral system, the winner was the Labour candidate, who got 21,881 votes, the Liberals got 19,756 votes, the Conservatives got 13,561 votes, UKIP got 929 votes and the Green Party got 823 votes. That's 21,881 votes for the winner and 35,069 votes for the losers, that's a majority of 13,188 for the losers, and there were no calls for another election, to achieve a different result.

The main question is, why would Nick Clegg agitate for a re-run of the United Kingdom European Union membership referendum (2016), which had 17,410,742 votes to 'leave' and 16,141,241 votes to 'remain', a majority of 1,269,501 votes, when he suggests that in politics, you 'live by the sword and die by the sword'? Is it because he has some emotional attachment to Europe, through his Dutch mother and his Baltic-German paternal grandmother, and her Russian grandfather, or possibly through his Spanish wife, Miriam Gonzalez Durantez? Or is it because he was a Member of the European Parliament (MEP) (1999 to 2004) and had previously worked for the European Commission? The arrogance of this former senior politician, a former deputy prime minister, to talk down to the leave voters, suggesting that they had been misled, and should have another opportunity (referendum) to change their minds, is breath-taking.

He has chosen to ignore the democratic 'will of the British people', or even the 'wisdom of the crowd', who voted to leave the European super-tanker, as it steams towards a United States of Europe. This referendum resulted in a decisive majority to leave the

Union, and the Conservative government must carry out their instructions, despite the 'resistance movement' of the arrogant political elite and the opposition parties and some members of the governing party. The government may have been given a 'poisoned chalice', but they must stay the course and ensure that we get a clean break from this dubious economic and political project, before it breaks up our United Kingdom, and its constituent countries become minor players in a multi-national super-state conglomerate.

Furthermore, high-profile senior citizens, like the former Deputy Prime Minister, Michael Heseltine (83), now Lord Heseltine, and billionaire businessman, Sir Richard Branson (67), are in the vanguard of resistance to the referendum result. Both these elderly citizens have questioned the long-term sustainability of the result, on the basis that the older people, who voted to leave, are dying off, and younger people, who voted to remain, are increasing in numbers. Isn't this always the case, after any parliamentary election? The question is, of course, how many older (define 'older') people voted to leave or remain? If it was a similar number, they cancel each other out, which destroys the argument.

Another prominent former senior politician to support the 'resistance movement' was the former prime minister, Tony Blair. Despite the fact that parliament approved the invocation of Article 50, to authorise the withdrawal agreement process, which means that we should have left on 29th March 2019 (now 31st October 2019), Mr Blair undermined the negotiations by supporting the 'resistance movement' and promoting a second referendum on the negotiated terms, in an attempt to overturn the 'will of the British people' to leave the European Union super-state.

This was the opinion of Tony Blair, when interviewed on the Andrew Marr show, BBC Parliament, Sunday 3rd March 2019: "Use the delay for a purpose. And the purpose should be to put to parliament; do you want a hard Brexit or a soft Brexit, and I believe that when parliament is faced with the choice, because a hard Brexit is (so) painful and a soft Brexit is (so) pointless, they (the people) will go for another referendum."

On the same programme, the pollster, Sir John Curtiss, said: "There's little sign of any recent increase in support for a second referendum. (The Delta Poll showed 43% in favour and 45%

opposed) The country doesn't want it. Parliament doesn't want it. Time to give up on it."

However, Tony Blair responded: "You say the country doesn't want it, 43% (to) 45%, that's pretty 'even Stephens'. The question for parliament is, what's the right thing to do and the risk of her deal is, we're going to leave in circumstances where we don't know what we're getting (and) by the way Theresa May promised continually, if you remember, we would know in sufficient detail, the future relationship with Europe, so that we could make a decision, because she can't get agreement in the Cabinet … for example, Liam Fox … is in favour of a hard Brexit. He's in favour of a Canada style free trade agreement; Amber Rudd and Phillip Hammond are well opposed to it and in favour of a Norway-style agreement. This is a fundamental question. You've got to resolve it before you leave. The message to Labour MPs is vote against the deal (and) use an extension to (get) a conclusion. Hard versus soft or back to the people. Understand that a hard Brexit is going to be deeply economically painful for the country and a soft Brexit means that we just become a rule taker. It's in those circumstances that I think you'll mobilise a majority in parliament to say look, the sensible thing in these circumstances, is to put it back to the people or pass her deal subject to a confirmatory referendum."

Furthermore, the *Telegraph* newspaper reported on 12th March 2019, under the headline: 'Tony Blair Secretly Advising Emmanuel Macron on Brexit' as follows: "Tony Blair has been accused of 'unacceptable' behaviour, after it emerged he has been briefing Emmanuel Macron on how to force Britain to stay in the EU. The former prime minister believes that if the EU stands its ground over the Brexit deal, parliament will cave in and accept a customs union – which would keep Britain yoked to Brussels – or a second referendum that could cancel Brexit altogether. He is reported to have told Macron to 'hold-firm' and wait for events to play-out in London, that end in Britain staying in the EU."

Another headline in the *Express* online was 'Blame Blair for the mess EU has made of Brexit' which included the following: "… EU insiders tell me that (Donald) Tusk, allowed himself to become convinced Brexit was going to be overturned after a plan was constructed between senior Brussels figures and British pro-Remain politicians, led by Blair, that seemed to be working perfectly. Part of the plan involved Brussels playing hardball in negotiations, so that the deal Theresa May was able to put in front of MPs was profoundly unappetising. That advice to Brussels was relayed by a stream of pro-Remain visitors from the heart of the British establishment. One of them, A. C. Grayling, was even caught on camera telling the European Parliament's Brexit chief, Guy Verhofstadt: 'What would help the Remain movement in the UK, is if the EU is very, very, tough and uncompromising on a deal.' And so, it came to pass, with the EU offering Britain almost no concessions but (the UK) being tied to the interminable 'Irish Backstop' with no unilateral right of escape."

Isn't it instructive that this discredited former prime minister, Tony Blair, who took the us into the disastrous Iraq War, which destroyed their infrastructure and killed, injured and displaced millions of people, and destabilised the Middle East, against the will of millions of people, worldwide, was again attempting to subvert the will of 17,410,742 people, who voted to leave the European Union super-state conglomerate?

Incidentally, Mr Blair was so keen to overturn the 'will of the people', by disrespecting the votes of 17,410,742 British citizens, with a majority of 1,269,501 to leave the European Union, but was very happy to accept the 'will of the British people' when they voted him into office on a supposed 'landslide' victory in 1997, when he told the unsuspecting British people that 'things could only get better'. Well Mr Blair became prime minister on 1st May 1997, under the 'first past the post' electoral system, when 13,518,184 people voted for New Labour, but 17,766,514 people did not vote for New Labour, they voted for another party, which is a significant majority against New Labour of 4,248,330 votes!

He was happy to accept this so-called 'landslide' victory, when there was a majority of 4,248,330 votes against his party, which is the nature of the 'first-past-the-post' electoral system, but wants to overturn the result of the Brexit referendum (2016), when the British people voted to leave the European Union by a decisive majority of 1, 269,501 votes.

If the Brexit 'resistance movement' can overturn the result of the Brexit referendum and ignore the 'will of the British people', and the people are required to vote in a second referendum, in the expectation of a different outcome, then our liberal western democracy will be 'dead in the water'.

Furthermore, those who called for another referendum on the negotiated exit terms, weakened the hand of the British negotiators and strengthened the hand of the Brussels negotiators, who were able to offer a poor deal for the British and a good deal for the Europeans, to force a change of mind, which benefits Brussels. It is, however, normal practice, after a referendum or election, for all parties to respect the 'will of the people' and work together in a spirit of co-operation in the public interest.

The final insult to those citizens who voted to leave the European Union, is to label them elderly or uneducated or working class or xenophobic or Islamophobic or white supremacist or racist or the radical right, without some detailed research to prove such spurious allegations. For instance, Professor Matthew Goodwin, speaking on Aljazeera's 'The Big Picture' (10/08/17) said: "UKIP and the Conservatives have mobilised an older, whiter, working-class, left-behind electorate, that delivers them victory, especially in economically struggling parts of England." He was followed by Professor Arun Kundnani, author of *The Muslims are Coming* who said: "Not everyone who voted leave was racist or Islamophobic or xenophobic, but the discourse of that movement was clearly mobilised around 'Islamophobia' and 'xenophobia' and 'racism'." Really!

It's quite disturbing that Professor Matthew Goodwin should describe those who voted to leave the European Union, this project of the political elite, as 'older, whiter, working-class and left-behind'. It would be very interesting to analyse the research, which produced those conclusions.

It's also disturbing that Professor Arun Kundnani should conclude that the discourse of the movement to leave the European Union, was clearly mobilised around 'Islamophobia' and 'xenophobia' and 'racism'. Is it necessary to inform an intellectual academic, that public concern about uncontrolled mass immigration is not necessarily a hatred of foreigners or hostility towards people of other races? It could be a genuine concern about the sheer numbers of immigrants and the lack of political control?

Surely, we should be able to expect that those who carry the title of professor, should make public statements based on factual research? Where is the evidence to support the claim that the leave movement was mobilised around 'Islamophobia, xenophobia and racism' and that they were 'older, whiter, working-class and (particularly) left-behind'?

It would also be appropriate for those senior politicians who accepted the 'first past the post' electoral system, which produces a winning party, based on a simple majority, over another party, when they have lost the 'popular vote' by a significant margin, to accept the 'will of the people' in a referendum, with a massive majority of 1,269,501 votes.

The Brexit 'resistance movement' are challenging the very foundations of our parliamentary democracy and cannot class themselves as democrats. They should be constantly reminded that the House of Commons passed the European Union Referendum Bill on 9th June 2015 by 544 to 53 votes, which is a majority of 491. A large majority of elected members wanted the British people to decide on our future relationship with the European Union, including our trading arrangements, and they voted to leave.

Furthermore, having voted to leave the European Union, the Members of Parliament voted by 494 votes to 122 votes to invoke Article 50 of the Lisbon Treaty, on 29th March 2017, to start the process to negotiate a Withdrawal Agreement, with the EU, over a two-year period, programmed to end on 29th March 2019, which would include a 'framework' of our 'future relationship' and a 'framework of a future trade deal'.

It's, perhaps, understandable that not every elected representative would be happy with the negotiated Withdrawal Agreement or the 'framework' for our future relationship, including our trading relationship, but if the EU refuse to amend the agreement, we can only leave on 29th March 2019 (now 31st October 2019), without an agreement and without a framework for our future relationship, including our trading relationship.

Members of Parliament should have been aware of the contents of Article 50 and should have known that it clearly decrees: "If negotiations do not result in a ratified agreement, the seceding country leaves without an agreement, and the EU treaties shall cease to apply to that country, without any substitute or transitional arrangements being put in place. As regards trade, the parties would likely follow World Trade Organisation (WTO) rules and regulations on tariffs." That is the legal position.

So far as the Brexit 'resistance movement' is concerned, the United Kingdom parliament approved the Brexit referendum and the people made their decision and parliament accepted that decision when they invoked Article 50 to start the negotiations towards a Withdrawal Agreement, and the government did their best, despite the obstruction of the opposition and the wider 'resistance movement', to get an agreement.

In the above circumstances, why would parliament not approve the Withdrawal Agreement, which includes the framework for our future relationship, including our trading arrangements, and a transition period to negotiate our future relationship and a mutually beneficial trade deal?

Those members who voted against the Withdrawal Agreement because they considered it to be a 'bad deal' for our country, must be able to offer an alternative agreement or accept the alternative is a 'no-deal' outcome.

Those members who voted against the Withdrawal Agreement because they don't want to leave the European Union, must accept that they are opposing the 'will of the people' and creating a 'no-deal' outcome, which could destabilise the British and European economies. More importantly, however, do they realise that they are acting as 'saboteurs' from within parliament, which means that they are intentionally causing damage?

It is, however, suggested that besides fighting against their home-grown, Westminster 'resistance movement', the British government negotiators were also fighting against a Brussels 'resistance movement', but covert resistance activities are extremely difficult to prove. So, let's consider any information available to show a Brussels 'resistance movement' existed.

15

THE BRUSSELS 'RESISTANCE

MOVEMENT'

The main question to consider, in this 'search for the truth', is how far will the European political elite go to frustrate the democratic 'will of the British people' to leave the European Union, as they've done after many other treaty referenda, which did not get the desired or required result?

We got some idea of this from a Channel 4 programme on Wednesday 30th May 2018 entitled 'Carry on Brussels', when we saw Liberal MEP, Catherine Bearder, promoting 'Exit from Brexit' and admitting to being part of a "remainer group of remoaners or whatever you want to call us, proud to be saboteurs". Does she really understand the meaning of the word 'saboteurs'? She also set up a monthly meeting of like-minded MEPs, with her special ally, Guy Verhofstadt, MEP, the European Parliament's chief Brexit negotiator, to debate how they can fight the referendum to stop Brexit. The meeting was said to allow a high level of exchange of intelligence and to generate new tactics to disrupt Brexit and discussions were said to be top secret. She was also seen introducing a British philosopher, A. C. Grayling, to her 'special ally' Guy Verhofstadt, and A. C. Grayling said; "What would help the remain movement in the UK (is) if the EU is very, very, tough, and uncompromising, on a deal".

The programme also showed Guy Verhofstadt, MEP, calling for a vote in the European Parliament, on the British negotiations (inexplicably,) to stop the negotiations moving to the next phase. This behaviour by Catherine Bearder, supported by Guy Verhofstadt, encouraging 'Exit from Brexit' is an attack on the very foundations of our liberal western democracy and disrespect for the 'will of the people', who voted by a majority of 1,269,501 to leave the European Union federal super-state.

So, who is Guy Verhofstadt, and why is he so keen to stop Brexit against the 'will of the British people'? He is a Belgian politician and Member of the European Parliament (MEP) since 2009 and a former Prime Minister (1999 to 2008) and Deputy Prime Minister (1985 to 1992) of Belgium. As a Member of the European Parliament, he leads the Alliance of Liberals and Democrats for Europe (ALDE) and founded the interparliamentary 'federalist' Spinelli group and is the parliament's representative in the controversial Brexit negotiations and advocates for a federal Europe.

The last great autocratic superpower, which bore some resemblance to the overregulated, protectionist European Union conglomerate, was the Union of Soviet Socialist Republics (USSR) or Soviet Union, which was a totalitarian, communist regime, with a dominant central government. Big centralised government is normally too powerful and too dominant and too remote from the ordinary decent people they are supposed to serve.

The Kremlin ruled the Soviet Union conglomerate with a 'rod of iron' and savagely stamped out any dissent. The thought of any state leaving the Soviet Union was repugnant and repellent. When the Hungarian people revolted in 1956 the Kremlin sent in the troops and tanks and killed 2,500 people and 200,000 fled as refugees. That was the response of the Soviet Union to the 'will of the Hungarian people' who were revolting against their own government and its Soviet-imposed policies.

In 1968 the Soviet Union savagely responded to the peaceful protest of the Czechoslovakian people, who were seeking some reform, by sending in 200,000 troops and 5,000 tanks and killing 100 people. The demands of the Czechoslovakian people included the introduction of democratic elections, the freedom of speech and religion, greater autonomy for the Slovakian people and an end to travel restrictions. Well the European political elite cannot stamp out public dissent with military force, but they have expressed their distaste, with a demand for a crippling 'divorce settlement', and the threat of a bad trade deal or a no trade deal, which would destabilise the economy of any member state wanting to 'jump ship', even when their people have voted to leave in a referendum.

Whilst there is no real comparison between the 'brutal' Soviet Union and the liberal democracies of the European Union, their obdurate resistance to any form of dissent are very similar. Certainly, Catherine Bearder and Guy Verhofstadt seemed determined to subvert the democratic result of the Brexit referendum and appeared to have little respect for the 'will of the British people', who voted to leave by a majority of 1,269,501 votes.

Incidentally, Guy Verhofstadt wrote a book entitled *The United States of Europe*, published in March 2006 by the Federal Trust, which said: "The Belgium Prime Minister, Guy Verhofstadt, does not mince words, he wishes to create a United States of Europe with all member states of the EU participating, if possible, with a group of pioneers if necessary."

He also wrote a book entitled *Europe's Last Chance. Why the European States Must Form a More Perfect Union* published in January 2017 by Basic Books, which said: "Guy Verhofstadt (the) former Prime Minister of Belgium and (the) current leader of the liberal faction in the European Parliament... offers a powerful vision for how the continent can change for the better. The key is to reform the European Union along the lines of America's federal government and called the United States of Europe."

Guy Verhofstadt is one of the most powerful members of the European Parliament and he appears to be determined to create a multi-national super-state called the United States of Europe, along the lines of the United States of America, the most powerful country in the world.

Another powerful official in the Brussels bureaucracy is Martin Selmayr, a German-Belgian civil servant, who has been Secretary-General of the European Commission since 1st March 2018. He was previously Chief of Staff to the President of the Commission, Jean-Claude Juncker. After taking office as Secretary-General, he was described in a debate in the Parliament as "the most powerful bureaucrat in the world." We are also told by Robert Hardman, in an article in the *Daily Mail* on 28th July 2018, that he is a fanatical European federalist, with an alarming headline: 'Brussels bully who wants to turn Brexit into a punishment beating'.

Do we really want to be run by 'brutal' European federalists, based in Brussels? Do we really want to be run by unelected foreign politicians, riding on the lucrative Brussels-to-Strasbourg Express? Surely, we want to be run by elected politicians who campaign for our support and promise to represent us in our parliaments and assemblies, and whom we can eject from power, when they don't deliver what they promised?

The Brussels 'resistance movement' strikes at the heart of our liberal western democracy and challenges the 'will of the British people', who were happy with the European Economic Community or Common Market but concerned about the 'stealth-like' movement of the European Union, 'juggernaut', as it 'thunders' towards a federal United States of Europe.

However, whilst the European Union 'resistance movement' undermined the negotiating power of the British 'Withdrawal Agreement' negotiators, it paled into insignificance, when compared with the terminal damage being inflicted by the British 'Remain Campaign' saboteurs, who are arrogantly dismissing the 'will of the British people' in the referendum.

The determination of the Remain Campaigns, to overturn the result of the referendum, has seriously damaged the ability of the British negotiators to achieve an orderly Withdrawal Agreement from the European Union and to negotiate our 'future relationship', particularly a good trade deal.

So, who are the Remain Campaigners who have undermined the British government's attempt to get the Withdrawal Agreement ratified by their parliament, and who have demanded a second referendum, or a 'People's Vote', with an option to remain, and overturn the express 'will of the British people', which has created parliamentary 'deadlock'?

16

THE REMAIN CAMPAIGNS

We were told (1/6/2018) that a 'grassroots' group of Jeremy Corbyn supporters and trade union leaders were to launch a major speaking tour, billed as a 'left-wing' campaign to remain in the EU. The 'Left Against Brexit' (LAB) tour would attempt to persuade their leader and his allies, of the 'left-wing' case for a pro-EU position and would argue that the party will reap the electoral benefits from a shift in policy.

Rajeev Syal of *The Guardian* reported on 5th September 2018 that "One of Britain's biggest unions has called for a vote on the final Brexit deal in a move that will increase pressure upon (MP) Jeremy Corbyn to adopt a similar line. Tim Roache, the General Secretary of the GMB, said that the public had a right to a public vote on a final deal… The union… backed remaining in the EU, although it admitted its members were divided."

Incidentally, there should be no controversy over the administrative process to leave the European Union or the agreement of a 'mutually beneficial' future relationship, under Article 50. The people decided to leave, in the Brexit referendum, and the government invoked Article 50, to start the leaving process. The controversy surrounding an agreement on a 'mutually beneficial' trade deal or the threat of a no-deal, is fuelled by the liberal media and the remain campaigns, and the EU negotiators saying such things as: 'We can't have our cake and eat it'.

This tortuous process has been carried out in the full glare of the liberal media headlights, and the British negotiations have been undermined at every turn by the remain campaigns and many of the opposition parties, which must be viewed as an attempt by the political elite to ignore the votes of 17,410,742 citizens and destabilise the democratic process.

For instance, three former cabinet ministers launched a cross-party alliance on 14th May 2018 to keep Britain in the 'single market', claiming that to do so would let the Brussels elite 'breathe a sigh of relief'. David Miliband, Nicky Morgan and Nick Clegg joined forces to demand that we continue with 'close ties' with Brussels, even after Brexit. David Miliband said that Brexit voters had not voted to leave the 'customs union' and the 'single market', but he must know that we can't remain in either, when we leave the Union. Even if we joined the 'European Economic Area', like Norway, which provides access to the 'single market', we would have to accept EU rules and regulations and pay into their budget and accept the 'free movement of people', without having a seat at the top table.

Furthermore, the *Daily Mail* revealed a 'plot to subvert Brexit' on Thursday 24th May 2018, which said that the pro-Remain group 'Best for Britain', backed by billionaire financier, Hungarian-born George Soros, had launched a six-month plan to stop Britain leaving the EU. They want to persuade MPs to vote against the final deal and 'throw Brexit into chaos' and persuade trade unions to change Labour's stance on Brexit.

The 'Best for Britain' website shows that they're 'fighting to keep the UK open to EU membership, which seems a direct challenge to the 'will of the British people'. They say that they want 'younger people' to steer Britain into the future, which is disrespectful to the more experienced 'older people', who have effectively cast their vote on behalf of the less experienced 'younger' people, who were not old enough to vote. The Best for Britain campaign is committed to finding a democratic way to stop Brexit. They want a final say for Parliament and a second referendum. They're fighting to stay in the European Union with no compromise deal. They clearly think that they know better than the 17,410,742 citizens what's best for Britain, which is arrogant and probably won't work.

Another campaign group, known as 'Open Britain', is leading the fight against a hard and destructive Brexit. They believe that we are stronger in Europe. They will campaign for a close relationship with Europe and for the government to change its hard Brexit approach and provide the country with more than just a 'bad deal' or a 'no deal'. They want to make a positive case for a closer relationship with the European Union.

Yet another campaign group, 'Britain for Europe', which is partnered with 'The European Movement', campaigns for continued membership of the EU. They claim that continued membership of the Union is recognised in public debate, as a legitimate option, and that most people want a vote on the final deal, with remaining in the union as the outcome, if the deal is rejected. The European Movement is an independent, 'cross-party', organisation committed to keeping the UK in the EU. Their belief is that there's no deal better for our country than full EU membership and their nationwide grassroots network is campaigning to keep our country at the heart of Europe. It was reported that the 'Open Society Foundation' had donated £303,000 to the 'European Movement' and 'Scientists for EU'.

The 'Open Society Foundation' was launched by billionaire George Soros in South Africa in 1979 and he has given over $32 billion for their work in over 100 countries. Interestingly, the Open Society Foundation's work is to 'build vibrant and tolerant democracies whose governments are accountable to their citizens', which is probably one of the principal reasons why so many British people voted to leave the European Union and regain our independence. Does George Soros really believe that the European Union, which is growing into a federal, multi-national super-state, probably called the United States of Europe, is a "vibrant and tolerant democracy, whose government is accountable to their citizens"?

We recently heard of the 'People's Vote' campaign, which has been joined by the former professional footballer turned journalist, Gary Lineker, who said that: "Some things in life are more important than football"!

The 'People's Vote' campaign held rallies across the country during the summer, culminating in a march in central London in October 2018, which they expected to be the biggest Brexit protest yet. Incidentally, on the two-year anniversary of the vote, more than 100,000 people joined a 'People's Vote' march in London, wanting a referendum on the final deal. Do the 'People's Vote' campaign leaders think that an organised march of 100,000 people should be able to overturn the 'people's vote' of 17,410,742 British citizens, with a majority of 1,269,501 votes?

Incidentally, Julian Dunkerton, the co-founder of the clothing brand 'Superdry' had, apparently, made a £1 million donation to the 'People's Vote' campaign, suggesting that the public knows that Brexit will be a disaster and he thought that they had a chance to turn this around. Well he's entitled to his views, but they are insignificant when compared with the views of 17,410,742 British citizens. Julian Dunkerton may be a successful businessman, but in a democracy, he has just one vote.

Do these high-profile celebrities not realise that the reason our country has not got a 'good deal' with the European Union, is because the 'resistance movement', of which they are part, has weakened the hand of the Westminster negotiators and strengthened the hand of the Brussels negotiators? The 'resistance movement' has effectively given licence to the European political elite to punish the 'naïve' British electorate and send a warning to the electorate of other member states, who may also want to leave the European Union. If it's so difficult for a country like the United Kingdom to escape from the European project, what chance have weaker member states got to escape from the grand project, particularly those which are inextricably linked to the project, through the Eurozone?

Furthermore, *The New European* is a weekly newspaper, which was launched in July 2016 in response to the 2016 EU referendum and aimed at a readership of those who voted to remain in the EU. Its circulation was reported in November 2016 to be about 25,000 and in February 2017 to be about 20,000, which pales into insignificance when compared with the number of votes cast in the referendum. On 30th September 2016, the newspaper won serial rights to the fifth volume of Alistair Campbell's diaries about the Blair government, which is serialised over three weeks. In March 2017 they announced that they had appointed Alistair Campbell as their 'Editor at Large'. Incidentally, the first extract of the Campbell diaries revealed that Prime Minister Tony Blair had thought of leaving No. 10 in 2004 and that he had harboured hopes of securing the European Commission presidency. Contributors to the New European newspaper, include such pro-Europeans as Richard Branson, Nick Clegg, Chuka Umunna, Professor A. C. Grayling, Alistair Campbell and Tony Blair.

If the European Union multi-national super-state was a 'vibrant and tolerant democracy, accountable to their citizens', which is implied by the support of George Soros and the 'Open Society Foundation', they would have listened to Prime Minister David Cameron, as he 'scuttled' around Europe seeking some minimal reforms to the project, and there would have been no need for a referendum and we would not now be leaving.

It was so embarrassing to watch a British prime minister being ignored by his European colleagues, in the European Parliament, when he just wanted them to consider some minimal reforms, particularly to the 'free movement of people' principle and the 'stealth-like' movement towards 'ever-closer union', which are, of course, 'code words' for their ultimate 'clandestine' destination of a federal 'United States of Europe'.

The European political elite should have realised that the uncontrolled 'free movement of people' across 'open borders' in the Schengen Area, could be unmanageable and a matter of concern for the people of the more successful economies, which attract more migrants, and should not be dismissed as racist or xenophobic. Incidentally, the area covers 26 EU, member states, that have abolished passports and all other types of border controls. The Schengen Area is classed as a single jurisdiction for international travel purposes, with a common visa policy. The area has a population of 400 million people and about 1.7 million people commute to work across 'open borders' each day. However, one downside to the 'free movement of people' across 'open borders' is that during the EU migrant crisis, the lack of border controls helped illegal immigration.

They should also have realised that their gradual progress towards 'ever-closer union' and a federal country called Europe, run by the unelected European political elite such as President Jean-Claude Juncker, is not particularly democratic and would inevitably lead to a public 'backlash'.

The question is, however, to what lengths would the 'remain campaigns' go, to keep the United Kingdom in the European Union, against the 'will of the British people', and to what lengths would the Brussels political elite go, to support the 'saboteurs', who thought they could overturn the demand of 17,410,742 citizens, to leave an overladen 'sinking ship'?

We do, however, want our European neighbours to know that the British people voted to leave the growing European Union conglomerate, as it moves towards a federal country called Europe, with the free movement of millions of people across open borders, but they are not leaving their European neighbours and business partners. British 'business-people', want to continue trading with their European business partners, as they always have done, and be supported, not hindered, by the political class.

The European political elite should not have conflated international trade relationships or an economic community, the Common Market, with the membership of a political union, the European Union, and the threat that wanting to leave the expanding political union will seriously damage the economic trading relationships and destabilise the economic community.

17

THE GREAT BRITISH

TRADING NATION

Industrious and entrepreneurial British businesses will continue to trade with their European partners, as they always have done, and that's why the people voted to remain in the European Economic Community (EEC) or the Common Market. There was, of course, no mention, at that time, of the burning ambition of the European political class to progress from the European Economic Community (EEC) or Common Market, to a federal country called Europe or a United States of Europe. The European political class were, of course, aware of the objective to create a federal country called Europe or a United States of Europe, but they did not choose to share that information with their citizens, until it was too late.

This deceit by the political elite was started on 30th April 1952 by one of the founding fathers, Jean Monnet, when he apparently wrote: "Europe's nations should be guided towards the super-state, without their people understanding what is happening. This can be accomplished by successive steps, each disguised as having an economic purpose, but which will eventually and irreversibly lead to federation." This means that the European political elite, created an economic community, with an ultimate (discrete) destination of a federal country called Europe.

So far as trade is concerned, the other twenty-seven EU member states, mainly the Western European countries, across the channel, export more goods to the UK, than the UK does to them. In other words, the UK has a significant trade deficit with the rest of the EU member states, so why would the unelected European Commission negotiators, supported by the elected European Parliament, make it so difficult to achieve a 'mutually beneficial' free-trade deal, to coincide with our leaving the Union?

Incidentally, the following is evidence of the strength of our trading nation: The United Kingdom was ranked seventh in the recent World Bank's 'Doing Business' report, as one of the best countries in the world to do business, coming behind New Zealand (1), Singapore (2), Denmark (3), South Korea (4), Hong Kong (5) and the USA (6) and leaving our closest European rivals, Germany (20) and France (31) trailing behind.

Even better than that, according to the Forbes Annual Survey (2017), Britain has been crowned the world's best country to do business with, after coming fifth in the previous year. The United Kingdom scored well on technology and education of the workforce but 'political risk' was thought to be a weakness. This could be explained by the rise of militant, unionised socialism, in the Jeremy Corbyn Labour Party, and their grassroots 'resistance movement', under the banner of Momentum, which could be a return to the nineteen-seventies and the 'Winter of Discontent', when we were known as the 'Poor Man of Europe'.

The Forbes top ten best countries to do business with (2017) were the United Kingdom (1), New Zealand (2), the Netherlands (3), Sweden (4), Canada (5), Hong King (6), Denmark (7), Ireland (8), Singapore (9) and Switzerland (10). Remarkably, the United States (USA) was ranked (12), Germany (13) and France (22). This is another reliable indicator that Great Britain (GB) or the United Kingdom of Great Britain and Northern Ireland, can flourish on the world stage, when they escape the restrictive trade practices and over-regulation of the bureaucratic European Union.

We must realise that social justice will only emerge from the foundation stones of commercial enterprise and economic success, between trading nations, and we must remember that 'when trade stops, wars start'.

Consequently, the distant Brussels autocrats should have worked with their long-standing British partners, to negotiate a mutually beneficial trade deal and accept the 'will of the British people' and realise that many other member states may vote to leave the Union in the future.

There is a welcoming process to join the Union and a vindictive process to leave the Union, and the latter must be changed to be conducted in a spirit of co-operation, to secure a mutually beneficial outcome for both parties. Furthermore, there is a process concerned with joining and leaving the Union and another process, concerned with negotiating trade deals, and they should not be conflated, as they're not directly related.

The unelected scribes of the European Commission, who conducted the negotiations with the British, used the threat of a bad trade deal or a no-trade deal, to achieve a punitive 'divorce' settlement, as they need the income from one of their biggest net-contributors. They've never had to negotiate a Withdrawal Agreement with any member state, particularly a net-contributor to the budget, and they made the negotiation process so difficult, to ensure that other member states won't consider leaving.

Incidentally, it's interesting to note that the EU has recently negotiated and signed a free trade deal with the Japanese (July 2017), yet they threaten one of their biggest member states, and one of their biggest trading partners, with a 'bad deal' or 'no deal', on the basis that it was the British people who wanted to leave and there will be consequences and 'we can't cherry pick' and 'we can't have our cake and eat it'.

However, we do know that the European Commission should conform to the requirements of Article 8 of the Treaty of Lisbon, to develop a special relationship with neighbouring countries and aim to establish an area of prosperity, characterised by close and peaceful relations, based on co-operation, and not stamp out dissent by damaging mutually beneficial trading relations with their immediate neighbours and former partners.

We should note that the Kremlin eliminated the dissent of the communist states of Hungary and Czechoslovakia, with tanks and troops and death, and Brussels eliminates dissent of member states, wanting to leave, with a punitive 'divorce settlement', including the payment of some employee pension liabilities and the threat of a bad trade deal or a no-trade deal and the distinct probability of seriously destabilising their economies.

Incidentally, the United Kingdom has been a member of the European Economic Community (EEC) or the Common Market and the European Union for more than 45 years, and has always been a net-contributor to the budget. They may need to pay a 'divorce settlement', based upon current budget commitments and they may need to finance some future pension liabilities but what about accrued assets? It has been suggested that the United Kingdom has contributed (or invested) more than £300 billion to the EU budget over the years, which means it should have accrued some tangible assets, such as buildings and equipment, which should be valued and set against the punitive 'divorce settlement' demand from the Brussels political elite, which was apparently agreed at circa £39 billion. Just imagine what the British government could do with a 'treasure chest' of thirty-nine thousand million, that's £39,000,000,000.

Those independent nation states waiting to join the European Union, such as Turkey, which would be a net-contributor to the EU budget, should watch this tortuous leaving process very carefully and ensure that a much more reasonable leaving process is available before they join.

When the British escape the 'clutches' of the European Union, they may find that other member states demand a change from the 'free movement of people' to the 'free movement of labour', with a basic rule that anyone moving to another member state must have a job or be able to maintain themselves (and their families) until they can find paid employment.

Furthermore, it may not be a bad idea for member states of the growing European Union, to demand that they return to the European Economic Community (EEC) or the Common Market, which the United Kingdom joined in 1973 and approved in a referendum in 1975. The ordinary people, who voted to join the European Economic Community or the Common Market, had no knowledge of the 'clandestine' motivation of the remote European political elite to create a federal country called Europe.

Having watched the Brexit referendum being played out on the world stage, the people of the other twenty-seven member states should have the opportunity to decide whether they want to remain as members of this burgeoning, multi-national, federal super state, or return to an economic community or common market or single market and customs union.

Should the reform take place and the European political elite were prepared to 'ditch' their grand project and return to a common market or economic community or a single market and customs union, then the British would probably be 'first in the queue' to rejoin but they won't hold their breath, because it's unlikely to happen, any time soon.

18

RETURN TO THE COMMON MARKET!

It would not be unreasonable for the dominant member states of the European Union, which are paying the bills, to suggest a return to the original concept of the Common Market or the European Economic Community (EEC) and reject the ambition of the Brussels political elite to create a country called the United States of Europe. However, looking at the structure of the European Commission, with a president, a vice president and twenty-six other commissioners and 32,000 permanent and contract employees, a return to the Common Market or the European Economic Community (EEC), will not happen any time soon.

The President of the European Commission, Jean-Claude Juncker (2019), and First Vice-President, Frans Timmermans, and the twenty-six other commissioners, are entrenched in a 'deep-state' European Union.

The European Commission is composed of a College of Commissioners of the twenty-eight members, including the president and vice-president, and one from each member state. How many European citizens know the six vice-presidents (2019) or their responsibilities, starting with the President, Jean-Claude Juncker or the First Vice President, Frans Timmermans, responsible for Better Regulation, Inter-institutional Relations, the Rule of Law and the Charter of Fundamental Rights; or Federica Maria Mogherini, the High Representative for Foreign Affairs and Security Policy; or Andrus Ansip, responsible for the Digital Single Market; or Maroš Šefčovič, responsible for Energy Union; or Valdis Dombrovskis, responsible for the Euro and Social Dialogue, Financial Stability, Financial Services and Capital Markets; or Jyrki Katainen, responsible for Jobs, Growth, Investment and Competitiveness?

Each commissioner is assigned responsibility for specific policy areas by the president but the reality is that few of us have heard of the twenty-one other commissioners, starting with Cecilia Malmstrom, responsible for Trade; or Pierre Moscovici, responsible for Economic and Financial Affairs, Taxation and Customs; or Marianne Thyssen, responsible for Employment, Social Affairs, Skills and Labour Mobility; or Dimitris Avramopoulos, responsible for Migration, Home affairs and Citizenship; or Elżbieta Bieńkowska, responsible for Internal Market, Industry, Entrepreneurship and Small and Medium Enterprises; or Vytenis Andriukaitis, responsible for Health and Food Safety; or Günther Oettinger, responsible for the Budget and Human Resources; or Tibor Navracsics, responsible for Education, Culture, Youth and Sport; or Violeta Bulc, responsible for Transport; or Carlos Moedas, responsible for Research, Science and Innovation; or Johannes Hahn, responsible for European neighbourhood Policy and Enlargement Negotiations; or Vera Jourova, responsible for Justice, Consumers and Gender Equality; or Mariya Gabriel, responsible for the Digital Economy and Society; or Neven Mimica, responsible for International Co-operation and Development; or Miguel Arias Cañete, responsible for Climate Action and Energy; or Christos Stylianides, responsible for Humanitarian Aid and Crisis Management; or Corina Crețu, responsible for Regional Policy; or Karmenu Vella, responsible for Environment, Maritime Affairs and Fisheries; or Margrethe Vestager, responsible for Competition; or Phil Hogan, responsible for Agriculture and Rural Development; or Julian King, responsible for Security Union. These commissioners may or may not be impressive civil servants, who are known in their own country, but they are virtually unknown to most people in the wider European Union.

The British people knew the former Foreign Secretary, Jeremy Hunt, but how many knew Federica Maria Mogherini, High Representative of the European Union for Foreign Affairs and Security Policy, since 2014, who is an Italian politician who served as Italy's Minister for Foreign Affairs and International Co-operation (2014) in the centre-left Renzi Cabinet.

The reality is, of course, that none of these politicians, who have been chosen to represent us on the world stage, have been elected by the people, and they cannot remove them from office at the next election.

Furthermore, we all knew the former Chancellor of the Exchequer, George Osborne, who controlled our economic and monetary affairs (2010 to 2016) but did we know of the powerful politician Olli Rehn, European Commissioner for Economic and Monetary Affairs (2010 to 2014)? He was a Finnish politician, who served as their Minister of Economic Affairs and later was the Governor of the Bank of Finland.

This is not a xenophobic attack on foreigners working in the European Commission, such as Federica Maria Mogherini or Elżbieta Bieńkowska or Vytenis Andriukaitis, it's just drawing attention to these powerful politicians, whom the British people did not select or elect and cannot reject, which undermines the foundation of our liberal democracy.

These unknown foreign politicians, who control our affairs from their secure Brussels and Strasbourg 'ivory towers', are a serious challenge to our treasured parliamentary democracy and the theory of the 'primacy of the people'. It is, therefore, essential, that the development of a federal country called Europe, governed from Brussels and Strasbourg, must be returned to a coalition of independent trading nations or common market.

Incidentally, to add to the confusion, the European Parliament met on Tuesday 2nd July 2019, the first meeting since the European Elections (June 2019), and selected some new leaders for a five-year term of office:

They elected a new President of the Commission, Ursula von der Leyen, currently the German Defence Minister, to replace Jean-Claude Juncker. She is a committed Conservative Europhile who has apparently voiced support for a United States of Europe, which is said to be the standard view of any mainstream German politician! They also elected a new President of the European Council, the Belgian Prime Minister, Charles Michel, to replace the former Polish Prime Minister, Donald Tusk. They also elected the Spanish Foreign Minister, Josep Borrell Fontelles, as the High Representative for Foreign Affairs and Security Policy to replace Federica Maria

Mogherini, previously Italy's Minister for Foreign Affairs and International Co-operation. They also elected Christine Lagarde, currently leader of the International Monetary Fund (IMF), to be President of the European Central Bank (ECB). The question is, of course, do the British people know anything about the German Defence Minister, Ursula von der Leyen, or the Belgian Prime Minister, Charles Michel, or the Spanish Foreign Minister, Josep Borrell Fontelles, who have been elected to these important positions in the European Union, which affect our lives, without any reference to the people of Europe?

Furthermore, an Italian MEP, David Sassoli, was elected President of the European Parliament, on 3rd July 2019, to replace an Italian politician, Antonio Tajani, and will serve until January 2022. He was appointed by the European Parliament and not by the people. He was up against three other candidates: Ska Keller from Germany, Sira Rego from Spain and Jan Zahradil from the Czech Republic and he won 345 votes out of the 667 valid votes in the second round. This was not a 'people's vote' and most of the people have probably never heard of any of the candidates, yet David Sassoli occupies such an important position in the European Parliament, which directly affects the lives of so many European people.

The distance between the unknown Brussels politicians and bureaucrats and the ordinary people of the member states, creates a huge democratic deficit, which can only be resolved by a return to an economic community of independent nation states and the people must 'derail' the Brussels-to-Strasbourg Express, as it 'thunders' towards a United States of Europe.

However, whilst it may make sense to return to the European Economic Community or the Common Market, rather than pursuing the ultimate dream of a United States of Europe, the vested interests of the twenty-eight commissioners and circa 32,000 civil servants, suggest that it will not happen anytime soon, because 'turkeys don't vote for Christmas'.

Even the 822 elected Members of the European Parliament (MEPs), who benefit from an extravagant, cosmopolitan lifestyle, on the Brussels-to-Strasbourg Express 'gravy train', won't vote for change, any time soon. We've seen many British MEPs vociferously working with the Remain Campaign 'resistance movement', attempting to protect their lucrative employment, and why would they not indulge in self-preservation?

It was relatively easy for the United Kingdom (UK) to join the European Economic Community or the Common Market in 1973, which, through a series of discreet treaties, morphed into the European Union (EU), with clear ambitions for a United States of Europe, but it's proven extremely difficult to leave, due to the obstructive attitude of the Brussels machine.

As a net-contributor to the budgets of the European Union for decades, the United Kingdom must accept their fair share of current financial commitments, in the 2015 to 2020 budget cycle, as well as some future pension liabilities, but they should have accrued many tangible assets, such as buildings and equipment, which are not being considered. The autocratic Brussels negotiators appear to have ignored accrued assets and have demanded an extortionate 'divorce settlement' or 'bill' to cover budgetary commitments and future pension liabilities, before they would discuss our future relationship, particularly our trading relationship. The EU negotiators said that the UK cannot expect to get the same free trade deal, after leaving the club, as it had when members of the club, and said that 'we can't have our cake and eat it', which is conflating an unhealthy 'deep-state', 'Fortress Europe' with healthy international 'free trade'.

The British government should honour current budget commitments (2015-2020) and future pension liabilities, and demand that they consider accrued assets. Furthermore, the European political elite must see the benefit of a mutually beneficial 'free trade' deal with the British, who have been net-contributors to their budget for decades and the EU export more goods to the UK than we export to them. It's in their own economic 'self-interest' not to conflate EU membership with trade and to negotiate a mutually beneficial free-trade deal in a spirit of co-operation.

It's suggested that the ordinary people of the more powerful member states, such as Germany and France, should hope that the European political elite heed the warning from the Eurosceptic British people, and demand that they return, as a matter of urgency, to the original sensible concept of the European Economic Community or the Common Market.

The British people were very comfortable with their membership of the Common Market or the European Economic Community but became uncomfortable as the European political elite took us into a process of 'ever-closer' union, treaty by treaty, towards a United States of Europe.

So, let's consider a United States of Europe and the adverse effect it would have on the independence and sovereignty of our great country.

19

A UNITED STATES OF EUROPE

As we watched the negative negotiating approach of our 'friends' in Brussels, towards our departure from the Union, many British citizens must have thought 'who needs enemies, with friends like these'. We'd been a net contributor to the EU budget for decades, yet they treated us like strangers, just because we wanted to recover our independence, as they moved inexorably towards a multi-national super-state, a United States of Europe, with a multitude of disparate countries, languages, currencies, economies, cultures, traditions, customs and religions.

To give some idea of the bureaucracy involved in creating a United States of Europe, with a federal government, an elected president, a common currency (the euro) and a central bank (ECB), we can look beyond the challenges of so many differences, and consider the sheer numbers of politicians and civil servants in 28 member states, parliaments, and the European Parliament (and Commission), besides regional and local government, all of which are expensive talk-shops for the political elite.

When we voted to remain in the European Economic Community (1975), it consisted of twelve parliamentary democracies of which Belgium had 212 members in the lower house, Denmark had 179, France had 577, Germany had 656, Greece had 300, Ireland had 166, Italy had 630, Luxembourg had 60, The Netherlands had 150, Portugal had 250, Spain had 350 and the United Kingdom had 650, and we now have another sixteen members, many of which were former members of the Soviet Union or USSR, with little experience of liberal western democracy.

There are now circa 822 Members of the European Parliament (MEPs) from 28 member states, in addition to their national parliaments. For instance, Germany, has 99 MEPs, in addition to 656 members in its state parliament, known as the Bundestag in Berlin. The UK has 82 MEPs in addition to 650 members in the national parliament, known as the House of Commons in London, and France has 79 MEPs in addition to 577 members of its own parliament, known as the National Assembly in Paris.

To make matters worse, they all have legislative Upper Houses, with more state legislators. For instance, Germany has the Bundesrat, which meets at the Prussian House of Lords in Berlin and represents the 16 Federal States (Lander) with 61 non-elected delegates. Inexplicably, the United Kingdom has circa 824 unelected 'Peers of the Realm' in the Upper House, known as the House of Lords, in London, which has more members than the European Parliament. Finally, France has 348 Senators in the Upper House, known as the Senate, which meets in Paris.

The conclusion about the growth of the European Commission and Parliament, must be that we already have too many expensive politicians in the upper and lower chambers of our national parliaments, who are remote from the people, without another layer of politicians in Brussels.

Most people in Europe must conclude that they have virtually no influence over the 822 elected members of the European Parliament or the twenty-eight unelected European Commissioners, or the 32,000 civil servants, riding on the Brussels-to-Strasbourg Express 'gravy train'.

Democracy is about the government of the people by the people or their elected representatives and its success depends upon transparency and accountability, which cannot be delivered from distant 'ivory towers'.

It's difficult enough for the politicians and bureaucrats to manage an independent nation state, with a liberal parliamentary democracy, but it is virtually impossible to govern a multi-national super-state, with so many disparate, independent nation states, and very little in common.

The identity of a nation state is based on shared culture, religion, history, language or ethnicity, which give rise to strong feelings of patriotism and nationalism. However, many prominent national politicians talk about the concept of globalism, whatever that means. French President Emmanuel Macron 'criticised nationalism as a betrayal of patriotism' in a speech to commemorate the 100th anniversary of the end of the First World War, on Sunday 11th November 2018, when he said: "A global order based on liberal values is worth defending against those who have sought to disrupt that system." He went on to reject the "Selfishness of nations only looking after their own interests because patriotism is the opposite of nationalism." Well, he's entitled to his opinion about the relationship between patriotism and nationalism, but 'charity begins at home'. It's important that nations get their own houses in order and live within their means and balance their books, before they can donate their accumulated wealth towards contrived, multi-national super-states or welfare states.

The United Kingdom was a net-contributor to the budget of the European Union, which was necessary to sustain this multi-national super-state or welfare state, this dubious project of the European political elite, yet they have more than two trillion pounds of national debt. That's a massive two million, million, pounds of national debt, together with large debt interest payments and a recurring annual budget deficit of billions, to add to their debt each year. Incidentally, Britain last ran a budget surplus in 2000-01 before Labour embarked on a socialist spending spree. The annual deficit hit a record £153 billion in 2009 but reduced to £39.8 billion by 2017, under the Conservatives, and was expected to fall to £25 billion in 2018.

Many member states have accumulated significant national debt burdens, yet they are often significant net-contributors to the EU annual budget, which is then redistributed to the poorer member states, which often don't carry so much national debt. In other words, these 'debtor' nations are financing donations from more debt. They are borrowing to donate.

Incidentally, Hugo Duncan, the Deputy Business Editor of the *Daily Mail*, reported on 24th October 2018, that Britain would be in the black in just three years if the prime minister secured a Brexit deal with the EU. He reported that the country will run a surplus of £6 billion in 2021-22, thanks to a 'deal dividend' boosting the economy and (associated) tax receipts, according to claims from research group 'Capital Economics'.

However, the following chapters show the annual budget contributions of member states and their unemployment rates and their national debt burdens, which questions the viability of this contrived, multi-national super-state or welfare state, run by the European political elite and their bureaucrats from their remote Brussels and Strasbourg 'ivory towers'.

How long can this European Union enlargement mentality continue, before they take their member states into serious financial debt and become too big to fail? That was the case of the brutal Soviet Union and the Kremlin, or the Union of Soviet Socialist Republics (USSR), which was thought to be 'too big to fail' until it collapsed under its own weight.

Building a United States of Europe is a very big deal. Big is not beautiful. It's much more likely to be unmanageable, uncontrollable, untransparent and unacceptable to the innocent electorate, those ordinary people, who watch this expensive political fiasco from the sidelines, a 'view from the street'. These ordinary people, who ask for very little but 'dare to dream'.

So, let's look at the state of the Union and the budget contributions of member states, contributing to the continued expansion of this multi-national 'welfare state' and the burden placed on the so-called 'richer' economies, financing their largesse from increased national debt.

When considering the state of the Union, it is perhaps useful to consider the following three factors: (1) membership budget contributions (2) the national debt (3) unemployment rates, particularly youth unemployment.

20

THE STATE OF THE UNION

Budget Contributions of Member States

When considering the viability of the European Union, it's interesting to consider each country's share of the contributions to the EU budget (2016), according to Statista: Germany contributed 19% of the EU budget; France 16.63%; the United Kingdom 13.45%; Italy 12.49%; Spain 8.55%; Belgium 4.47%; Netherlands 3.71%; Poland 3.26%; Sweden 2.45%; Austria 2.36%; Denmark 1.83%; Ireland 1.61%; Finland 1.56%; Portugal 1.35%; the Czech Republic 1.3%; Greece 1.29%; Romania 1.15%; Hungary 0.82%; Slovakia 0.58%; Bulgaria 0.34%; Croatia 0.33%; Slovenia 0.32%; Lithuania 0.31%; Luxembourg 0.25%; Latvia 0.19%; Estonia 0.16%; Cyprus 0.14%; and Malta 0.07%. This is very much the model of a multi-national welfare state, where the so-called 'richer' countries provide financial support to the so-called 'poorer' countries, to stimulate industrial and commercial growth.

There's no wonder that the people of the 'poorer', mainly East European member states, which are beneficiaries of EU largesse, voted to join the Union in 2004. Some had public referendums with the following results: Malta had a vote of 53.6% in favour, on a turnout of 90.9%. Slovenia had 89.6% in favour, on a turnout of 60.2%. Hungary had 83.8% in favour, on a turnout of 45.6%. Lithuania had 91.9% in favour, on a turnout of 63.4%. Slovakia had 93.7% in favour, on a turnout of 52.1%. Poland had 77.5% in favour, on a turnout of 58.9%. The Czech Republic had 77.3% in favour, on a turnout of 55.2%. Estonia had 66.8% in favour, on a turnout of 64.1% and Latvia had 67.5% in favour, on a turnout of 71.5%. The positive voting of the people of the above countries, mainly former members of the Soviet Union, feels like a 'stampede' to join the club.

It could be argued that the European Union is very much a multi-national 'welfare state', which takes from the 'richer' countries and gives to the 'poorer' countries, to stimulate industrial and commercial growth and to increase employment opportunities and to provide the essential funding for infrastructure projects and to provide agricultural subsidies.

The dilemma is, however, how does the investment from the more industrial and commercial member states, to the less industrial and commercial member states, to stimulate industrial and commercial growth, match the demands of the global warming or climate- change campaigns, to reduce carbon emissions from power stations and motor vehicles, which increase with industrial and commercial growth?

Surely, the journey from agricultural to industrial societies must increase carbon emissions and contribute to global warming and climate change, and create more social turmoil, as the global warming and climate change campaigners take to the streets. Perhaps the Brussels political elite should reconsider their enlargement ambitions, to accept 'poorer' countries and give them the finance to grow their economies, which increases the standard of living of their people, but simultaneously increases carbon emissions and contributes to global warming and climate change, which is the biggest concern of the younger people.

Furthermore, as the European Union continues to enlarge, and takes in less industrial or commercial countries, which need financial support to stimulate industrial and commercial growth and infrastructure projects and agricultural subsidies and increased employment, how will that affect the economies and unemployment rates in the existing member states?

However, should the European Union, this project of the political elite, experience high levels of unemployment, as they attempt to stimulate industrial and commercial growth, particularly amongst young people, this multi-national super-state project will inevitably suffer increased social turmoil on the streets, as it has already done in Greece.

Unemployment Rates in the European Union

Another measure of the viability or sustainability of the European Union project, is the unemployment rates in member countries (June 2018), according to Statista as follows: Greece had an unemployment rate of 20.2%; Spain had 15.2%; Italy had 10.9%; France had 9.2%; Croatia 9.2%; Cyprus 8.2%; Finland 7.6%; Latvia 7.4%; Slovakia 6.9%; Lithuania 6.8%; Portugal 6.7%; Sweden 6.2%; Belgium 6%; Slovenia 5.6%; Luxembourg 5.2%; Ireland 5.1%; Denmark 5%; Estonia 4.9%; Bulgaria 4.8%; Austria 4.7%; Romania 4.5%; United Kingdom 4.1%; Malta 3.9%; Netherlands 3.9%; Poland 3.7%; Hungary 3.6%; Germany 3.4%; and the Czech Republic 2.4%. The level of unemployment in some of the south European member states is particularly unsustainable and is bound to lead to some adverse reaction, as the people take to the streets.

Even more concerning are the youth unemployment rates, which show Greece with 43.2%; Spain with 33.8%; Italy with 31.9%; Croatia with 23.6%; Portugal 20.8%; France 20.4%; Finland 18.4%; Slovakia 17.9%; Belgium 17%; Romania 16.8%; Sweden 15.5%; Luxembourg 14.2%; Lithuania 12.2%; Ireland 12%; Great Britain 11.5%; Bulgaria 11.2%; Poland 10.9%; Latvia 10.7%; Austria 10.2%; Slovenia 10.1%; Denmark 10.1%; Hungary 9.4%; the Czech Republic 7.6%; the Netherlands 6.9%; Estonia 6.8%; Germany 6.1%; and Malta 4.8%. It is a responsibility of the political class, to create an environment in which commercial activity can flourish, including agriculture and fisheries, and provide a wide pool of employment for our young people, as they leave education.

One would think that being a member of the European Union and the single market and customs union and single currency, would provide significant security, but the Greek tragedy suggests otherwise. How can a country survive, with an unemployment rate of 20.2% and a serious youth unemployment rate of 43.2%? The world's premier investing publication, Barrons, had this to say about Greece on 24th August 2018: "Greece's bailout was a disaster for Greece. The

European Stability Mechanism disbursed its final tranche of loans to the Greek government on Aug 6. On August 20, the program officially ended, although the loans are not expected to be fully repaid for another half-century. If their purpose was to support the Greek economy, the emergency loans must be considered a failure. Since 2008, the Greek economy has shrunk by a quarter, and more than 400,000 Greeks have emigrated…"

Furthermore, so far as the unemployment rates are concerned, the 'free movement of people' principle allows dependent unemployed people and their families to move from those member states with higher levels of unemployment, such as Greece, Spain and Italy, to other member states, with lower levels of unemployment, such as Germany, France and the United Kingdom, regardless of whether they have the skills to match the employment opportunities. There needs to be a more organised approach to the 'free movement of people' for employment, which matches the skills needed for the work or jobs, with the skills of the job-seekers, and takes account of the needs of the vulnerable job-seekers and their dependent families, for accommodation, public services and language differences.

When the unemployment rates in member states are so high, particularly youth unemployment, it suggests that their economies are not in good shape and they are probably increasing their national debt and annual deficits, and they are not able to subsidise other member states. The following gives some idea of the serious levels of national debt in some member states, many of which are still subsidising other member states.

The National Debt in Member States

Another measure of the viability of the European Union project, is the national debt in member states (1st quarter of 2018) in relation to their Gross Domestic Product (GDP) according to Statista as follows; Greece had a national debt of 180.4% of GDP; Italy had a national debt of 133.4% of GDP; Portugal had a national debt of 126.4% of GDP; Belgium had a national debt of 106.3% of GDP; Spain had a national debt of 98.8% of GDP; France had a debt of 97.7% of GDP; Cyprus had a debt of 94.7% of GDP; the United

Kingdom had a debt of 85.5% of GDP; Austria had a debt of 77.2%; Croatia had a debt of 76.2%; Slovenia had a debt of 75.1% of GDP; Hungary's debt was 75.1% of GDP; Ireland's debt was 69.3% of GDP; Germany's debt was 62.9% of GDP; Finland's debt was 59.8% of GDP; the Netherlands debt was 55.2% of GDP; Poland's debt was 51.2% of GDP; Slovakia's debt was 50.8% of GDP; Malta's debt was 50.4% of GDP; Sweden's debt was 37.9% of GDP; Lithuania's debt was 36.3% of GDP; Denmark's debt was 36.2% of GDP; Latvia's debt was 35.8% of GDP; the Czech Republic's debt was 35.8% of GDP; Romania's debt was 34.4% of GDP; Bulgaria's debt was 24.1% of GDP; Luxembourg's debt was 22.2% of GDP and finally, Estonia's debt was 8.7% of GDP. European Union standards require that member states should restrict their national debt to no more than 60% of their Gross Domestic Product and that does not appear to be the case in many of the so-called 'richer' member states.

There are five members of the European Union which have national debts of more than one trillion euros (that's more than a million, million euros): the United Kingdom, Italy, Germany, France and Spain. Whilst their economies may be strong, they carry serious national debt, and these are the countries which bear the brunt of economic migration.

The 'free movement of people' principle has no regard for the fact that many of the receiving countries are in serious debt, and any migration of dependent people and their families will be financed from more debt.

Whilst the European Union operates like a 'welfare state', taking from the so-called 'richer' member states, to give to the so-called 'poorer' member states, to stimulate industrial and commercial growth, many of the 'richer' countries have a serious national debt and should not be required to subsidise the 'poorer' member states from debt. The 'richer' countries borrow 'other people's' money, increasing their national debt burden, to subsidise the 'poorer' countries, which carry much less debt.

As the European Union 'juggernaut' trundles towards the United States of Europe, with a federal government, a single currency and a central bank, they must accept that many of the 'richer' member states are living beyond their means and that they must reduce their national debt and 'balance their books' and 'live within their means' or the United States of Europe will emerge onto the world stage as a debt-ridden super-state.

One thing is certain, in this age of uncertainty, the European political elite are creating a United States of Europe, which will consist of a group of 'debtor' nations, amongst their so-called 'richer' member states, and they should urgently reconsider their unsustainable multi-national 'welfare state' project and return to the European Economic Community (EEC) or the Common Market or a Commonwealth of Independent States (CIS), similar to the Russian Federation. If 'poorer' member states want to expand their economies and increase the living standards of their people, they should seek financial investment on the open market and not expect subsidies from other member states.

The European Union is a project of the European political elite and has very little to do with the 'will of the ordinary people'. Their 'clandestine' ambition to create a multi-national super-state, called the United States of Europe, and the operation of a multi-national welfare state, taking from the so-called 'rich' and giving to the so-called 'poor', is a very 'high-risk' strategy, which could end in financial disaster, with member states living well beyond their means and creating unsustainable debt.

So, let's examine the behaviour of the political elite, as they 'dragged' the cynical British electorate 'kicking and screaming', from an 'innocent' economic community or common market of independent nation states, to a 'sinister' political and economic union of subordinate member states, with the ultimate 'clandestine' objective of a United States of Europe.

21

THE POWER OF

THE POLITICAL ELITE

If only Prime Minister John Major had given the British people a referendum on the Maastricht Treaty (signed 7/2/92 and effective from 1/11/93), formally known as the Treaty on European Union (TEU), which created the euro and the three pillars structure of the Union, we may not have got bogged down in this multi-national 'welfare state' quagmire.

One of the obligations of the treaty was to keep fiscal policies, with debt limited to 60% of GDP and annual deficits no greater than 3% of GDP, which feels very much like the dictate of a federal government. The treaty also established a legally separate European Union, which comprised of the renamed European Economic Community and the inter-governmental policy areas of foreign policy, military, criminal justice and judicial co-operation in civil matters and paved the way for further developments, such as the Treaty of Amsterdam and the Treaty of Nice and others.

The ratification of the Maastricht Treaty was fraught with difficulties. In Denmark, the first Maastricht Treaty referendum, held on 2nd June 1992, rejected the treaty by a margin of 50.7% to 49.3% on an 83.1% turnout. Alterations were made to the treaty, which lists four Danish exceptions, and the treaty was then ratified by the Danes, on 18th May 1993, after a second referendum, by a margin of

56.7% to 43.4% on an 86.5% turnout.

Isn't it instructive, that the Danish referendum, on the game-changing Maastricht Treaty (which created the European Union from the Common Market or the European Economic Community), which rejected the treaty by 50.7% to 49.3% votes, was not accepted by Brussels, yet they accepted the French referendum on the Maastricht Treaty, which accepted the treaty by 50.8% votes to 49.2% votes, and no mention of a 'narrow margin' or 'slender margin' or the need for another referendum!

The stark reality is, that if the treaties concerned with the development of the European Union are 'accepted' by a narrow margin, then that's fine with the political elite. However, if the people have the temerity to 'reject' a treaty by a narrow margin, they receive some minor concessions and a second referendum, to achieve acceptance. In other words, nothing will be allowed to slow down this European-registered 'juggernaut', as it thunders towards its ultimate destination of a United States of Europe.

Whilst no one appears to have questioned the validity of the French referendum on the Maastricht Treaty (September 1992), which approved the change from the European Economic Community (EEC) or Common Market to the European Union (EU), on a slender margin of 1.6%, based on 50.8% in favour to 49.2% against, so many people from the remain campaign, in the United Kingdom Brexit referendum, have made so much of the 'margin' of 3.78%, based on 51.89% to leave and 48.11% to remain. If the people had been consulted on the Maastricht Treaty and had been told of the change from the Common Market trading group, to the European Union super-state, they may have voted against the treaty.

Incidentally, if the British people had been consulted by New Labour on the Treaty of Nice (signed on 26/2/2001 and effective from 1/2/2003), which reformed the institutional structure to withstand eastward expansion, they may have prevented the 'exodus' of people from the Eastern European countries to the Western European countries, which was one of the reasons for them voting to leave the European Union.

Furthermore, had the unelected Prime Minister, Gordon Brown, consulted the British people on the Treaty of Lisbon (Reform Treaty, signed on 13/12/2007 and effective from 1/12/2009), which created a long-term president of the European Council and a High Representative for Foreign Affairs and Security Policy (and gave members the right to leave and the procedure to do so), they may have voted against the treaty and slowed down the enlargement process and they may not have needed the United Kingdom European Union membership referendum in 2016.

More importantly, had Prime Minister Ted Heath informed the people about the 'small-print' objective of the architects of the European Union project, to create a United States of Europe, when he took us into the European Economic Community (EEC) or the Common Market (1973), we may not have approved the subsequent referendum (1975) to approve continued membership, authorised by Prime Minister Harold Wilson.

The disproportionate power of the Westminster political elite, when compared with the impotence of the British people, is illustrated by the undemocratic approach of the three prime ministers who took the people into, what appeared to be, an eminently sensible economic community or common market and then failed to consult them about the 'clandestine' transition to a political union, through a series of sinister treaty changes.

The creation of the European Union is a project of the European political elite and has little to do with the 'will of the people'. When the people vote in favour of a treaty by a small margin, their decision is accepted, but when they vote against a treaty by a small margin, their decision is rejected. This totalitarian behaviour by the European political elite is an attack on the foundation stones of our cherished liberal democracies.

So far as the Brexit referendum is concerned, it may not have been necessary, had the arrogant European political elite, in their Brussels and Strasbourg 'ivory towers', listened to the concerns of the British people and introduced some limited reform, particularly concerning the principle of the 'free movement of people'. All they needed to do was ensure that the multitude of economic migrants were able to maintain themselves and their families until they found employment and could not depend on the 'overstretched' public services of the receiving countries.

All the British people wanted, was some limited reform to the 'free movement of people' principle and some reassurance that the economic community or common market, was not gradually moving from a trading group to a political union, with ambitions to become a multi-national super-state, with a federal government, an elected president, a single currency, a central bank and a standing army. Neither did they want to be a satellite state of a multi-national super-state, with a multitude of disparate countries, languages, cultures, traditions and religions and managed by unknown politicians they did not elect and cannot reject.

However, despite the best efforts of the political elite to disguise their creation of a multi-national super-state, the British people became aware that those they elect to represent them in the 'corridors of power', were 'dragging' them towards a United States of Europe, without their permission or consent, and all they had wanted was some limited reform.

22

THE BRITISH JUST WANTED

LIMITED REFORM

Despite the political deception, which 'dragged' us towards a United States of Europe, had the European political elite respected the concerns of the British people and listened to Prime Minister David Cameron as he 'scuttled' around Europe, seeking some support for limited reform, particularly to the 'free movement of people' principle and the gradual movement towards 'ever-closer' union, we may have voted to remain.

In early 2014 Prime Minister David Cameron outlined the changes he wanted to agree with the other members of the European Union. These included additional immigration controls, especially for citizens of new member states; tougher immigration rules for existing EU citizens; new powers for national parliaments to collectively veto proposed EU laws; new free trade agreements and a reduction in business bureaucracy; a reduction in the influence of the European Court of Human Rights on the police and the courts; more power for individual member states and less power for the European Union, and the abandonment of the objective of 'ever-closer union'. He wanted to achieve agreement for limited reform, with other leaders, and then put the result to the people, in a referendum.

In November 2014, he gave an update on his negotiations and clarified his objectives, which included that Eurozone laws should not necessarily apply to non-Eurozone members and the latter would not have to 'bail out' troubled Eurozone economies; and for the UK to be exempt from the objective of 'ever-closer' union and for national parliaments to be able to collectively veto proposed EU laws; and for EU citizens working in the UK to be unable to claim social housing or in-work benefits until they had worked for four years, and not send child benefits overseas. We were happy with economic migrants in search of work but not welfare benefits.

The outcome of the negotiations was announced in February 2016, which included some limits to 'in-work' benefits for EU immigrants but these limits would apply on a sliding scale over four years and would be for new immigrants only and members would need to get permission from the European Council to introduce the restrictions; child benefit payments could still be sent overseas but these would be linked to the cost of living in the receiving country; the UK was reassured that it would not have to participate in 'ever-closer' union; and it would be made easier for member states to deport EU nationals for public policy or public security reasons.

However, they had just payed lip service to the concerns of the British people, and in the wake of the referendum vote to leave the Union, David Cameron resigned and sparked a leadership contest which was won by Home Secretary Theresa May, who promised to make Brexit a reality, saying that 'Brexit means Brexit'. To her credit, whilst she had voted to remain, she respected the 'will of the people' and said that there would be no second referendum, as had occurred in other member states.

Whilst David Cameron had failed to get the Brussels negotiators to introduce some meaningful reforms and having then called a referendum on our continued membership, he should not have resigned and handed a 'poisoned chalice' to his successor, Theresa May, who had voted remain.

He should not have campaigned one way or the other and let the people decide. However, having 'nailed his colours to the mast' and campaigned to remain, he lost the vote and resigned and left his successor to deal with the obstinate Europeans, to sort out the mess that he'd created.

Incidentally, until Article 50 of the Lisbon Treaty emerged, there was no formal mechanism to leave the European Union and we are told that the article was written with the intention that it would never be used. Since the result to leave was announced, the leavers have suffered obdurate resistance from the opposition parties and the many remain campaigns, blatantly wanting to overturn the result through a second referendum.

Having passed the Lisbon Treaty (Reform Treaty) 2007, which authorised member states to leave the Union and the mechanism to do so, why would they make it so difficult to leave at the first hurdle? We got the message, during the passage of the many European treaties, when any negative referendum result was sent back to the member state to hold a second referendum, to get a positive result. We got the message, when a 'narrow result' against a treaty, was unacceptable, but a 'narrow result' in favour of a treaty was accepted. We got the message when they would not start to negotiate a withdrawal agreement until we had agreed to pay them a substantial 'divorce settlement'. We got the message when they said that we voted to leave and there would be consequences. We got the message when they said that 'we can't have our cake and eat it'. We got the message, that they won't tolerate 'truculent' member states wanting to leave, when they immediately made the withdrawal agreement process so unpalatable, to discourage others from making the same (stupid) mistake!

Article 50 of the Lisbon Treaty introduced an exit clause for members wanting to leave the European Union, which requires a member state to inform the European Council before it can terminate membership and a 'withdrawal agreement' must be negotiated within two years of giving notice, unless the period is extended by mutual agreement. It all sounds easy, but the approach of the Brussels negotiators was to declare that it was the British who voted to leave, so they can't expect a trade deal like the one they had as members, as they 'can't have their cake and eat it'.

Whilst the people just wanted some limited reform, particularly to the 'free movement of people', their request was not taken seriously by the European political elite, which led to the Brexit referendum and a large majority of 1,269,501 votes to leave, which was inexplicably described by our former prime minister, John Major, as the "tyranny of the majority".

23

THE "TYRANNY OF THE MAJORITY"

The most disturbing reaction to the result of the Brexit referendum was from two prominent former prime ministers, John Major and Tony Blair.

John Major's response to the result of the Brexit referendum was to describe it as the "tyranny of the majority", which flies in the face of democracy, which recognises the 'will of the people' through a simple majority vote. Incidentally, John Major won the 1992 General Election on a minority vote, which is the very nature of the 'first past the post' electoral system and could be referred to as the 'tyranny of the minority'.

Tony Blair called on the Remain campaign to 'rise up' in defence of their beliefs and suggested that the electorate voted without knowledge of the true terms of Brexit and as the terms become clearer, it would be their right to change their mind. This is a man who informed the people, in the last New Labour manifesto, that they would give the people their say on the Lisbon Treaty and his successor Gordon Brown failed to do so. This is the man who took us to war in Iraq, on a false prospectus, resulting in thousands of people being killed and seriously injured and a refugee crisis greater than the Jewish diaspora. He ignored the voices of millions of people who marched the streets against the dubious Iraq war. The Blair government sent our troops into harm's way without knowing the real consequences to the soldiers and millions of innocent civilians. He was the leader of our country who started a war without an exit strategy.

This is the prime minister who allowed unlimited immigration from the former communist countries, Poland, Slovakia, the Czech Republic, Hungary, Estonia, Lithuania and Latvia, when the political leaders of other West European member states, imposed restrictions, which was one of the reasons why the sceptical British people voted to leave the Union.

Incidentally, the hypocrisy of Tony Blair, who may still have ambitions to become the first elected president of the European Union, should be a matter of public concern. He has challenged the decision of 17,410,742 citizens to leave the European Union (EU), yet when he campaigned to become a Member of Parliament (1982-83), his personal manifesto said: "We'll negotiate withdrawal from the European Economic Community, which has drained our natural resources and destroyed jobs."

Another disturbing reaction to the democratic decision of the British people was from the former Deputy Prime Minister and leader of the Liberal Democrats, Nick Clegg, who lost his seat in parliament and wrote a book entitled *How to Stop Brexit*. This is an attack on the principles of the British democratic and electoral process, from someone who worked for and benefits from the Brussels-to-Strasbourg 'gravy train'.

He said in his book: "If we want to understand Brexit today, we need to acknowledge the distinct circumstances in which we joined the European club in the first place. Our original decision was shaped by a sense of national decline." The 'European club' was, of course, otherwise known as the European Economic Community (EEC) or the Common Market, a group of independent trading nations, and we were probably right to join in 1973 (without a referendum) and right to confirm our membership, in a referendum in 1975. Had the 'European club' continued to be a group of independent trading nations, instead of adopting the principles of 'ever-closer union' and the 'free movement of people' across 'open borders', effectively a federal country called Europe, we would not have needed a referendum, or if we'd had one, we may not have voted to leave.

The blatant hypocrisy of the two former prime ministers and the former deputy prime minister, and many other prominent politicians and former politicians, is breath-taking. They all held high public office, as a result of a 'first past the post' electoral system, which expected losers to accept the result, with a constructive opposition, and not a destructive 'resistance movement' actively campaigning to change the result.

In fact, the hypocrisy is even worse when one considers that general elections, under the 'first past the post' electoral system, are usually won on a minority vote, with the majority voting for the losing parties.

These former senior politicians accepted the results of general elections, which they won, knowing that more people voted against them than for them, yet they have the audacity to challenge the result of the Brexit referendum, which produced a significant majority of 1,269,501 in favour of leaving the European Union. Tony Blair suggested that the people voted without knowledge of the true terms of Brexit and as the terms become clearer it would be their right to change their minds. Surely, this is the case in most elections or referenda, where the people are exposed to misleading 'campaign' information, but they are unable to call another general election to change the result. Does Tony Blair want our elections and referenda to be decided on the 'best of three' or just keep repeating the electoral process until the politicians get the result they want?

Many of the older and wiser citizens who voted to leave the growing European Union, as it moves inexorably towards a federal country called Europe, had witnessed the discreet change from an eminently sensible European Economic Community (EEC) or Common Market, towards a European Union super-state, without being consulted. This is a project of the European political class, and very little to do with the 'will of the people', who are being carried along on a wave of misinformation or a deliberate lack of 'candour' or 'honesty' about their ultimate objectives.

In particular, the behaviour of these two former prime ministers, who accepted the 'first past the post' electoral system, is damaging the foundations of our liberal western democracy, by demanding a second referendum, to change the result, and keep us in this growing European super-state conglomerate. So much for the electoral system delivering on the 'will of the people' when a former prime minister refers to a majority of 1,269,501 as the 'tyranny of the majority' and the other referred to the result as a 'small margin'. Do we really need to inform these two former prime ministers, that a majority of

1,269,501 voters is significant and is almost as many people as live in the two cities of Leeds and Bradford?

If the arrogant political elite had achieved a second referendum, the divisive electoral process would have damaged our liberal western democracy and destroyed the concept of the 'will of the people', who voted, for whatever reasons, to leave the European project as it moves towards a federal country called Europe or a United States of Europe.

Incidentally, whilst so many former prime ministers and deputy prime ministers and the 'resistance movement' were demanding a second referendum, to change the result of the first referendum, on 15th March 2019, parliament voted by 334 to 85 votes (in an 'indicative vote') to 'crush' any suggestion of a second referendum or a 'People's Vote'.

Surely, an indicative vote of such clarity should have silenced those who want our country to have a second referendum and remain in the Union.

So, let's look at the multitude of reasons why a significant majority of the people voted to leave the European Union and challenge the suggestion that they were influenced by extreme thoughts of racism and xenophobia.

24

WHY WE VOTED TO LEAVE

THE EUROPEAN UNION

Let's now look at the multitude of reasons why 17,410,742 British people voted to leave the European Union project. We probably needed to leave, just because it's inexorably moving towards a United States of Europe, consisting of twenty-eight disparate countries. The first six countries of the original European Economic Community (EEC) or the Common Market, were Belgium, France, Germany, Italy, Luxembourg and the Netherlands (1951); followed by Denmark, Ireland and the United Kingdom (1973); then Greece (1981); then Spain and Portugal (1986); then Austria, Finland, Sweden, the Czech Republic, Slovakia, Hungary, Poland, Slovenia, Estonia, Latvia, Lithuania, Malta and Cyprus (1995); then Bulgaria and Romania (2007) then Croatia (2013), with Serbia, Montenegro, Macedonia and Albania waiting to join (32) and Turkey waiting in the wings (33), when the vast majority of the land mass of Turkey is not even part of Europe. Furthermore, Brussels has apparently promised Kosovo and Bosnia and Herzegovina the prospect of joining in the future (35). Is there any limit to the enlargement ambitions of the EU?

This multinational super-state, of twenty-eight (shortly to be twenty-seven) disparate countries, with plans for expansion, can only function effectively with a federal government, a central bank, and a single currency, which means that individual member states will erode their national identities and economic independence, and this should only happen, when their unsuspecting citizens have spoken in a referendum.

Whilst the creation of a multinational super-state by the remote political elite is reason enough to leave the growing European Union, there are many other reasons to leave this political construct, which threatens the independence of nation states and the ability of their people to select and elect and reject their politicians, which is the basis of our democracy.

In the first instance, the European Commission has not had an annual budget audit passed for more than twenty years, which would not be tolerated had it been a private company. For many years the European Union auditors refused to endorse the spending on large parts of the EU budget. Whilst the auditors found problems with the way the EU spends its money, they declared them to be reliable. However, the European Court of Auditors (ECA) said that they had misspent about seven billion euros (£5.5 billion) in 2013, that's 4.7% of its annual budget. They also said that the budget should be focussed on achieving results, rather than just getting funds spent. The most error-prone spending areas in 2013 were regional policy, including energy and transport (6.9% error rate) and rural development, which includes the environment, fisheries and health (6.7% error rate). They agreed an EU budget (2014-20) of 960 billion euros, which is the maximum they can spend. The money allocated to the EU budget includes 325 billion euros to support those countries and regions that are economically 'lagging behind' other member states and 278 billion euros to aid farmers and help maintain rural communities and 15.7 billion euros for the fight against international terrorism and to deal with asylum seekers and refugees. This financial mismanagement, concerned with money being misspent and a lack of focus on results and error prone spending, is probably a consequence of remote corporate governance, getting involved in matters which should have been devolved through 'subsidiarity' to the lowest practical level in member states.

Furthermore, on 26th September 2018, *The Times* newspaper reported: "If more proof were needed that institutions of the European Union are insular, hypocritical, amoral and blind to political imperatives, they provided it yesterday. The ruling by the European General Court... that the European Parliament was right to decline requests for information about members expenses, is a charter for political corruption. Unless the ruling is overturned... MEPs will be allowed... expenses allowances worth more than 4,000 euros a month, in addition to their 8,611 euros, monthly salaries... without receipts or public disclosure of how the money has been spent. That this spending has been subject to so little (public) scrutiny was already a scandal. That an opportunity arose to remedy the situation, only to be rejected by the European Parliament and one of the European Union's highest courts, is unconscionable..."

If the European Union is to continue towards a United States of Europe and accept ever more new member states, they must take the concept of subsidiarity (the devolvement of power to the lowest practical level) more seriously and develop a smaller and more efficient federal government in Brussels and much stronger and more independent member states.

A more practical approach to the European Union project would be to abandon the 'covert' objective to create a United States of Europe, with a federal government, an elected president, a central bank and a single currency and return to the early construct of the European Economic Community (EEC) or the Common Market, which was an economic or commercial union of independent, Western European, trading nations.

Another reason to leave the European Union super-state, is the principle of the 'free movement of people' which resulted in uncontrolled economic migration from the 'poorer' agrarian Eastern European countries to the 'richer' industrialised Western European countries. This flawed social concept resulted in the net immigration of circa 333,000 migrants and refugees into our country from the rest of the Union and the 'war-torn' Middle East, and North and West Africa and elsewhere during 2015.

Whilst the United Kingdom must accept its international obligations to accept a proportion of the world's refugee population, it has no control over the numbers arriving from other EU countries. The unplanned and uncontrolled arrival of hundreds of thousands of economic migrants and vulnerable refugees, when employment and accommodation may not be available, cannot be absorbed by most countries and could have serious economic and social consequences and put pressure on public services.

So far as the EU is concerned, it should be no surprise that citizens from the much 'poorer' countries will be attracted to the 'richer' countries and arrive regardless of whether there is enough housing or employment, and many 'dependent' families throw themselves onto the oversubscribed health, education and welfare services of the receiving countries. This is a challenge for the authorities, when many immigrant families do not speak their language, and is a more serious challenge for the education authorities, when the 'innocent' children cannot speak the language.

A series of papers released by the Office for National Statistics (ONS) on 24th May 2018 showed that the migrant population in our country had reached 9.4 million last year – a 3% increase on 2016. It showed that the Poles were the largest population of non-British nationals (2017) with 1,021,000, followed by Romanians with 411,000, then Eire with 350,000, India with 346,000, Italy with 297,000, Portugal with 235,000, Lithuania with 199,000, Pakistan with 188,000, Spain with 182,000, France with 181,000, Germany with 154,000, China with 147,000, USA with 133,000, Latvia with 117,000, Nigeria with 102,000, Hungary with 98,000, Netherlands with 97,000, Australia with 87,000, Bulgaria with 86,000, Bangladesh with 84,000. According to the ONS, England's population is expected to rise by 5.9% to 58.5 million by 2026.

Incidentally, whilst the UK may be the fifth largest economy in the world it is also a debtor nation and is trying to reduce its penchant for spending 'other people's' money. In 2017 the national debt reached circa £1.72 trillion, while the annual deficit was circa £68 billion (March 2017) with no sign of a budget surplus on the horizon. The interest alone, to service the debt (2017/18) was circa £49 billion, which is more than we spend on our defence. The constant flow of hundreds of thousands of dependent refugees and economic migrants, into a debtor nation, where there may be no employment opportunities or available accommodation, means that any additional costs will be financed from more borrowed money or debt.

Furthermore, the people should not be labelled right-wing nationalists, because they want to recover their independence and don't want to be part of a European Union conglomerate. Neither should the people be labelled xenophobic because they are concerned about the numbers of foreigners coming from the EU and elsewhere, and they should not be labelled racist because they are worried about the unsustainable level of refugees and economic migrants, who happen to be black or brown.

How can so many individual nation states with diverse languages, cultures, mores, religions, currencies and economies, form a European super-state, like the United States of America, which has one main language (English), one currency (dollar), one central bank (Federal Reserve), one federal government and one elected president? It's quite exhausting to follow the presidential election campaigns across the fifty states of the USA, every four years, with two main political candidates and one main language. Just imagine a European presidential election campaign, across so many disparate countries, with different languages and presidential candidates, who may only speak their native language.

Even a country like Belgium has three different languages – Dutch, French and German. Citizens of Cyprus speak Greek, Turkish and English. Estonians speak Estonian and Russian. Latvians speak Latvian and Russian. Lithuanians speak Lithuanian and Russian. Luxembourg has three languages – Luxembourgish, German and French. Finland has two languages, Finnish and Swedish, and remarkably Spain has four different languages – Castilian, Catalan, Galician and Basque, and the Catalans are desperate to break away from Spain and become an independent nation.

For those concerned with EU expansion into Eastern Europe, they should question the application of Turkey, a country of circa 79 million people, mainly Muslim, when most of the land mass is in Asia and it shares its southern border with Syria, Iraq and Iran. If Turkey is accepted as a full member of the Union, with most of its land mass in Asia, why would they not consider applications from Syria, Iraq and Iran and others, which are also in Asia, and form a Eurasian Union? However, before expanding into Asia, what about the accession of Moldova, Belarus and Ukraine (Crimea), which are already part of Europe, as is a large part of Russia, and its capital city, Moscow, and most of the Russian population? Surely, even supporters of globalism can see the nonsense of creating a multi-national super-state across Europe, let alone a Eurasian conglomerate.

It's suggested that the people of the world who believe in democracy and the 'will of the people', should reject the academic concept of globalism promoted by the political elite, and demand the retention of independent nation states, working and trading together, for the common good. The ordinary people, who have just one vote, must promote the concept of 'smaller government, bigger people and stronger society' and reject the concept of European or Eurasian multi-national governance, which appears to be the desire of the unaccountable European political elite.

The best example of a country in crisis, from their disastrous venture with European Union multi-national governance, and the single currency, is Greece, which is suffering the humiliation of enormous national debt and worklessness and homelessness and survival on external bailouts. That beautiful Mediterranean country, with 'wall-to-wall' sunshine, should be the tourist destination of the world and it should be flourishing as an independent nation, with its own currency, without being reliant on the financial largesse 'bailouts' of their dominant European Union partners.

Being a member of the European Union multinational super-state, has probably terminally damaged the ability of the Greek people, and their political representatives, to control their own affairs and chart their own future, rather than being dependent on European financial largesse. If there was ever a reason for a member state to leave the European Union conglomerate, and their monetary union and single currency, it must be the recent tragedy of Greece, floundering in the shadow of Brussels.

This dangerous expansionist mentality of the Brussels political elite has created a union of interdependent nation states, which is too big to fail. This has been shown by their determination to pump money into the Greek economy, which was effectively bankrupt, as it could not settle its debts. Greece was bailed out by the European Commission (EC), the European Central Bank (ECB) and the International Monetary Fund (IMF) to the tune of 110 billion euros, and in return they were required to take drastic austerity cuts to their public expenditure and reduce their annual budget deficit and liberalise their markets, to avoid bankruptcy.

During this economic crisis in Greece, there were violent street protests and increased suicide rates and increased homelessness and changes of government. On 5th July 2015 a referendum was held on the bailout conditions, in the Greek government debt crisis, resulting in 61.3% of the people voting against the conditions, on a turnout of 62.5%, but the result was ignored, and the weak Greek government had to accept the bailout with even harsher conditions than the ones rejected by the people. If this economic tragedy does not illustrate the power of the European political elite over their dependent Eurozone member states, then nothing does.

Yanis Varoufakis, the former finance minister of Greece, said in his book, *And the Weak Suffer What They Must* published by Vintage in 2016: "By the summer of 2015 the writing was on the wall: Greece would be locked into a debtor's prison and I, refusing to sign the surrender documents, resigned my ministry. The EU would again pretend it had solved a crisis by throwing new debt into the bottomless pit of unpayable older debts. And the peoples of Europe would lose what little confidence they had left in the European Union's institutions."

Finally, Matthew C. Klein reported on barrons.com on 24th August 2018 that "Greece's 'bailout' was a disaster for Greece" and went on to say: "The European Stability Mechanism disbursed its final tranche of loans to the Greek government … although the loans are not expected to be repaid for another half-century. If their purpose was to support the Greek economy, the emergency loans must be considered a failure. Since 2008, the economy has shrunk by a quarter and more than 400,000 Greeks have emigrated. House prices are down 43%. Bank credit to the private sector contracted by a third … Greek residents spent far more than they earned, with the result that the current account deficit ballooned from about 5% of gross domestic product in 1999 to 10% by 2006 and to 14% by 2008. Had Greece been a country with its own currency… the central bank could have plugged the funding gap and prevented an abrupt collapse in spending. Membership of the euro area removed that option… The textbook response would have been for the government to default on its debt and get a loan from the International Monetary Fund (IMF) to help smooth out the adjustment. That option was blocked by a coalition of Greece's 'European partners' and the USA… Their concern was not about what a default would do to Greece but what it would do to them…"

Surely, we should have learned the weakness of the Eurozone through the Greek tragedy, but the Brussels autocrats are more determined than ever to achieve their ultimate objective. The 'stealth-like' movement towards 'ever-closer' union, has no regard for the 'will of the people', who are being 'frog-marched' towards a United States of Europe, with a single federal government, a central bank, a single currency, an elected president and their latest obsession, to create a European army.

The expansion of the European Union, from the small beginnings of the Western European Common Market (the 'twelve democracies of Belgium, Denmark, France, Germany, Greece, Ireland, Italy, Luxembourg, the Netherlands, Portugal, Spain and the United Kingdom') towards a United States of Europe, should have been a matter of concern to those who favour liberal democracy and the concept of limited government.

The British people were concerned about the creation of a European Union super-state, and the expansion into Eastern Europe, and the 'free movement of people' across 'open borders', and the lack of transparency and accountability of the remote European political class, which led to the popularity of the United Kingdom Independence Party (UKIP), and the unexpected (Brexit) referendum result, to leave the European Union.

It's difficult enough for ordinary people to have confidence in national and regional governments but it's virtually impossible for them to have confidence in an unaccountable European super-state conglomerate.

So, let's look at the lack of accountability of this expanding monolithic institution, the European Union, which is managed by an army of elected (MEPs) and unelected politicians and officials, based in Brussels, most of whom we do not know and did not select or elect and cannot reject.

If there was ever a reason to leave the European Union conglomerate, it's the lack of transparency and accountability of the many European institutions and politicians and officials, who are presiding over our affairs, and there's not a damned thing we can do about it. Whilst we have an army of elected and appointed politicians and officials in Westminster, Edinburgh, Cardiff and Belfast, representing the people, in national and regional parliaments and assemblies, the ultimate legal authority is vested in the European Union constitution and institutions.

Does anyone really know what happens in the European Parliament or the European Council or the Council of the European Union (or Council of Ministers) or the European Commission or the Court of Justice of the European Union or the European Central Bank or the Court of Auditors?

This is a taste of the extent of bureaucracy which exists in the European Union institutions, as it moves, inexorably, towards a country called Europe or a United States of Europe, and it's virtually unstoppable. It's very similar to an Exocet missile: 'you can hear it coming, you can see it coming, but there's not a damned thing you can do about it'!

The European Parliament acts together with the Council of the European Union, as a legislature, and has budgetary powers and exerts democratic control over the many institutions, including the European Commission.

Does anyone know the President of the European Parliament, Antonio Tajani (2019), an Italian politician, who presides over debates and activities of the European Parliament and represents the parliament within the Union and across the world? He previously served as one of the fourteen Vice-Presidents of the European Union and was European Commissioner for Industry and Entrepreneurship and Vice-President of the European Commission and European Commissioner for Transport. Incidentally, we need to pay attention. President Antonio Tajani was replaced by another Italian politician, David Sassoli, on 3rd July 2019.

The European Council provides a summit for the Heads of Member States or Governments, with the President of the European Council and the President of the European Commission. It gives the political impetus or stimulus for the further development of the European Union and sets its general objectives and priorities but does not legislate. The President of the European Council, Donald Tusk, a former Polish Prime Minister, has just (2019) been replaced by Belgian Prime Minister, Charles Michel.

It's interesting to learn that the French President, Nicolas Sarkozy, recommended Tony Blair, Jean-Claude Juncker and Felipe Gonzalez, as candidates for the post of President of the European Council, with Tony Blair being a front-runner. However, he faced opposition for being from a large member state outside the Eurozone and the

Schengen Area, as well as being the leader who entered the Iraq War, which split Europe.

It's suggested that this former prime minister of the United Kingdom still harbours an ambition to be the first elected president of the burgeoning European Union, which may explain why he opposed the result of the referendum to leave the European Union and advocated for a second referendum. As a senior representative of the European political elite, he opposed the 'will of the British people' to leave the European Union and risked terminal damage to the fabric of our liberal western democracy. In other words, the personal ambitions of the political elite, are more important than the 'will of the people', whose opinions are ignored.

Furthermore, the Council of the European Union, informally known as the 'Council of Ministers', is composed of twenty-eight ministers from member states, who act together with the Parliament as a legislature, and shares the budgetary powers and ensures the co-ordination of the broad economic and social policies, and sets out guidelines for the Common Foreign and Security Policy and concludes international agreements.

The Chancellor of Austria, Sebastian Kurz, was the rotating president of the Council of the European Union (2017), working with the presidents of Estonia and Bulgaria, to set long-term goals and produce an agenda on major matters to be considered by the Council, and they focussed their attention on migration and asylum and protecting external borders and fighting radicalisation, terrorism, organised crime, digital security and protecting European values. Sebastian Kurz was replaced on 1ˢᵗ January 2019 by the little-known Romanian Prime Minister, Viorica Dăncilă

The European Commission is the executive branch of the European Union, under the leadership of President Jean-Claude Juncker, former Prime Minister of Luxembourg, which submits proposals for new legislation to the Parliament and Council of the European Union and implements policies and administers the budget and ensures compliance with European law, and is 'guardian' of the treaties and negotiates international agreements. President Jean-Claude Juncker has just been replaced (2019) by Ursula von der Leyen, the German Defence Minister, who is a staunch supporter of a federal United States of Europe, and the creation of a European

Army, which should be a matter of concern.

Incidentally, Michel Barnier, a former French politician, was appointed by the European Commission as their chief negotiator, in charge of the preparation and conduct of the (Brexit) negotiations with the United Kingdom, under Article 50 of the Treaty on European Union (TEU). This is a very powerful role performed by an unelected French politician who told the British 'leavers' that they 'can't have their cake and eat it'.

The reality is that so long as we are members of the European Union, we are governed by such people as the former Italian politician, Antonio Tajani, and the former Prime Minister of Poland, Donald Tusk, and the former Prime Minister of Luxembourg, Jean-Claude Juncker, and the Chancellor of Austria, Sebastian Kurz and their replacements, the Prime Minister of Romania, Viorica Dăncilă and the German Defence Minister, Ursula von der Leyen and the Belgian, Prime Minister, Charles Michel.

They may all be respected senior politicians in their countries of origin, but they are virtually unknown to most European citizens, who have not had the opportunity to select or elect them and they certainly can't reject them: they are virtually unaccountable to the majority of the people.

We are also being controlled by other influential foreign politicians and officials, such as the former Belgian Prime Minister, Guy Verhofstadt (MEP), and the little-known, German-Belgian Secretary General of the European Commission, Martin Selmayer, who are European federalists and supporters of the ultimate objective of the United States of Europe.

Democracy is about political representation, preferably by local people, who state their case and seek your vote and are under threat of removal, should they not deliver for the people. Even governance from distant Westminster, Edinburgh, Belfast or Cardiff, challenges the concept of transparency and accountability but control by strangers from their remote Brussels and Strasbourg 'ivory towers', is a 'stretch too far' and the British people were right to 'throw in the towel' and 'call it a day'.

Whilst the sceptical British people eventually 'saw the light', the people of the other member states are still anchored to the deck of this multi-national super-tanker, storming across the choppy seas towards the perceived security of a country called Europe. They would be well advised to follow the example of the perceptive British and 'jump ship', before it reaches its ultimate destination of a United States of Europe.

It would also make sense, if the European political elite accepted the democratic deficit of remote governance and relinquished their obsession with a United States of Europe and returned the project to the security of an economic community of independent and sovereign nation states.

Incidentally, Roger Bootle, winner of the Wolfson Economic Prize, in his book entitled *The Trouble with Europe*, published by Nicholas Brealey Publishing (2016), said: "The EU hasn't delivered the prosperity and growth it promised, the euro has turned out to be a disaster, and the EU's share of GDP is set to fall. Moreover, no one is clear what the EU is for, or how 'ever-closer' union can be matched with expanding borders and huge disparities of income and culture. The EU is the most important thing that stands between Europe and success. Prime Minister David Cameron's 'renegotiation' produced nothing substantive. It now looks like the EU cannot and will not willingly embrace fundamental reform… Brexit could provide the spur for the European Union to either reform or break-up (and) the Brexit vote can lead the way to a better Europe."

However, as we watched the tortuous process to extricate the United Kingdom from the European Union, and the behaviour of the 'resistance movement', which included the Scottish Nationalists, it perhaps reminded the people that we continue to risk the break-up of the United Kingdom.

Whilst the United Kingdom has been a member of the Common Market or the European Economic Community (EEC) since 1973 and a member of the European Union (EU) since 1992 (when we signed the Maastricht Treaty or the Treaty on European Union), it has been a 'unified state' since 1707, with the political union of the Kingdoms of England and Scotland, followed by the Act of Union 1800, which added the Kingdom of Ireland, to create the United Kingdom of Great Britain and Ireland.

However, in 1922, Ireland seceded to become the Irish Free State and a day later Northern Ireland seceded from the Free State and returned to the United Kingdom of Great Britain and Northern Ireland. The main point, however, is that our association with the European Economic Community and the European Union, is a recent event, compared with our unification as a United Kingdom, and 'we the British people' must do whatever is needed to prevent a break-up of these proud island nations.

It's certainly the case, so far as these island nations are concerned, that our people are deeply integrated and we are a good example of a united nation, despite the bellicose rhetoric of the Scottish Nationalist Party, which is determined to achieve independence from the United Kingdom but inexplicably, wants to be a very small fish in a big European pond.

So, let's examine the political climate in the 'Not So' United Kingdom and the bellicose language of the Scottish Nationalists, who appear to despise the dominant English. They do so, despite so many Scottish-born people, having been prime ministers and senior ministers in the United Kingdom government. They do so, despite so many of their fellow citizens being prominent political media commentators and influential leaders, in many professions across the rest of the United Kingdom.

25

THE 'NOT SO' UNITED KINGDOM

To introduce a further complication to our constitutional arrangements, when the British people voted by 51.89% to 'leave' the European Union and 48.11% to 'remain', the bellicose leader of the Scottish Nationalist Party (SNP), Nicola Sturgeon, threatened another Scottish independence referendum, with the intention of leaving the not so United Kingdom and subsequently applying to re-join the European Union, when they would have to adopt the single currency (the euro) and the European Central Bank (ECB) and leave the pound sterling and the Bank of England.

However, in the interests of democracy, should the SNP achieve their ambition to have another independence referendum, to leave the United Kingdom, the electoral rules should include the votes of the registered voters within the circa 800,000, who live elsewhere in the United Kingdom. This was an anomaly at the last Scottish independence referendum (2012) which allowed foreigners, resident in Scotland, to vote on independence, but 'did not seek the approval of the Scottish-born citizens, resident in England, Wales or Northern Ireland, with a patriotic interest in their beloved homeland remaining as part of the United Kingdom.

There is a recent precedent for such action, when the recent abortion referendum (2018), in the Irish Republic (Eire), allowed Irish citizens from elsewhere in the world to return to vote on that important issue.

It's rather disappointing, however, to accept that Scottish Nationalists would rather have a political union with the former communist states of Estonia, Lithuania, Latvia, Poland, the Czech Republic, Slovakia, Hungary, Slovenia, Croatia, Bulgaria and Romania, than a secure union with their island neighbours, England, Wales and Northern Ireland, the adopted homelands of so many Scottish-born citizens and their families, besides the many millions whose ancestors were born in Scotland.

Furthermore, a vote for Scottish independence would mean that they would start a process to leave the United Kingdom and the Bank of England and the pound sterling and establish a new Scottish currency, presumably under the Royal Bank of Scotland (RBS), and then start a protracted period of uncertainty, in an attempt to rejoin the European Union (EU) and the Eurozone and the European Central Bank (ECB).

This would mean that the Scottish Nationalists would rather have a political and currency union with Austria, Belgium, Finland, France, Germany, Ireland, Italy, Luxembourg, Netherlands, Portugal, Spain and Greece, which use the euro, and a political union with Sweden, Poland, Slovakia, the Czech Republic, Hungary, Slovenia, Estonia, Latvia, Lithuania, Malta, Cyprus, Bulgaria, Romania and Croatia, which do not use the euro, and Serbia, Montenegro, Macedonia, Albania, Kosovo, Bosnia and Herzegovina and Turkey waiting to join, rather than a union with their island neighbours in England, Wales and Northern Ireland.

It's more than obvious that the United Kingdom of Great Britain and Northern Ireland, these island nations, are bonded together, through generations of integration and assimilation of a common people, who share the same language (English) and currency (pound sterling) and have similar cultures, customs, conventions and traditions, and through the 'free movement of people' and 'intermarriage', have cemented a deeply integrated union of English, Scottish, Welsh and Irish people.

It's so disappointing that the Scottish Nationalists are so bitter and divisive about our union, which has survived more than three hundred years of living and working and fighting together, for the common good.

The natural cohesion of these island nations, which have bonded together through decades of the free movement of people and extensive integration through intermarriage and a common language and similar cultures, customs, conventions and traditions, is not remotely the same as the political and social construct of the European Union, with a multitude of diverse languages, cultures, customs, conventions, traditions and much less integration through intermarriage, across widespread nation states.

For instance, there has been so much intermarriage between the people of Scotland and England and Wales, on the island of Great Britain, with the same language and religion, which cannot be said about the diverse countries of Latvia and Romania or Hungary and Holland or Spain and Slovakia, which are located so far apart, on the continent of Europe.

Should the Scottish Nationalists (SNP) achieve another independence referendum, which would precede any application to re-join the EU and the euro, it is doubtful whether the Scottish electorate would vote to leave the security of the United Kingdom and the pound sterling, where they have virtual independence. Why would they want to be a very small fish (circa 5 million people) in a very big pond (circa 500 million people) and have limited political influence and no control over the free movement of people, which would impose strains on their essential public services?

Incidentally, Scotland's trade with the rest of the United Kingdom, at £49.8 billion (2015) was four times more than with the European Union, at £12.3 billion and there is a risk that independence could damage their trade with the rest of the United Kingdom, particularly England, which is their biggest trading partner by a country mile. Whilst the patriotic Scots want independence from the 'dominant' English, why would they not just want virtual independence, within the security of the United Kingdom, rather than become a fragile 'minnow' in a European 'super-pond'?

The United Kingdom of Great Britain and Northern Ireland is a very successful economic and political union of virtually independent nation states, with a central government and devolved administrations, with a central bank, a single currency, a single market and customs union and the free movement of goods, services and people, across open borders.

Why would the Scottish people want to leave the security of an economic and political union with their island neighbours and trading partners?

The Scottish people should heed the words of John Mackay, who was the chief executive of the Whole Foods Supermarkets in the USA, who said; "Business people are truly the heroes, they are the value creators in the world, and they lift humanity out of poverty and create prosperity."

As mentioned above, the Scots did a significant £49.8 billion trade with the rest of the United Kingdom, and an insignificant £12.3 billion with the rest of the European Union (2015), which should focus the minds of Scottish voters, when deciding on their future in the United Kingdom.

Nothing is more important than industrious commercial activity and free trade arrangements, which provides employment for the people and creates the wealth, through taxation, to fund essential public services.

So, let's consider the importance of free trade, in the context of leaving Fortress Europe and stimulating the British economy and making free-trade deals with our European partners and the rest of the world.

26

THE IMPORTANCE OF FREE TRADE

The European Commission have made it clear that the United Kingdom must accept the 'free movement of people' if they want access to the Single Market and the Customs Union, when they leave the Union. This is quite perplexing, because 'business-people' instinctively do business with 'business-people' across the world, and business transactions should have nothing to do with the 'free movement of people'. In fact, business transactions should have little to do with governments, except for the collection of taxes. Government officials impose import taxes, export taxes, value added taxes, personal taxes, corporation taxes and capital gains taxes, despite the fact they add little or no value to any business transactions. It's suggested that government bureaucracy should not get involved in business transactions and let traders trade. The more trade that's created by traders, the more taxes are available for governments to fund the public services. Furthermore, the more jobs created by increased trade, means less unemployment and less demand on welfare services.

The remote Brussels autocrats should heed the words of John Mackay, who was the CEO of Whole Foods Supermarkets (USA) and Raj Sisodia, in the book, entitled *Conscious Capitalism* published by Harvard Business School (2014) who said: "Every business has the potential for a higher purpose besides making money. Doctors have a higher purpose, they heal people, teachers educate people, architects design buildings and business (people) create value for everyone with whom they trade; value for their customers, employees, suppliers, investors and value for the community. Business-people are truly the heroes, they are the value creators in the world, they lift humanity out of poverty and create prosperity."

In other words, it's not 'talk-shop' politicians, who 'lift humanity out of poverty', it's industrious commercial enterprise, which creates jobs and taxation revenues, to feed the government machine. We must, therefore, respect our enterprise economy, which creates employment opportunities and generates taxation revenues, to finance government and essential public services and it should be viewed as 'altruistic capitalism' and the seed-corn for social improvement, community renewal and social justice.

We must stop criticising industrious entrepreneurs and support them as 'value creators' who lift humanity out of poverty and create prosperity.

The reality is that we cannot keep expanding government institutions and essential public services, which increases annual budget deficits and the national debt mountain, and through increased business taxation, reduce business investment and reduce business growth, effectively biting the commercial hand that feeds the avaricious government machine.

What we need in our enterprise economy, is a more liberal approach to fiscal conservative governance, which through lower taxation revenues, stimulates investment for business growth (and employment creation), which increases taxation income, to finance more efficient government services and welfare support, a 'safety net' for those in genuine need.

The world doesn't need the diversity of multi-national, multi-cultural, multi-racial super-states, such as a United States of Europe, it needs individual nation states, with unique cultures, traditions, customs and industrious commercial enterprise, trading with their neighbours, just like the former European Economic Community or Common Market.

The world needs enterprising and industrious and independent nation states (with smaller and more efficient governments), making things and building things and trading with their neighbours and 'punching above their weight', because history suggests that when trade stops, wars start.

It's, therefore, interesting to consider the United Kingdom's top ten trading partners, between January and November 2016, according to HM Revenue and Customs:

Imports: Germany £58.91 billion; United States £36.44 billion; China £35.65 billion; Netherlands £31.37 billion; France £22.47 billion; Switzerland £21.93 billion; Belgium £21.19 billion; Italy £15.64 billion; Spain £14.87 billion and the Irish Republic £12.03 billion. Exports: United States £41.45 billion; Germany £29.68 billion; Netherlands £17.55 billion; France £17.48 billion; Eire £15.39 billion and China £12.18 billion; Belgium £10.81 billion; Switzerland £9.67 billion; Italy £8.91 billion and Spain £8.55 billion.

It's also interesting to note that the United Kingdom had a trade deficit with Germany of £29.23 billion, which means that Germany, the biggest net-contributor to the EU budget, should be concerned about a bad trade deal or a no-trade deal, with the United Kingdom. We also have a trade deficit with the Netherlands of £13.82 billion and Belgium of £10.38 billion and Italy of £6.73 billion and Spain of £6.32 billion and France of £4.99 billion. That's a trade deficit of £71.92 billion with these six Western European trading nation partners, who were members of the European Economic Community (EEC) or the Common Market.

With regard to our significant trade with Germany, France, Italy, Spain, the Netherlands and Eire, why didn't the political and industrial leaders of these countries not support our negotiations for a free-trade agreement with the European Union? The UK business regulations are already harmonised with Europe, which means that there should be no obstacles to striking a mutually beneficial free-trade agreement, as an independent nation state and former member of the 'single market'.

It, perhaps, needs to be mentioned that the Withdrawal Agreement process, which included a Political Declaration, with a framework of our future relationship, including a future trade deal, to be negotiated after withdrawal during a two-year transition period, was not intended to negotiate a free-trade deal during the first phase of the negotiations.

If the United Kingdom politicians (mainly 'remainers') had ratified the Withdrawal Agreement and the Political Declaration, then the United Kingdom would have been able to leave the European Union on 29th March 2019 (extended to the 31st October 2019) and remain in the Single Market and the Customs Union, while they negotiated a free-trade deal.

This would have been infinitely better than the alternative of parliament failing to ratify the Withdrawal Agreement and Political Declaration, and the government negotiators not being able to move into the transition period to negotiate our future relationship and future trade deal from the positive framework included in the text of the Political Declaration.

This has been characterised as 'crashing out' of the Single Market and the Customs Union, without having had the opportunity to negotiate our future relationship, including a future trade deal (whilst remaining within the rules and regulations of the Single Market and the Customs Union), which 'Project Fear' campaigners suggested would be 'catastrophic' for our business community and created fear in the minds of the voters.

Even without the ratification of the Withdrawal Agreement (first phase) and without being able to move into the Political Declaration (second phase) and discuss our future relationship and a future trade deal, with some 'goodwill' on both sides, the EU and the UK could still come to some agreement about our future relationship and our future trade deal, to avoid logistical disruption to our respective business communities.

The political and commercial leaders of Germany, France, Italy, Spain, the Netherlands and Eire, should have demanded unrestricted access of their goods and services into the United Kingdom, after 31st October 2019. However, the Eurocrats may have another agenda, concerned with preventing a potential 'break-up' of the Union. It may be more important to the Eurocrats to maintain the integrity of their European project, than striking a mutually beneficial free-trade deal with the Eurosceptic British.

Why did it feel like the British negotiators were 'fighting a losing battle' against the 'stubborn' Brussels negotiators and appeared to be getting no real support from their main trading partners across the channel?

However, there appears to be one notable exception, the Italian Deputy Prime Minister and Minister of the Interior (from 1st June

2018), Matteo Salvini, who was an Italian Senator from March 2018 and a Member of the European Parliament (MEP) for North West Italy, from 2004 to 2018, who had the experience to comment on the state of the European project.

Matteo Salvini was interviewed by Stephen Sackur of the television programme HARDtalk on Sunday 16th September 2018 and he said: "On more than one occasion in the past… when citizens voted against the wishes of Brussels, they made citizens vote again until they got what they wanted. There is, typically, an attempt on the part of Brussels to punish. They are not negotiating. They want to punish a government and a people that voted against their expectations. If you sit at the negotiating table, you start with some political goodwill. If you start with the idea of punishing or attacking, you're not going to be a good negotiator." He also said the following: "We have to foster good relations, and nobody should be punished. The Italian government is on the side of the UK government, in our mutual interests." When asked if he would consider taking Italy out of the EU he replied: "No, my goal is to remain within the EU and to change the rules, to go back to the original spirit of the European Community (the Common Market) before Maastricht."

Whilst Matteo Salvini, is dismissed by the European political elite as a Eurosceptic, with critical views of the European Union, particularly the euro, they should probably take him much more seriously and reject the dream of a United States of Europe and return to the pre-Maastricht European Community or European Economic Community, or Common Market, comprising of a free-trade group of independent nation states.

Whilst it may be 'wishful thinking', the author believes that common sense should prevail, and the Eurocrats and Europhiles must see the importance of a mutually beneficial free-trade agreement between the European Union and an independent United Kingdom, one of their biggest and closest trading partners, just across the English Channel.

One thing is certain, traders will not obstruct a free trade deal between the European Union and the United Kingdom. Obstruction can only come from the Brussels political elite, who want to make an example of the obdurate British, for having the audacity or the temerity or the cheek to vote to leave the burgeoning European

Union super-state, and send a strong message to other member states, not to make the same mistake!

Well according to the British Prime Minister Theresa May (2016), 'Brexit meant Brexit' and Britain would leave the European Union on 29th March 2019 (extended to 31st October 2019) 'deal or no deal' and leaving with no deal was better than leaving with a bad deal.

However, the inability of the government to get parliament to ratify the Withdrawal Agreement led to the resignation of the prime minister, which created a Conservative Party leadership contest, in which the final two contenders both confirmed that we would leave on 31st October, with or without a deal. Whilst leaving without an agreement is the legal position should we not ratify the agreement, some parliamentarians are determined to derail the project and have voted against leaving (or 'crashing out') without an agreement, which they suggest would be 'catastrophic' for our economy. However, they've not explained why it would be 'catastrophic'. Surely, we would not be 'crashing out' and it would not be 'catastrophic', if both sides wanted to minimise commercial uncertainty and commercial disruption in their mutual interests?

However, one thing is certain, in this age of uncertainty, there may be some short-to-medium-term disruption to trade, caused mainly by the obstinate Brussels machine, but Great Britain will survive and thrive, as an industrious independent nation state, trading on the world stage.

This is now a battle between the 'will of the people' and their elected representatives (those they select and elect to represent them in the 'corridors of power') and the result will be a defining moment in the context of our liberal western democracy, so admired across the world.

Do 'we the people', want to live in a country, where the political power rests with their elected representatives, who call a 'people's vote', on a major constitutional matter, and when the 'people have spoken' they attempt to overturn the result and disregard the 'will of the people'.

Is there any chance that our elected representatives, those we elect to represent us in the 'corridors of power', may realise that they have 'overstepped the mark' and may suffer a serious 'backlash' from the people?

The essence of any liberal democracy is the extent to which the elected representatives respect the views of the people (they are there to serve) and accept the elementary political concept of the 'power of the people'.

Whilst parliamentarians may accept that they are elected to represent the will of the people, by using their best judgement, they must be in touch with the views of the people and they must respect their instructions, particularly when they express their views in a 'people's vote'. So, let's now look at the 'power to the people', in an independent sovereign state, when we have released ourselves from the restrictive 'shackles' of the European Union, as it powers towards a United States of Europe.

27

'POWER TO THE BRITISH PEOPLE'

When we have released ourselves from the 'shackles' of Fortress Europe, the next big challenge facing our elected government, is to 'drain the Westminster swamp', starting with those elected representatives who voted against the Withdrawal Agreement legislation and defied the 'will of the people'. They should then turn their attention to the unelected House of Lords, which defeated the elected government multiple times in the Withdrawal Agreement legislation, and defied the 'will of the people'.

To his credit, Baron Andrew Lloyd-Webber, a member of the House of Lords, criticised Remain-backing peers for attempting to undermine Brexit and defying the 'will of the people'. He also said that peers were 'wrong' to vote for 'wrecking amendments on key Brexit legislation'.

It also came as Jeremy Corbyn, leader of the Labour Party and Her Majesty's Loyal Opposition, made voting for the abolition of the Upper Chamber a condition for the appointment of new Labour Peers.

The future of our liberal western democracy and the primacy of the British people, as opposed to the dictate of the distant political elite, in the Brussels and Strasbourg 'ivory towers' and the Westminster 'bubble', depends on our ultimate escape from the 'stranglehold' of the European Union 'juggernaut' as it thunders towards a United States of Europe.

We must heed the words of President Abraham Lincoln, when he said in his Gettysburg speech (1863): "The nation was conceived in liberty and dedicated to the proposition that all men are equal and that the future of democracy in the world would be assured that 'government of the people, by the people, for the people' shall not perish from the earth."

We must, therefore, elect strong leaders who are prepared to challenge the establishment and oppose the autocratic political elite and return the political power to the ordinary people. The British people, to their credit, have taken the first step in this process of independence by voting to leave the Brussels-to-Strasbourg Express, which is 'charging' towards a United States of Europe, as we witness the slow death of independent nations.

Incidentally, when we finally overcome the resistance of the European political elite, and attempt to 'drain the Westminster swamp', particularly the unelected and aristocratic 'Upper Chamber', which appears to have no regard for the 'will of the people', we must understand that 'draining the Westminster swamp' is an interesting concept, but making it happen will be very difficult, as 'turkeys don't often vote for Christmas'.

The controversial President of the United States of America (USA), Donald J. Trump, promised to 'drain the Washington swamp' but has been met with an obdurate 'resistance movement', which has brought politics to a standstill. He has difficulty getting any legislation through Congress and achieves change through presidential 'Executive Orders'. American politics is so polarised and divided that it's no longer seen as the 'shining city on the hill' and a beacon of liberal western democracy.

On a similar basis, the difficulty of negotiating our withdrawal from the European Union, when faced with the resistance of parliament and the remain campaigns, played into the hands of the European political elite and created a constitutional crisis and economic uncertainty, which is not what's expected of our elected representatives, who should respect the 'will of the people', when expressed through a 'people's vote'.

However, whether it's the United States of America or the United Kingdom or the European Union, the people must ensure that our elected representatives are 'brought to heel' and made to respect the 'will of the people' and are prepared to 'drain the political swamps', to re-establish the principle of 'government of the people, by the people, for the people' and recreate the notion of our once Great Britain being a 'beacon of democracy' and seen across the world as the 'shining city on the hill'.

When we are released from the 'shackles' of the European Union super-state, we can then turn our attention to a more efficient United Kingdom federal government and the devolvement of more power, on the principle of subsidiarity, to more transparent and accountable regional and local government, with representatives much closer to the people they serve.

It's, therefore, instructive to note that the founding fathers of the United States of America (USA) wrote the Tenth Amendment to the Constitution to specifically limit the powers delegated to the federal government. The Tenth Amendment, which is part of the Bill of Rights, ratified on 15th December 1791, was intended to confirm that powers not granted to the federal government were reserved for the states or the people, as the founding fathers deeply distrusted (federal) government power. The Tenth Amendment was written to emphasise the limited nature of the powers delegated to the federal government. It said that when states and local communities take the lead on policy, the people are that much closer to the policy makers and the policy makers are that much closer and more accountable to the people they serve. Adherence to the Tenth Amendment is the first step towards ensuring liberty through decentralisation.

It's also interesting to note that the adoption of the Constitution (1787) was opposed by many well-known patriots, including Thomas Jefferson, who argued that the Constitution would eventually lead to a stronger centralised state power, which would destroy the individual liberty of the people. Many in this movement were classed as being Anti-Federalists and the Tenth Amendment was added to the Constitution because of the intellectual influence and persistence of that libertarian movement.

However, nothing can be more undemocratic and unaccountable than the European Union or their ultimate objective of a United States of Europe. The sceptical British people were right to say YES to the Common Market or the European Economic Community and they were right to say NO to the European Union, before the European political elite arrive at their ultimate destination of a United

States of Europe, run from Brussels.

If we are interested in the 'power of the people', the British people voted to leave the European Union, and we must resist the clamour for another referendum, to reverse the inconvenient result of the first referendum, and the European political elite should return to an economic community or a common market, consisting of independent nation states. In fact, it would be more sensible if the whole grand project could be slowed down and turned around and recreated as an economic community, similar to the Commonwealth of Independent States (CIS) based in Minsk, Belarus, with an Assembly of Member Nations and an Executive Director, which was founded by the Russian Federation, Belarus and Ukraine (1991).

There is, of course, no doubt that the European Union (EU) is a project of the political elite and has nothing to do with the 'will of the people'.

The creation of this monolithic conglomerate, by the European political elite, appears to be irreversible, as the absolute power is vested in the political class and not in the people. In fact, whenever the people got an opportunity to vote on the growth of the project, in the form of treaties, their opinion was only accepted if they voted in accordance with the views of the political class. However, when the sceptical British people were given the opportunity to vote on their relationship with the project, they voted to leave, which shocked the Brussels establishment and started a 'resistance movement' to change their minds and get them back on side.

This is the illiberal behaviour of the European political elite, which can be contrasted with the more liberal approach of the Russian Federation, which emerged from the ashes of the former Soviet Union, which created a more democratic economic community of independent nation states!

Consequently, we must always remember the words of Thomas Jefferson, President of the United States of America (1801 to 1809), who said: "The will of the people is the only legitimate foundation of any government and to protect its free expression should be our first objective." We must also remember the words of President Abraham Lincoln, in his Gettysburg Speech (1863) who said: "The nation was conceived in liberty and dedicated to the proposition that all men are equal and that the future of democracy in the world would be assured that 'government of the people, by the people, for the people', shall not perish from the earth."

Certainly, the Westminster parliamentarians need to consider the words of Thomas Jefferson and Abraham Lincoln, when they reflect on their undemocratic behaviour, subsequent to the Brexit referendum, when so many of them blatantly ignored the express 'will of the people', to leave the European Union, and like 'saboteurs', attempted to overturn the decision of the people and keep our country in the European Union.

The worst example of undemocratic parliamentary behaviour, bordering on 'sabotage', is the behaviour of the Liberal Democratic Party, under the new leadership of Ms Jo Swinson, which is determined to wreck the leaving process and overtly proclaims that their policy is to 'Stop Brexit'.

How can elected representatives of the people, who are elected by the people, to represent their views in the 'corridors of power', disrespect and disregard the 'will of the people', in a 'people's vote', and attempt to 'wreck' the electoral process and overturn the decision of the people?

It's normal practice in our liberal western democracy for the people to elect a government with a majority of electoral seats but a minority of the overall votes, and the people accept that electoral process and the opposition then hold the government to account on behalf of the people.

Why are we so tolerant of the 'first past the post' electoral system, which produces a government with a minority of the votes, yet we are so intolerant of the express views of the people, when they respond to an uncomplicated choice of 'leave' or 'remain' in the European Union?

The dubious behaviour of many of our elected representatives has been so undemocratic that they cannot now claim to be democrats and cannot remain as parliamentarians and must be held to account by the people, as those who 'live by the sword' must be prepared to 'die by the sword'!

CONCLUSION

Our choice at the 2015 General Election was between the Conservatives, who wanted to reform our relationship with the European Union, and then provide a referendum on our membership of the European Union, and the United Kingdom Independence Party (UKIP), which wanted to leave the European Union, but could not provide a referendum, and a Labour Party, 'sitting on the fence', with a leader 'genetically' opposed to our membership of the European Union, according to his track record.

Well the Conservatives, under Prime Minister David Cameron, won the 2015 General Election and pursued the promise to negotiate reform of the European Union, particularly the move towards 'ever-closer union', which are effectively code-words for a United States of Europe, and the uncontrolled 'free movement of people' across the twenty-eight member states. Sadly, the Eurocrats did not take him seriously and he returned with some derisory reforms and he gave the people the referendum he had promised. He then campaigned to 'remain' but his hollow message fell on deaf ears and the Eurosceptic British people voted to 'leave'.

The Conservatives won the general election, which was held on 7th May 2015, with the following results: The Conservatives won 331 seats and 11,334,920 votes or 36.0% of the electorate. The Labour Party won 232 seats and 9,347,326 votes or 30.4% of the electorate. The result suggests that the British people voted for the Conservatives, because they wanted a public referendum on our future relationship with the European Union, after the prime minister had attempted to negotiate some meaningful reform, particularly the perpetual movement towards 'ever-closer union' and the unmanageable 'free movement of people' across 'open borders'.

What Prime Minister David Cameron should have done, was, attempt to negotiate some meaningful reform and then be candid with the people about his lack of success. Furthermore, he was right to give the people a referendum, but he should not have got involved in the campaign. When the people voted to 'leave', he should have remained as prime minister and led the Withdrawal Agreement negotiations, to extricate our country from the rules and regulations of the European Union, and not expect someone else to do his 'dirty work' and accept a 'poisoned chalice'.

The European Union Membership Referendum (2016), known as Brexit, was held on 23rd June 2016, with the following result: There was a large turnout of 46,500,001 voters or 72.21% of those eligible to vote, and a massive 17,410,742 (51.89%) voted to 'leave' and 16,141,241 (48.11%) voted to 'remain'. This result was a victory for the 'leavers' and was not a 'slender margin' or a 'small majority', as suggested by the 'remainers'. The majority for 'leave' was 1,269,501 votes, which is almost the number of people who live in the two northern cities of Leeds and Bradford. Just imagine attempting to change the minds of so many 'leave' voters, in a second referendum or a 'people's vote', to get a win for 'remain', with the same majority. The 'remainers' would have to retain their 16,141,241 votes and convert 1,269,501 votes, to win by the same 'slender margin' or 'small majority'. The 'bottom line', however, is that the 'remainers' would need to retain their 16,141,241 voters and change the minds of 634,751 voters, to win by a majority of one vote. Having regard to the controversy in parliament, it's suggested that many 'remain' voters may change their minds in the interests of democracy. Despite the fact they lost the referendum, they may believe that the result should be honoured and that we should leave the European Union, preferably with a deal.

However, in the wake of the defeat, the prime minister resigned and the Home Secretary, Theresa May, won the leadership election and became the new prime minister and promised to accept the 'will of the people' and said that 'Brexit means Brexit' and that no deal is better than a bad deal. However, she may have underestimated the determination of the Westminster and Brussels 'resistance movements' and the 'remain campaigns', to undermine the negotiations and overturn the decision of the people, but to her credit she respected the 'will of the people' and worked to get a

Withdrawal Agreement and deliver our independence.

Whilst the country was divided over the result of the referendum, it was hoped that the politicians would support the new prime minister, who respected the 'will of the people' and attempted to release our country from the 'shackles' of the European Union, and to re-establish Great Britain as an independent nation, trading with Europe and the world.

The British government spent over two years attempting to negotiate an acceptable Withdrawal Agreement and a Political Declaration, which included a 'framework' of our future relationship and a future trade deal, and the final documents were signed by both parties to the agreement. However, whilst the European Commission got the agreement and declaration documents ratified by the other twenty-seven member states, in their parliament, the British government could not get the agreement and declaration documents ratified in the United Kingdom parliament.

After the shock result of the referendum (2016) and the resignation of Prime Minister David Cameron, his successor, Theresa May, called a general election (2017), to get an increased majority and a stronger mandate for the withdrawal negotiations process. However, whilst the Conservatives won the general election, they got a smaller majority, and they formed a minority government, with the support of the Democratic Unionist Party (DUP) of Northern Ireland. The result of the election was as follows: The Conservatives won 318 seats and got 13,636,684 votes (42.4%) and to the surprise of the prime minister and her advisors, the socialist Labour Party, won 262 seats and got 12,877,918 votes (40%).

This unexpected result meant that the Conservatives got more votes but less parliamentary seats, than they got at the previous general election (2015). Their votes increased from 11,334,920 to 13,636,684, yet their seats reduced from 331 to 318. Furthermore, the socialist Labour Party, under the leadership of Jeremy Corbyn, increased their votes from 9,347,326 to 12,877,918 and increased their seats from 232 to 262.

It should, of course, be no surprise that parliament, which included the Conservatives with 318 seats and Labour with 262 seats (a total of 580 seats), who both promised to honour the result of the referendum, should be ready to invoke Article 50 of the Lisbon

Treaty (2009) and start the withdrawal process. As expected, parliament voted to invoke Article 50 (7th September 2015) by a massive 461 votes to 89 votes, and Article 50 stated: 'At the end of the withdrawal negotiations, the seceding country would leave on 29th March 2019 (extended to 31st October 2019), 'with or without an agreement'. If a Withdrawal Agreement was ratified by both parliaments, there would then be a transition period to negotiate our future relationship and a future trade deal. However, it must be noted that Article 50 made it clear that should we leave without an agreement, we would have to trade under World Trade Organisation (WTO) rules.

However, the British government put the Withdrawal Agreement before parliament on three separate occasions and the parliamentarians, who were mainly 'remainers', refused to ratify the agreement and voted to stop the government leaving without an agreement, which created 'deadlock'. Did our parliamentarians not realise that if they refused to ratify the Withdrawal Agreement we would have to leave without an agreement, and should they then vote to stop the government leaving without an agreement, it would just create parliamentary deadlock or stalemate?

They also voted (indicative vote) on 1st April 2019, on whether to revoke Article 50 and remain in the European Union, and the vote failed by 292 votes (against) and 191 votes (for), with 151 abstentions. This was a vote which made it clear, that despite their opposition to leaving the European Union, particularly without an agreement, our elected representatives were not prepared to revoke Article 50 and stop the withdrawal process.

Neither was parliament ready to support a second referendum or a so-called 'People's Vote'. On 15th March 2019, 334 members voted against having a second referendum and 85 voted for a second referendum. This would have been the ultimate 'slap in the face' for the voters, had they voted to reject the first referendum and have a second referendum, and hope to reverse the unexpected and inconvenient decision of the people.

Furthermore, in a second round of indicative votes, held on 1st April 2019, parliament voted on whether to hold a 'Confirmatory Public Vote' on the final deal and 280 members voted for a confirmatory public vote and 292 members voted against with 62 abstentions. It is unsatisfactory that 280 elected representatives voted to have a re-run of the plebiscite, when the details of the Withdrawal Agreement were known, in the hope of reversing the democratic decision and remaining in the European Union.

The above votes against having a second referendum or a so-called 'people's vote' and against having a 'confirmatory public vote' on the final deal or no-deal, should have put the idea of a second referendum to bed, but Jeremy Corbyn later announced at the Labour Party conference (24/09/19) that they would renegotiate the Withdrawal Agreement and put it to a confirmatory public vote, should they win the next general election.

However, these parliamentary 'manoeuvres' resulted in the resignation of Prime Minister Theresa May, which started a Conservative Party leadership contest, which was won on 23rd July 2019 by Boris Johnson (MP), who was a 'leaver', who had vowed to get us out of the European Union, by 31st October 2019, 'deal or no deal'. He won the contest, with the Foreign Secretary, Jeremy Hunt, by 92,153 to 46,656 votes, cast by members of the Conservative Party and not by the British electorate.

Had Jeremy Hunt won the Conservative leadership contest, things would have been much different. He is a much less controversial character, with a more stable personality and he would have approached the challenge of the controversial withdrawal process in a more collegiate manner.

As the Conservative leadership contest came to a close, the European Union made it clear that: "The United Kingdom reached an agreement with the European Union and the European Union will stick with that agreement." They also warned that a 'no-deal' exit would be a 'tragedy'.

Isn't it instructive that the European Commission refused to amend the agreement, to enable the British government to get it through parliament, which meant that we would have to leave without an agreement, which parliament won't approve, and the EU consider would be a 'tragedy'?

Wouldn't it have been refreshing if the European and British politicians could have come together in a spirit of 'goodwill' and 'compromise', to 'get this thing done'. It may, however, have been easier said than done, as the British parliamentarians were 'spoiling for a fight' and they were, no doubt, being supported by their European Union 'cheerleaders'.

However, the politicians were entrenched and the choice was between leaving with no deal, as they couldn't get the agreement ratified in parliament, or having a second referendum or a 'people's vote' on the final deal or the 'nuclear option' of revoking Article 50 and remaining as a member, and all three options had already been rejected by parliament.

Incidentally, the Irish Taoiseach, Leo Varadkar, speaking on Sky News on Thursday 25th July 2019, said: "It seems to me that there is a strong majority in the House of Commons, that wants to avoid a no-deal and certainly we don't want to see no-deal happen but I would say that if no-deal does occur, nobody can blame Ireland or the European Union. No-deal can only ever be a British decision because there are many ways by which no-deal can be avoided: Either by revoking Article 50 or by seeking a further extension or by ratifying the withdrawal agreement."

Did Leo Varadkar not understand that the British parliament was in 'deadlock' because they would not ratify the Withdrawal Agreement in its present form, particularly concerning the Northern Ireland 'backstop' arrangements, and the European Union would not amend the Withdrawal Agreement, which had been ratified by their parliament? Couldn't he see that the British government was in an impossible situation, due to the Westminster and Brussels 'resistance movements' and the lack of 'goodwill' and support of our nearest 'friends' and neighbours in Dublin?

The main concern was, of course, should the new prime minister, Boris Johnson, get no positive response from Brussels, and he can't get the current agreement though parliament, he'll have no choice but to leave the European Union on 31st October 2019, without an agreement and trade under WTO rules, in accordance with Article 50. However, whilst this may be the legal position, so far as Brussels is concerned, the British parliament had voted to stop the United Kingdom leaving without a deal, creating parliamentary deadlock and public frustration and annoyance.

Whatever the shenanigans of the 'saboteurs' in parliament, to frustrate the 'will of the people', we must say farewell to the autocratic European Union, and its inexorable move towards a United States of Europe, and stamp our trademark on the world stage, as an independent trading nation, 'punching above our weight', and trading throughout Europe and across the world, because the message is: 'when trade stops, wars start'.

So far as trade is concerned, we must remember the words of John Mackay, the CEO of Whole Foods Supermarkets (USA), who said: "Business-people are truly the heroes, they are the value creators in the world, they lift humanity out of poverty and create prosperity." It is, of course, 'business-people' who create employment and wealth and tax revenues, not 'talk-shop' politicians, who add no value to the economy.

So far as the future of our once proud nation is concerned, we may be 'jumping out of the frying pan into the fire' if we are not very careful.

Our inability to withdraw from the European Union, under the terms of Article 50, could lead to a general election and a 'backlash' from the people. Another general election could produce a 'nightmare' coalition, between a socialist Labour Party, under the leadership of Jeremy Corbyn and his Momentum 'street-fighters', wanting to 'keep the red flag flying' here, and the Scottish Nationalist Party (SNP), vociferously demanding another independence referendum to break up the United Kingdom.

The people just need to watch the negative behaviour of the socialist Labour Party opposition and the truculent behaviour of the Scottish Nationalist Party (SNP), in parliament, to realise that a Labour/SNP coalition would break up our United Kingdom and make our divided nations subordinate satellite states of a United States of Europe.

Many people believe that we'll never leave the European Union and many politicians are working hard to ensure that we don't. However, the author believes that we will eventually release our once proud country from the 'shackles' of Fortress Europe, as it moves inexorably towards a federal Europe, and we'll create a vibrant enterprise economy, as an independent nation state, trading with Europe and across the world.

He also believes that as we leave the European Union, 'with or without' an agreement, despite all the parliamentary shenanigans, we could be seen as a 'beacon of democracy' by other member states, who are also concerned about the ultimate destination of the project and value their independence and realise that it's possible to leave 'Fortress Europe'.

It is, however, imperative, despite the 'sovereignty of parliament', that the people start a democratic process to move away from the reality of a sovereign 'parliamentary democracy', towards the concept of a sovereign 'people's democracy', where elected representatives must respect the 'will of the people', as we strive to be the 'shining city on the hill'.

However, with every cloud there's usually a silver lining and the speech of Ursula von der Layen, the candidate for President of the European Commission, to the European Parliament, on 16ᵗʰ July 2019, should have given us hope of a better relationship with our European 'partners' and this is an extract from that speech: "I cannot talk about Europe without I talk about our 'friends' from the United Kingdom. For the very first time in 2016, a member state decided to leave the European Union. This is a serious decision, we 'regret' it, but we 'respect' it. Since then … the EU has worked hard to organise an orderly departure … The withdrawal agreement … provides certainty, where Brexit created uncertainty (and) in preserving … peace and stability on the island of Ireland ... However, I stand ready for (a) further extension of the withdrawal agreement, should more time be required for a good reason. In any case the United Kingdom will remain our ally, our partner and our friend."

If the European Union genuinely considered the British people to be their 'partner' and 'friend' and they 'respect' their decision to leave the Union and they wanted an 'orderly departure', all they had to do was remove the Northern Ireland 'backstop' text from the Withdrawal Agreement and transfer it to the discussions on our future trade relationship, mentioned in the Political Declaration, and then parliament may have ratified the agreement. In fact, why could they not have achieved a consensus by creating an independent commission to examine the 'backstop' text, during the transition period, and recommend alternative solutions?

Sadly, this sorry saga continued in parliament and the new 'defiant' prime minister, Boris Johnson, was faced with an uphill battle with the staunch 'remainers' from his own party and opposition parties, who have formed a formidable 'resistance movement' to obstruct us leaving the European Union. The legal position appeared to be that we must leave the European Union on the extended leaving date of 31st October 2019, under the terms of Article 50 (which was approved by parliament) with or without an agreement (or deal) but the parliamentarians, supported by the Speaker of the House of Commons, introduced legislation to stop the government leaving without an agreement. This meant that the new prime minister was in a 'catch 22' constitutional crisis. We can't leave with an agreement, because parliament will not ratify the current agreement, and the European Union will not change the agreement, which they have ratified in the European Parliament, and we can't now leave without an agreement (which is included in the terms of Article 50) as parliament has introduced legislation to prevent the government from doing so.

Being in an impossible 'catch 22' situation, the new prime minister asked parliament to approve an early general election, to enable the people to unlock this debilitating parliamentary 'deadlock', but only 293 Members of Parliament (out of 650) voted in favour of an early general election.

Parliament also introduced legislation to mandate the government to request a further three-month extension to the Article 50 leaving date (31st October 2019) if there was no agreement by 19th October 2019. Ironically, there could be an agreement with the European Union by 19th October 2019, but the parliamentarians would probably vote it down.

Incidentally, the prime minister had already proclaimed that he would rather 'die in a ditch' than ask for another extension to Article 50 and the EU made it clear that there must be a 'purpose' for any future extension. The only meaningful purpose for any further extension, would be to get an agreement ratified by parliament, to allow us to leave in an orderly fashion, and that's unlikely as the EU will not revisit the agreement.

So the prime minister is now mandated by parliamentary legislation to request a three-month extension from 31st October 2019, if there is no agreement by 19th October 2019, to prevent us 'crashing out' without a deal, which the parliamentarians consider would be 'catastrophic' and the European Union consider would be a 'tragedy'. The question must be asked: If Article 50 of the Lisbon

Treaty allows member states to leave 'with or without' an agreement, and leaving without an agreement would mean trading under World Trade Organisation (WTO) rules, why would it be 'catastrophic' or a 'tragedy'? If these assertions are correct, why would the European Union include such an eventuality in their treaty, which is the only way to leave their grand project. Could it be that they wrote Article 50 with the expectation that it would never be used?

Incidentally, if the European political elite believe that leaving their project without an agreement and having to trade under WTO rules would be 'catastrophic' or 'tragic', it suggests that they should have known this outcome, when they wrote Article 50, and it was, therefore, written with the intention of deterring any member state from leaving their project. This is more relevant to member states in the eurozone.

Furthermore, the Europhile 'remainer' parliamentarians, with the active support of the Europhile 'remainer' Speaker of the House of Commons, no doubt encouraged by their Brussels 'cheerleaders', have 'tied our minority government in knots' and made it virtually impossible for them to leave the European Union, in accordance with the 'will of the people' and the legal terms of Article 50 'with or without' an agreement.

Incidentally, parliament was prorogued by the new prime minister, Boris Johnson, following his sixth parliamentary defeat in six days, as Members of Parliament blocked his attempt to call a general election, to break the 'deadlock', and they would have resumed 'hostilities' on Monday 14th October 2019. However, the matter was referred to the Supreme Court and they handed down a landmark judgement on 24th September 2019, which said: 'The decision to prorogue parliament was unlawful because it had the effect of frustrating parliament'. The United Kingdom's eleven most senior judges found that the prime minister had given unlawful advice to the Queen, when he asked her to prorogue parliament. They said that the prime minister's decision to ask the Queen to shut down parliament for five weeks was 'unlawful, void and of no effect' and that 'the effect upon the fundamentals of our democracy was extreme'.

Incidentally, the case was brought to the Supreme Court by the arch-remainer Gina Miller and supported by former Prime Minister Sir John Major, which was an assault on a successor prime minister and leader of his own political party. It is, therefore, appropriate to mention that in 1997, when he was prime minister, John Major controversially prorogued parliament, at a time that avoided parliamentary debate of the Parliamentary Commissioner's report on the controversial 'cash-for-questions' affair. On that occasion the prorogation was on Friday 21st March and was followed by a general election on 1st May, resulting in the arrival of the New Labour Prime Minister, Tony Blair, who told the unsuspecting British people that: 'Things could only get better'.

This can be compared with the prorogation of parliament by Prime Minister Boris Johnson, on 10th September 2019, to the opening of a new session on 14th October 2019, stating that it was to allow the new government to lay out its agenda. Whilst this may seem a long period, parliament was due to have a three-week recess for the party conference season and the prorogation would apparently have added about four days to the recess. So, it appears to the people, that it was very much a 'storm in a tea-cup'!

The remainers immediately alleged that he was trying to stop Members of Parliament passing legislation to thwart his Brexit plans and delay Brexit further. The deputy leader of the Labour Party, Tom Watson, called the prorogation 'an utterly scandalous affront to our democracy'. The former Attorney General, and arch-remainer, Dominic Grieve, called the prorogation an 'outrageous act' and John Bercow, the Speaker of the House, called the prorogation a 'constitutional outrage'. Why would they make such exaggerated statements, when parliament would have been in recess for the party conferences for most of the prorogation period?

The media reported a further assault on the UK government, attempting to get us out of the EU, from a group of members of the European Parliament representing all of the mainstream political groups, who planned to trigger an inquiry about the suspension of parliament as a breach of Article 2 of the Treaty on European Union, under a process outlined under Article 7 of that treaty, which requires member states to act in accordance with the rule-of-law standards and fundamental rights.

The government must feel that it is being attacked from every angle as it strives to deliver on the 'will of the people', to get us out of the European Union. The numerous arch-remainers want to stop us leaving, without an agreement (or deal) or more accurately, stop us leaving under any circumstances, and they could bring this sorry saga to a close by voting to revoke Article 50 and remain. However, whilst parliament has previously voted not to revoke Article 50, this is now the policy of the Liberal Democrats, under their new leader Jo Swinson, should they win the next general election and form a government. In fact, according to their latest Labour 'defector', Chuka Umunna, their foreign affairs spokesperson, they would apply to re-join the European Union (and would not rule out joining the euro) if we ever manage to leave.

No one knows what will happen during the next few months but if the 'saboteurs' get their way and parliament votes to revoke Article 50, and we remain a subordinate state in an expanding European Union, our country will be a 'democracy in crisis'. They could, of course, introduce a vote of 'no confidence' in the impotent minority government or the beleaguered prime minister and trigger an early general election, which would further polarise the electorate and divide our once proud country.

However, the leader of the Labour Party, Jeremy Corbyn, will not invoke a vote of 'no confidence' in the government or the prime minister and will not vote for an early general election, until the prime minister has got an extension to the leaving date of 31st October 2019, to ensure we do not crash out without a deal, which he believes would be 'catastrophic'.

This parliamentary obfuscation will create a constitutional battle between the 'will of the people' or the concept of a 'people's democracy', and the alternative reality of a sovereign 'parliamentary democracy', with the 'power of the people' subordinated to their own elected representatives, those they have elected to represent them in the 'corridors of power'.

This is the modern version of the 'Battle of Britain', where the people are fighting for their independence against their own elected representatives.

We must always remind the ordinary, decent people, that according to Thomas Jefferson, President of the United States of America (1801-1809), the 'will of the people' is the only legitimate foundation of any government and to protect its free expression should be our first objective. Furthermore, according to President

Abraham Lincoln, in his Gettysburg Speech (1863), "The nation was conceived in liberty and dedicated to the proposition that all men are equal and that the future of democracy in the world would be assured that 'government of the people, by the people (and) for the people', shall not perish from the earth."

The British people must remember these wise words, as they attempt to extricate their country from the 'shackles' of the expanding European Union, and demand that our elected representatives, respect the 'will of the British people' or they must be 'brought down to earth' with a crash!

This is the defining battle between a genuine 'people's democracy' and a sovereign 'parliamentary democracy' and the real winners must be the ordinary people, with just one vote, who ask for little but 'dare to dream'.

Incidentally, should we struggle to leave the European Union and we are confronted with a second referendum or a general election, the people should respect the government for respecting the 'will of the people' and attempting to extricate us from the 'shackles' of Fortress Europe against all the odds. Finally, those who are concerned about the future of our fragile liberal democracy, should save their retribution for those who disrespected the 'will of the people' and campaigned to Stop Brexit!

So, where do we go from here? The picture is far from clear. However, the people have decided. They voted to leave the European Union. That was the 'will of the people' and their elected representatives, those they elect to represent them in the 'corridors of power', must deliver on the 'people's vote' and get our country out of the European Union, before it reaches its ultimate 'discreet' destination of the United States of Europe!

We joined a Common Market of Western European trading nations, not a European Union, with ambitions to become the United States of Europe!

The people have spoken!

Watch this space!

POSTSCRIPT

It's one thing voting to leave the European Union but it's an entirely different thing negotiating the formidable withdrawal process. It's also one thing getting the evidence to support leaving but it's an entirely different thing ascertaining who is behind the well organised 'resistance movement' to prevent us leaving.

One thing is certain, in this age of uncertainty, the political power is with the European political elite, who are ready to resist any dissent towards their grand project. The influential Belgian, MEP, Guy Verhofstadt, has revealed that this is more than a continental, super-state, project, it's a global enterprise, leading to a 'world order of empires', and like the Exocet missile: 'you can hear it coming, you can see it coming, but there's not a damn thing you can do about it'!

However, the sceptical British people have 'seen-the-light' and are fighting for their independence but they are up against the European political class, their political masters, working behind the scenes, playing a waiting game, and ready to stamp-out dissent, whilst sending a dire warning to any other member states wanting to leave their grand project. The message is, that you are 'either with us or against us', and if you want to leave, there is a process, and there will be consequences! Should we be successful in this tortuous process of leaving this European, super-state, project, others may follow. However, should we fail to escape, the journey to failure is so destabilising, that it will deter others from trying and the people will have been over-ruled by their political masters.

The most alarming aspect of our withdrawal from the European Union is that our parliament asked the people, whether we should 'remain' or 'leave' and the people voted by a significant majority to leave, yet more than three years later we're still members of the club.

Whilst the European Union must shoulder much of the blame for the delay, the main criticism must go to many of our elected representatives who have rejected the 'will of the people' and obstructed our leaving 'with or without' an agreement. They refused to ratify the withdrawal agreement, despite the European Union refusing to change the agreement, and they introduced legislation to stop us leaving without an agreement, which they said would be 'catastrophic', creating parliamentary deadlock, yet we don't know the 'driving-force' behind this well organised 'resistance movement'.

At the recent Labour Party Conference (2019), their leader, Jeremy Corbyn, who has always been vehemently opposed to our membership of the European Union, pronounced that the next Labour government would renegotiate another agreement and then have a second referendum with an option to remain and would campaign to remain. This is a 'slap-in-the-face' to the people, from the militant socialist Labour Party, which claims to be the 'party of the people'!

Consequently, we must remind ourselves of the comments of Jeremy Corbyn, when speaking to an audience of Irish activists, the year after they rejected the controversial Lisbon Treaty (2009) by 53.4% to 46.6%, and prior to a second referendum, as follows: "Don't scrap your posters, don't recycle them, because you're going to need them for a third referendum. Because I've got a feeling, they're going to keep on voting until they get the answer they want. If you succeed in getting a no vote here (second referendum), that will be such a boost to people like us, all over Europe, who do not want to live in a European Empire of the twenty first century. I'm pleased you're having a referendum. I wish we were having one in Britain." This is political hypocrisy on a grand scale, which cannot be accepted by the ordinary people in our liberal western democracy, which demands honesty, integrity, accountability and consistency.

Even worse than that: at their recent party conference, the new leader of the Liberal Democrats, Jo Swinson (a Scottish MP), said that should they win the next general election (which is unlikely), they would immediately revoke Article 50, and we would remain in the European Union. And Chuka Umunna, who had defected from Labour, would not rule out joining the Euro, which would cement our membership, against the 'will of the people'. This is a very undemocratic and illiberal approach from a political party called the

Liberal Democrats!

Incidentally, when their new leader, announced their intention to revoke Article 50 and ignore the 'will of the people' she was faced with the wise words of her former leader, Lord Ashdown, now deceased, when interviewed on ITV News, after the Brexit polls had closed, who said: "I will forgive no one who does not accept the sovereign voice of the people. When the people have spoken, we do what they command." That was the voice of a true liberal minded democrat!

Furthermore, the well-respected and controversial historian David Starkey, having watched the divisive party conferences and parliamentary shenanigans, claimed that the Liberal Party is an 'extremist party', and that: 'liberalism is extremist, anti-popular, anti-democratic (and) it is utterly intolerant'.

Many Conservative, members of parliament, were also opposed to leaving the EU without an agreement (despite the fact parliament would not ratify the agreement and the European Union would not amend the agreement) and they supported an opposition motion to prevent us leaving without an agreement, creating parliamentary deadlock. Consequently, twenty one Conservative, members of parliament, including the 'Father of the House', Kenneth Clarke and the former Chancellor of the Exchequer, Philip Hammond, lost the party whip for voting against their own government, to seize control of the House of Commons, and force a vote to stop them leaving 'without an agreement' and that they request the European Union to extend the deadline of 31st October 2019, to 31st January 2020, if there was no agreement by 19th October 2019.

Furthermore, the following, Conservative, Members of Parliament, Sarah Woolaston, Heidi Allen, Sam Gyimah and Phillip Lee, resigned from the party, and joined the Liberal Democrats. They left their party of government, which was attempting, 'against all the odds', to deliver on the 'people's vote', and joined the so-called Liberal Democrats, which promised that, should they form a government (which is unlikely), they would revoke Article 50 and remain in the European Union, without another public referendum, which is profoundly undemocratic. The Liberal Democrats also welcomed the following defectors from the Labour Party: Chuka Umunna, Angela Smith and Luciana Berger.

Having prorogued parliament, through a period which included the party conference season, and the Supreme Court decreeing that the prorogation was unlawful, the politicians returned to the chamber on Wednesday 25th September, to enable the angry opposition parties to 'vent-their-spleen' against the prime minister, which was not a pretty sight. The twisted faces of some politicians on the Labour benches, attacking the prime minister for his choice of words, such as 'surrender' and 'humbug', which they alleged 'provoked violence against them', was disturbing. Incidentally, many of those complaining, had obstructed the withdrawal agreement process, which may have angered their 'leave' voting constituents, and sadly some had resorted to threats of violence and damage to property. It may have been their obstructive behaviour, which had caused the threats of violence and damage, more than the words of the prime minister. The noise coming from the opposition benches was like an angry mob of saboteurs, determined to wreck the withdrawal process and bring down the government (which was trying to deliver the 'will of the people'), regardless of the serious damage they were doing to the reputation of our parliamentary democracy.

The alarming events of the past few months have thrown our parliamentary democracy into meltdown, which can only be reversed when the people assert their authority through the ballot box. The survival of our liberal democracy depends on our elected representatives respecting the 'will of the people' or the people must respond by voting them out of office. Liberal democracy can only survive when those we select and elect to represent us in the 'corridors of power', conduct themselves with honesty and integrity and respect those they are there to serve. In a liberal western democracy, a sovereign parliament (and the parliamentarians) receives its authority from the sovereign people.

Whilst our elected representatives must make judgements on behalf of the people (those who elevate them to the 'corridors of power'), they must take account of the views and the mood of the people. This is particularly important when they are considering such important constitutional matters as our future relationship with the European Union, and the people had been asked to decide.

Incidentally, those elected representatives, who are comfortable with the direction and speed of travel of the European project, should heed the words of Larry Siedentop, in his book 'Democracy in Europe', published by Allen Lane, the Penguin Press (2000), as follows: "The danger of premature federalisation in Europe – of the rush to political integration, which turns federalism into little more than a mask for a unitary super-state – is that it could put at risk the complex textures of European societies. For these textures have developed in alliance with nation states, endowed with distinctive political cultures. It is far from clear that they could long withstand the sudden subordination of those states to a centralised rule-making agency…" That is the nature of the risky federalisation of so many independent nation states, as the European Union, which emerged from the Common Market, moves inexorably towards a federal country called Europe or the ultimate ambition of a United States of Europe.

However, the reactionary behaviour of our elected representatives, particularly those who have opposed the 'will of the British people' in a public referendum or a 'people's vote', has raised many more questions than answers.

Why would the 'great' leader of the radical, socialist, Labour Party, want to renegotiate the withdrawal agreement and let the people decide in a second referendum, with an option to remain, and campaign to remain, when he was always such a 'staunch' opponent of the European Union and the people had already voted by a large majority (1,269,501) to leave this dubious project?

Why would the leader of the Liberal Democrats create a policy to revoke Article 50 of the Lisbon Treaty (2009) and remain in the European Union, without another referendum, when her former 'respected' leader, Lord Paddy Ashdown (now deceased), said: "I will forgive no one who does not accept the sovereign voice of the British people, once they have spoken, whether it's by one per cent or twenty per cent… When the people have spoken you do what they say."?

Why would so many respected Conservative, members of parliament, join the, so-called, Liberal Democrats, who campaigned to Stop Brexit, against the 'will of the people', and 'stooped' to wearing bright yellow t-shirts with the words 'Bollocks to Brexit', when at the last general election (2017), they stood on a Conservative manifesto pledge, to leave the European Union, and their own party in government was attempting to deliver on that manifesto pledge?

To show the resistance from some members of parliament, the

following is the statement of Anna Soubry, elected as a Conservative, member of parliament, for Broxstowe, in the East Midlands, and now the leader of the 'Independent Group for Change', at Prime Ministers Questions, on Wednesday 2nd October 2019: "The government talks about the will of the people and the need to restore the trust in democracy, when it comes to Brexit, whilst completely forgetting that over sixteen million people voted remain and thirteen million chose to abstain and one and a half million youngsters weren't eligible to vote and they want a say about their future. So, on that basis, surely the way to protect democracy, is to put any deal to a confirmatory referendum, because if we don't have that people's vote, we'll leave without the consent of, the majority of, the people of this country." Conversely, when we consider the people's 'trust in democracy', Anna Soubry is the elected representative of Broxstowe, which voted 29,672 (45.4%) 'remain' and 35,754 (54.6%) 'leave' and the best way to restore 'trust in democracy', is for our elected representatives to accept the unexpected result and support the government, attempting to deliver on the people's decision.

Furthermore, why would the Scottish Nationalists be so aggressive to the government, as it attempts to extricate us from the shackles of the European Union, in response to the result of the referendum? Granted, the Scots voted to remain, but this was a vote of the citizens of the four countries of the United Kingdom. There aggressive behaviour in parliament, which helps to support the European 'resistance movement', particularly from their leader Ian Blackmore, is disturbing. Incidentally, why would the Scots demand another referendum on independence from their island neighbours (and biggest trading partner), with an ambition to leave the United Kingdom and apply to re-join the European Union (and join the euro), and accept governance from Brussels rather than Westminster? Would the Scottish people rather be a satellite state of a United States of Europe, run by the European political elite, than a significant partner in the United Kingdom, which has been a unified state for more than 300 years, and for many of those years was run by Scottish born ministers? In fact, David Cameron, who got us into this mess, was the son of a Scottish immigrant.

However, despite the obstruction from the opposition parties, the government was determined to leave on the scheduled deadline date of 31st October 2019, despite the fact that parliament had passed legislation to stop the government from doing so, and mandating them to seek a further extension to the deadline date, should a withdrawal agreement not be reached by 19th October 2019.

As we approached the leaving date of 31st October 2019 the Conservative government was determined to leave in accordance with the instructions of the people, 'deal or no deal', which was the only sensible negotiating position to take, yet many of our elected representatives were determined to block us leaving 'with or without' a deal, which put Brussels in the 'driving-seat'.

The European Union (Withdrawal) (No 6) Bill 2019, known as the 'Benn Act', sponsored by Labour MP Hilary Benn, stopped the government from leaving without an agreement and demanded that the government request an extension to the leaving date of 31st October 2019, should no agreement be reached by 19th October 2019, which made it difficult for the government to leave without a deal, and would lead to further parliamentary deadlock.

Incidentally, the former Labour politician, Anthony Wedgewood Benn, father of Hilary Benn, was a staunch proponent of democracy and was quoted as saying: "When I saw how the European Union was developing, it was obvious what they had in mind was not democratic. In Britain, you vote for a government, so the government must listen to you, and if you don't like the government, you can change it." Those wise words are the foundations of a 'people's democracy'.

Furthermore, as we approached the leaving date of 31st October 2019, the government tried to resolve the main blockage, the Northern Ireland 'backstop', which was part of the withdrawal agreement text. The government negotiators submitted 'alternative arrangements' to avoid a hard border on the island of Ireland, in accordance with the Belfast Agreement. This meant that the trading arrangements of the United Kingdom (the fifth largest economy in the world) and the well-being of their people, were at risk, due to the controversy over the customs arrangements on the border between Ulster and Eire. Surely it was not beyond the ability of the two parties to the agreement to remove the 'backstop' text from the Withdrawal Agreement (which is binding) and transfer it to the Political Declaration (which is non-binding) for detailed discussion during the transition period, when the two parties would negotiate our future relationship, including a trade deal? This would have allowed our parliament to ratify the Withdrawal Agreement, minus the controversial 'backstop' text, and then move 'seamlessly' into the transition period, to discuss the 'backstop', alongside our future trading relationship, to prevent us 'crashing-out' with no deal, which the 'resistance movement' suggested would be 'catastrophic' to our economy.

As we approach the 'end-game' of this political saga, wouldn't it have been nice for our two former prime ministers, Tony Blair and Sir John Major, and our two former deputy prime ministers, Lord Heseltine and Sir Nick Clegg, to have conformed with the sentiments of John Major, when he left office (1997) and said: "When the curtain falls, it's time to get off the stage, and that's what I propose to do." Furthermore, his intervention into the Brexit saga, undermined the governments negotiating position, yet he once said: "Whether you agree with me, disagree with me, like me or loathe me, don't bind my hands when I'm negotiating on behalf of the British people." Well his intervention did 'bind the hands' of his own political party in government, as they wrestled with an obstinate European Commission and an obdurate British parliament.

Incidentally, Guy Verhofstadt, the leader of the Alliance of Liberals and Democrats in the European Parliament and their Brexit negotiator, attended the Liberal Democrat Conference on Sunday 15th September 2019, and posed with Liberal Democrat MEP Catherine Bearder, holding a bright yellow t-shirt with the words 'Bollocks to Brexit', which is disturbing. During his speech to the party conference, he talked of a 'world order based on empires' and said: "In the world order of tomorrow, the world order of tomorrow is not a world order based on nation states or countries, it's a world order based on empires". In conclusion, he said: "The world of tomorrow, is a world of empires, in which we Europeans, and you British, can only defend your interests, your way of life, by doing it together, in a European framework, and in a European Union." This seasoned Belgian politician is the ultimate Europhile, who passionately believes in a United States of Europe, and insists that member states must lose some of their valued independence and sovereignty, to deliver their grand project.

Furthermore, Guy Verhofstadt, is a very influential member of the European Parliament and has written a book entitled 'The United

States of Europe' which was published by the Federal Trust for Education and Research (2006) and a review said: "The Belgian Prime Minister, Guy Verhofstadt does not mince words. He wishes to create a 'United States of Europe' with all member states of the European Union participating, if possible, with a group of pioneers, if necessary." He also wrote a book entitled 'Europe's Last Chance', which was published by Basic Books, New York (2017) and a review said: "The key is to reform the European Union along the lines of America's federal government, a United States of Europe, strong enough to stand with the United States of America, in making a better (and) safer world."

Whether he achieves his ambition of a United States of Europe or a 'world order of empires', the British people don't want to be involved, and want to be an independent nation state, trading with Europe and the world, as they always have done. However, the unexpected and inconvenient decision of the British people, to leave the European Union, as it moves towards a United States of Europe, produced a formidable 'resistance movement', which worked hard to keep us in the European club, and in doing so, has deeply divided our people. Those responsible, particularly our own politicians, must be held to account by the people for opposing the democratic 'will of the people' in a referendum.

This is a defining moment in a battle between the 'sovereignty' of parliament and the 'primacy' of the people. This is also a defining moment between the 'sovereignty' of independent nation states and the ultimate authority of the European political class, who are prepared to resist any dissent to their grand project, and the influential Guy Verhofstadt makes no secret of the fact that we must all lose some of our independence and sovereignty for the greater cause.

The Eurosceptic British, started the dissent, with the Brexit referendum, but there are many more Eurosceptics, waiting to reform or leave, such as the French 'National Front', under Marine Le Pen; the 'Party for Freedom' in the Netherlands, under Geert Wilders; the 'Austrian Freedom Party', under Norbert Hofer; the Polish 'Law and Justice Party', under Jaroslaw Kaczynski; the Italian 'Northern League' under Matteo Salvini; the Danish 'People's Party', under Kristian Dahl; the Dutch 'Forum for Democracy' under Thierry Baudet; the 'Sweden Democrats' under Jimmie Akesson and the Eurosceptic Hungarian, Prime Minister, Viktor Orban, who 'takes no prisoners'.

The question is, of course, who will win these crucial constitutional battles and common sense suggests that the European people must control their elected representatives and independent and sovereign nations must define the ultimate destination of this ambitious political project of the European political elite.

The people of Europe must now be on a mission to establish the principle of the 'people's democracies', where the people are more powerful than their elected representatives, and the principle of independent, nation states, as part of an economic community or a common market and reduce the ambitions of the European political elite to create an economic and political union, a Fortress Europe, across the European continent and well beyond.

However, we must not 'hold our breath' because the European political elite are continuing to expand (accession talks started with Albania and Northern Macedonia) and the influential Guy Verhofstadt is talking about a 'world order of empires' and his views were applauded by the delegates at the recent Liberal Democrat Conference. So, we now have the Liberals wanting to Stop Brexit and remain a member of the European Union, as it moves towards a United States of Europe, with ambitions to become part of a 'world order of empires'! It's perhaps, appropriate to repeat the words of the Labour Party leader, Jeremy Corbyn, the 'ultimate protestor', when he told an audience of Irish activists, that 'we do not want to live in a European Empire of the twenty first century'!

It's also appropriate to mention the enlargement ambitions of the European Union, which are mentioned in the book entitled: 'why Europe will run the 21st century' by Mark Leonard, published by Fourth Estate (2005), under 'Keeping the Door Open' as follows: "Today the list of prospective members is long. Romania, Bulgaria and Turkey are already engaged in accession negotiations. The Western Balkans (Albania, Bosnia and Herzegovina, Croatia, Macedonia and Yugoslavia) are preparing for membership. The Ukrainian and Georgian governments have declared their intention of pursuing accession; Morocco has twice expressed an interest in joining; Silvio Berlusconi, held out the prospect of full membership to Russia on a recent visit…" The book also said: "The former

President of the European Commission, Romano Prodi, has spoken of turning (a) potential zone of instability on the EU's fringes into a 'ring of friend's'. He said that these countries would be offered everything short of membership. The strategy, which the European Commission published, lists fifteen incentives, from 'more effective political dialogue' to 'perspectives of integration into transport, energy, communications networks and enlarged and improved assistance." Furthermore, under the heading 'Europe at Fifty', the book said: "As the former French Finance Minister, Dominique Strauss–Kahn says: 'After opening to the East, Europe must now turn to the South. We will have to think about how to make it possible for countries from the ex-Soviet Union and the Mediterranean Basin, such as those of the Maghreb (Algeria, Libya, Mauritania, Morocco and Tunisia) to join our political area. It might be too early to start preparing for a European Union that stretches from the icebergs of the Arctic North to the sand dunes of the Sahara, with the Mediterranean in their midst. But it would be criminal to rule it out."

It's clearly time for the independent member states of the European Union, to heed the warning from the United Kingdom and take back control from the European political class, who appear to have enlargement ambitions, well beyond the borders of Europe. The people should now take the comments of the influential, Guy Verhofstadt, more seriously, when he talks about a 'world order of empires' and the loss of independence and sovereignty of member states.

Furthermore, the European political elite have made it very difficult for the United Kingdom to leave their grand project, stating that they 'can't have their cake and eat it' and it would be nice to know who is behind the well organised 'resistance movements', which have attempted to overturn the unexpected and inconvenient result of the Brexit referendum and reject the 'will of the people'.

Whether or not, the United Kingdom, leaves the European Union, 'with or without' an agreement remains to be seen, but one thing is certain, we are standing at the bar of the 'last-chance-saloon'. The level of resistance to our leaving the European Union, as it moves towards its ultimate destination of a United States of Europe, presumably within a framework of a 'world order of empires', is a frightening prospect. Once an independent country has become a subordinate state of the European Union and reduced its independence, there's no going back! The question is, however, how can the ordinary, decent, people of the European Union 'turn back the tide' before it becomes an uncontrollable 'tsunami', created by the dubious ambitions of their remote political masters?

Remember the words attributed to Jean Monnet, one of the founding fathers of the United States of Europe, that: "Europe's nations should be guided towards the super state, without their people understanding what is happening. This can be accomplished by successive steps, each disguised as having an economic purpose, but which will eventually and irreversibly lead to federation."

However, as the people realise that we have been constantly deceived by our elected representatives or our political masters, we should remember the wise words of the well-respected, Mikhail Gorbachev, former General Secretary of the Communist Party, of the Soviet Union, when he said: "The most puzzling development in politics, during the last decade, is the apparent determination of Western European leaders, to recreate the Soviet Union in Western Europe."

So far as the British people are concerned, leaving the European Union may prove to be very challenging, mainly due to the intransigence of the European political elite, and many of our own elected representatives, but leave we must.

The British people, voted by a significant majority to leave the European Union, as it moves inexorably towards a United States of Europe, within a 'world order of empires.' They voted to regain their independence and sovereignty and it is now up to the government to deliver on their manifesto pledge but they are fighting against an obdurate European political class and an organised 'resistance movement', which wants to overturn the people's decision to leave.

No one knows how this will transpire but should we regain our independence and sovereignty, the electorate should remember those elected representatives who accepted the 'will of the people' and fought for our withdrawal and those who rejected the will of the people and attempted to 'sabotage' the negotiations.

At the next general election, in the very near future, the electorate must respect those political parties and politicians who accepted the decision of the people in the Brexit referendum and reject those political parties and politicians who ignored the decision of the people and attempted to 'sabotage' the negotiations with our European partners and did what they could to Stop Brexit in its tracks.

Our political parties and our politicians must be told by the people that they are our elected representatives and that they must work on behalf of the people who selected and elected and elevated them to the corridors of power. This simple contract, between the people and their elected representatives, is the foundation of our liberal democracy, which is non-negotiable and must be 'set-in-stone.'

It is hoped, that this 'search for the truth' and this 'view from the street', has revealed some of the realities of our membership of the European Economic Community (EEC) or as it was known, the Common Market, which morphed into the European Union (EU), and has reassured the great British people, that they made the correct decision to leave the Brussels to Strasbourg Express, as it thunders towards its 'clandestine' destination of the 'United States of Europe', which would then be part of a 'world order of empires', whatever that means!

The 'Final Showdown'

Prime Minister, Boris Johnson, who had always insisted that we would leave the European Union, 'with or without' an agreement or deal, on the extended leaving date of 31st October 2019, struck a new withdrawal agreement with the European Union, which had insisted that they would not revisit the original withdrawal agreement, ratified by the leaders of the other member states.

The new withdrawal agreement, announced on Thursday 17th October by the President of the European Commission, Jean-Claude Junker and the United Kingdom, Prime Minister, Boris Johnson, includes 'alternative arrangements' to the Northern Ireland 'backstop' text and should have satisfied the doubters who were not happy with the previous arrangements. Incidentally, the leaders of the other twenty-seven member states of the European Union approved the new agreement, putting the 'ball in the court' of our parliamentarians to ratify the new agreement, and then move to the transition period, to discuss our future relationship, including a future trade deal, or reject the new agreement and continue with parliamentary prevarication and obfuscation and deadlock.

However, the new withdrawal agreement did not meet with the approval of the Democratic Unionist Party (DUP) of Northern Ireland, and the government would have problems getting the agreement ratified by parliament. The 'final showdown' was scheduled for Saturday 19th October 2019, which left twelve days to the scheduled leaving date of 31st October 2019, when we were due to leave 'with or without' a deal, according to Article 50 of the Lisbon Treaty.

The final showdown arrived on Saturday 19th October 2019 when the Prime Minister, Boris Johnson, presented parliament with the main changes in the new withdrawal agreement, previously agreed with the European Union, with the intention of having a 'meaningful vote' on the government motion. Had the government won the vote, we could have then left the European Union on 31st October 2019 and moved into the transition period to discuss our future relationship, including a trade deal, and avoid economic turbulence.

However, the new withdrawal agreement got a negative response from the opposition parties, particularly the Labour Party, the Scottish Nationalists and the Liberal Democrats. The inept leader of the Labour Party, Jeremy Corbyn, dismissed the new agreement as being worse than the previous agreement, which had been voted down on three occasions, and instructed his members to vote against the agreement. The combative leader of the Scottish Nationalist Party, Ian Blackmore, criticised the government for giving concessions to the people of Northern Ireland (who voted to remain) but giving no concessions to the people of Scotland (who voted to remain) and twice said the government had 'shafted' the people of Scotland. The leader of the Liberal Democrats, Jo Swinson, just wanted another referendum, to overturn the result of the first referendum and remain in the European Union and promised that should they form a government, they would immediately revoke Article 50 and 'Stop Brexit'.

This would have made it difficult for the government to win a majority in a 'meaningful vote'. However, despite a comprehensive debate, the government did not pursue a 'meaningful vote' on the new withdrawal agreement, because of an amendment tabled by Sir Oliver Letwin, which passed by 322 to 306 votes.

The motion tabled by the government said: "That in light of the new deal agreed with the European Union, which enables the United Kingdom to respect the result of the referendum on its membership of the European Union and to leave the European Union on 31 October with a deal… this House approves the negotiated withdrawal agreement… " However, the Letwin amendment to the government motion removed the wording after the word deal… and said: "this House has considered the matter but withholds approval unless and until implementing legislation is passed." The passing of this amendment meant that the government did not get their motion passed by 19th October 2019, which, therefore, triggered the instructions in the 'Benn Act', for the government to write to Brussels to request a further extension, beyond 31st October 2019.

We were told that the government sent a letter to the European Union, asking for an extension to the leaving date of 31st October 2019 on the instructions of parliament and the prime minister sent a separate letter to confirm that it was not government policy to extend the matter beyond the scheduled leaving date.

The next significant event in parliament, was on Tuesday 22nd October 2019, when parliament, passed legislation to ratify the new withdrawal agreement by 329 to 299 votes. This allowed parliament to start a debate on the withdrawal agreement legislation, within a strict timetable, to allow the legislation to be approved by parliament and allow us to leave on 31st October 2019. However, a second government motion to approve the strict timetable for debate on the agreement failed by 322 to 308 votes and parliament was again in deadlock.

The problem was that the failure to approve the strict timetable and start the debate, meant there would not be enough time to debate the agreement before the leaving date of 31st October 2019. The prime minister then 'paused' the process to await a response from the European Union on a further extension beyond 31st October 2019. It was understood that he wanted a short extension, to complete the withdrawal agreement debate, but he would not accept a longer extension, which would inevitably lead to further parliamentary prevarication.

Incidentally, the President of the European Commission, Jean-Claude Junker, was reported to have said to the European Union leaders in Strasbourg, as they discussed another extension, that Brexit was a 'waste of time and energy."

The 'Final Curtain'

As we approach the final curtain of this tortuous saga, the following quote from the influential Belgian, MEP, Guy Verhofstadt, 8th September 2019, shows just how much these Eurocrats are prepared to interfere in our internal politics: "Foreign Minister Le Drian (France) is right, yet another extension for Brexit is unacceptable unless the deadlock in London is broken. Let it be a second referendum, new elections, a revocation of Article 50 or the approval of the (agreement) deal but not todays helpless status quo."

So, 17,410,742 British people voted to leave the European Union and more than three years later an influential member of the European Parliament, suggests that if we can't reach an agreement, we should have a second referendum or a general election or revoke Article 50 and remain as a member of the European club and, effectively, disregard and disrespect the 'will of the British people'!

Well, should the outcome of this tortuous political obfuscation be a general election, which needs the approval of parliament, the electorate must vent their frustration on those political parties (and politicians), which have thwarted the government's attempt to deliver on the instructions of the British people.

Should the outcome be a second referendum on the final agreement, the people should confirm their desire to leave the European Union, as it moves inexorably towards a United States of Europe, and not be deflected by the many Remain Campaigns, suggesting that leaving would be 'catastrophic' to our economy.

Furthermore, should we have a second referendum, the question must be: 'Do you want to 'leave' or 'remain' in the European Union as it develops 'ever-closer' political and monetary union and completes its journey to a United States of Europe, with enlargement ambitions, beyond its current borders.

The prime minister decided to ask parliament on Monday 28th October 2019 to approve a general election on 12th December 2019, in an attempt to break the deadlock, but he knew that the Labour Party leadership would not support the motion until the government agreed to take 'no deal' of the table. Under the Fixed-Term Parliament Act, the government would need the support of 434 members of parliament. The result of the vote for an early general election, was that 299 voted 'yes' and 70 voted 'no' and 280 'abstained', which did not reach the target of 434 votes needed to change the Fixed-Term Parliament Act.

In the meantime, the European Union agreed another extension to the Article 50 deadline, from 31st October 2019 (the original deadline was 29th March 2019) to 31st January 2020. This meant that if parliament cannot approve the new withdrawal agreement by the new date, we would have to leave without an agreement, in accordance with the terms of Article 50, unless parliament passed legislation to stop us leaving without an agreement and the European Union were asked to grant another extension, which would be bordering on farcical!

To show that the government was determined to break the deadlock and seek approval for an early general election, it apparently agreed with the Liberal Democrats and the Scottish Nationalists, to table legislation to amend the Fixed-Term Parliament Act, which would mean that the government would only need a simple majority to secure a general election, which could be achievable.

However, some members of parliament wanted amendments to allow 16 year olds and EU citizens, resident in this country, to vote in a general election and others wanted an amendment, to change the proposed general election date of 12th December 2019 to 7th May 2020, provided a second referendum had taken place on 26th March 2020. Is there no end to the determination of the 'remain campaigners', to 'engineer' a second referendum, to overturn the result of the first referendum? What they don't seem to understand, is that even if they won a second referendum, there would then be demands from the 'leave campaigners' for a third referendum, the 'best of three' concept, which would be a nonsense.

However, inexplicably, amidst all the political obfuscation, at eleventh hour, on 29th October 2019, parliament voted by a massive 438 votes to 20, a majority of 418, to have an early general election on Thursday 12th December 2019.

So, where do we go from here? We missed the 29th March 2019 deadline and the 31st October 2019 deadline and we now have a new deadline of 31st January 2020, when we will (again) leave 'with or without' an agreement, in accordance with Article 50, unless the agreement is ratified before then, and we now have a general election on 12th December 2019, as we approach the festive season.

Having extended the deadline for leaving the European Union to 31st January 2020 and having approved a general election on 12th December 2019, with no prospect of ratifying the withdrawal agreement before the election, it is hoped that one of the political parties can form a majority government, rather than a coalition, after the election and pass whatever legislation is in their manifesto.

A majority Conservative government would be able to pass the withdrawal agreement and we would leave on 31st January 2020 or before and the move, seamlessly, into a transition period, to discuss our future relationship, including a trade deal, and avoid any unnecessary commercial and economic turbulence.

It would, however, be sensible for the Conservative Party to agree an electoral pact with the Brexit Party, which could otherwise 'split the vote' and prevent them from winning sufficient seats to form a majority government and, by default, let in the socialist Labour Party or a coalition between them and the Scottish Nationalist Party or the Liberal Democrats and the saga will continue.

If we think that the withdrawal process is a problem under the Conservatives, who want to deliver for those who voted to leave, just imagine a pact between Labour and the Liberals or the Scottish Nationalists, who want to remain!

A majority Labour government would attempt to negotiate a third withdrawal agreement with the European Union and then put the complex legal text of the withdrawal agreement to a referendum or public vote and campaign to remain.

A majority Liberal Democrat government would revoke Article 50 and 'Stop Brexit' and remain a member of the European Union, without referring the matter back to the people in a referendum, which would be very divisive.

We are clearly a 'democracy in crisis', as the exhausted people watch the obdurate Westminster and Brussels 'resistance movements' and 'Remain Campaigns' obstruct our departure, through political obfuscation and parliamentary prevarication, and there appears to be no end in sight!

However, the elected representatives have partly redeemed themselves by voting for a general election, which will be a plebiscite on the Brexit controversy, and the people will be able to endorse those politicians who supported the 'will of the people' and reject those politicians who thwarted the 'will of the people'.

Finally, 'all good things must come to an end'. It's not now intended to continue to catalogue these depressing political events. Wherever this tortuous journey takes us, over the next few months, one thing is certain, the people must bring their politicians 'down to earth' and ensure that those we elect to represent us in the 'corridors of power', do not get carried away with their own importance, and remember that they are elected to represent the 'will of the British people'.

Independence Day is now 31st January 2020, but we must accept that nothing will stop the vociferous 'resistance movement', particularly the Liberals, from blocking the withdrawal process, in an attempt, to 'Stop Brexit' in its tracks.

Whether one voted to 'leave' or 'remain', we had the referendum and the majority voted to leave and we should have all got behind the protracted process, to ensure that we could leave with minimal economic turbulence.

FOOTNOTE

Democracy Day: 12th December 2019.

Independence Day: 31st January 2020.

We are 'standing at the bar of the last chance saloon'!

Breaking News!

We have already started the 'nasty' pre-election discourse. The liberal media are already attacking the government for their austerity measures and the state of the nation. This will be the most important general election of the twenty-first century. Those of us, who have been around for some time must do the right thing for our grandchildren and great-grandchildren. This will be a very nasty general election, dominated by the Brexit conundrum and the adverse effects of austerity measures. The 'bitter' socialists have already started to wage 'class-warfare' on the 'posh' Conservatives. Their aggressive Momentum 'street-fighters' will be on our doorsteps and in our faces. They will promise 'justice for the many and not the few', as if they had a monopoly on compassion. They will promise to nationalise everything, in line with their Marxist obsession, but like the last New Labour pretence, they will break the bank. Remember the note from Liam Byrne, the outgoing chief secretary to the treasury, to his successor, which said: "Dear Chief Secretary, I'm afraid to tell you, there's no money (left), Kind Regards, Liam Byrne, Shadow Chief Secretary to the Treasury."

The people must be informed, particularly the young people, that the reason why the government had to introduce austerity measures, was to sort out the 'car-crash' left by their predecessors, who 'ran out of other people's money', as they always do. And if we thought that the New Labour pretence played 'fast and loose' with 'other people's money', they will be 'innocents at large' when compared with the Corbynista revolutionary guard, called Momentum. If the former 'discredited' prime minister, Tony Blair, had wanted to redeem himself, he should have attempted to recover his beloved Labour Party, which has been taken over by the extreme left-wing, rather than attempting to overturn the result of a democratic 'people's vote', which has further damaged his already tarnished reputation. This is a plea to the great British people from the author, who suffered the Labour 'car-crash' of the nineteen seventies, when dead bodies were not being buried and litter was not being collected and the lights went out: Please 'don't give the keys to the people who crashed the car."

So far as the so-called Liberal Democrats are concerned, they are now far from being liberal and they are certainly not democratic, as they promise to 'drive a coach and horses' through our democratic and electoral process, which was the envy of the world. They just want to revoke Article 50 and 'Stop Brexit', with a disgusting slogan 'Bollocks to Brexit', and remain members of the European Union, despite 17,410,742, ordinary, decent, people voting to leave. The great British public had 'seen the light' and wanted to recover our independence and sovereignty, from this monumental, European, super-tanker, which is 'crashing towards the rocks' This is a democratic election, a 'people's vote', where the ordinary, decent, people, vote for an 'elected representative', and they should not vote for the so-called Liberal Democrats, whose policy is to disregard and disrespect the views of the people in the last election (referendum). They are not democrats and they are not worthy of our vote. We must remember the views of their former leader, Lord Paddy Ashdown (now deceased) who said: "I will forgive no one who does not accept the sovereign voice of the British people, once they have spoken, whether it's by one percent or twenty percent… When the people have spoken you do what they say."! That's real democracy!

The liberal media and the opposition or 'resistance movement', may attack the government for their austerity measures, when they were trying to 'fix the roof when the sun was shining'. They may attack them for attempting to reduce our penchant for spending 'other people's money' and creating an enormous debt mountain. They may attack them for their stubborn determination to deliver on the result of the referendum, or the 'people's vote', despite all the dire warnings of 'catastrophe' and 'tragedy', but they are now the real 'party of the people'.

We are now standing at the bar of the 'last chance saloon'. If we don't vote for the politicians who believe in democracy and respect the 'will of the people', as opposed to those who disrespect the people, then democracy is virtually dead.

Finally, when we are concerned about our fragile liberal western democracy and wonder which political parties and politicians to support, we should reflect seriously on the following wise words of the two former respected presidents of the United States of America (USA), Abraham Lincoln and Thomas Jefferson:

The 'Will of the People'

"The will of the people is the only legitimate foundation of any government and to protect its free expression, should be our first objective."

Thomas Jefferson, President of the USA (1801 -1809)

'Government of the people, by the people, for the people'

"The nation was conceived on liberty and dedicated to the proposition that all men are equal and that the future of democracy in the world would be assured that 'government of the people, by the people, for the people', shall not perish from the earth."

The Gettysberg Speech (1863) of President Abraham Lincoln (USA)

The 'People have Spoken'!
That is the 'Will of the People'!
I rest my case!

EPILOGUE:

2020 UPDATE

The run-up to the 2019 General Election

The Westminster Resistance Movement

As we approached the general election (12th December 2019), the knives were out for the Brexiteers. The Europhile big beasts were circling the Eurosceptic wagons and wanting to destroy the hopes and dreams of 17,410,742 people waiting to leave the European Union and return to an independent, democratic and accountable United Kingdom, trading with Europe and the world.

The Europhile big beasts, our former political masters, included Lord Michael Heseltine, former deputy prime minister, Sir John Major, former prime minister, and Tony Blair, former prime minister, who probably still harboured ambitions to be president of a federal European super-power, or United States of Europe.

Inexplicably, Lord Heseltine urged voters to vote for the Liberal Democrats to stop the prime minister's 'great delusion' on Brexit. Speaking at a campaign event in Beaconsfield, prior to the general election, he told voters to vote for the Conservative defectors, such as Dominic Grieve and David Gauke, or for the (Bollocks to Brexit) Liberal Democrats. The Conservative grandee said: "Mr Johnson's 'Get Brexit Done' slogan was a great delusion which would herald 'years of further negotiations on trade' and an 'uncertain future' for Britain."

Surely, a Lord of the Realm and former deputy prime minister knew that the withdrawal process, under Article 50 of the Lisbon Treaty 2009, required the negotiation of a withdrawal agreement and a political declaration, which included a framework for our future relationship and future trade deal, to be negotiated after we leave? That means the European Union legislation requires 'years of further negotiations' to establish a future relationship and a future trade deal, which, by definition, creates an 'uncertain future', and that is the legal requirement of the European Union, not the seceding country. This is the legal pathway to leave the European Union and parliamentarians should have been aware of the legislation when they approved the Brexit referendum and when they voted to invoke Article 50 to start the withdrawal process.

Sir John Major branded Brexit as the 'worst foreign policy decision in his lifetime', as if our cabinet government had made the decision themselves, and he ruled out backing the Conservatives in the general election. Surely, a Knight of the Realm and a former prime minister, knew that Brexit was not a 'foreign policy decision' made by our cabinet government? The decision was delegated to the British people in a referendum or a 'people's vote' and 17,410,742 people voted to leave the European Union, and despite a formidable Westminster and Brussels resistance movement, the Conservative government was determined to honour the 'people's vote', which is the essence of our liberal democracy.

He also wanted a second Brexit referendum, to overturn the inconvenient result of the first referendum, which he called the 'tyranny of the majority'. This is bizarre, coming from a senior statesman, who accepted the results of so many general elections, won on a minority of votes under the 'first past the post' electoral system, which could be characterised as the 'tyranny of the minority'.

He also urged voters not to back the Conservatives in the general election, because of the way they'd handled Brexit. Did he mean their determination to deliver on the result of the referendum, something he denied the British people, when he approved the Maastricht Treaty, which changed the Common Market trading group into the political and economic European Union (EU), despite a clamour from his Conservative colleagues to consult the British people?

It's disturbing that some of our former political leaders should disrespect the will of the people (those who elevated them to the corridors of power) and disregard the essential principle of 'loser's consent'. Without the acceptance of the electoral principle of 'loser's consent' the democratic process cannot work effectively, as our elected governments are immediately confronted with an obdurate resistance movement, attempting to overturn the result of an election and overthrow the elected government, rather than accepting the tradition of Her Majesty's Loyal Opposition holding the elected government to account.

Neil Hamilton, a former Business Minister in John Major's government, being interviewed on LBC Radio, 7th December 2019, said: "I think that what we are seeing now is a rise in spontaneous opposition amongst the people of the global political class, of which John Major is a supreme example, and Tony Blair, perhaps the president of the globalist community worldwide. The people are in revolt, open revolt, against all this. These people, who think they know better than the rest of us and talk-down to us, their day is increasingly over."

Incidentally, Prime Minister Theresa May made the following statement about 'citizens of the world', shortly after coming to power in the wake of the Brexit referendum: "Too many people in positions of power behave as if they have more in common with international elites than with the people down the road… but if you believe you are a citizen of the world, you are a citizen of nowhere, you don't understand what citizenship means." Some of our representatives get carried away with their own importance in the corridors of power and are more comfortable on the European or world stage, having an academic discourse on multi-nationalism and globalism, than engaging with their local communities.

So far as Tony Blair is concerned, how ironic that he shared a pre-general election platform with Lord Heseltine and Sir John Major at Beaconsfield, under the banner 'Vote For A Final Say', where he had previously campaigned for election to parliament (1982/3) and his electoral leaflet said: "Above all, the EEC takes away Britain's freedom to follow the economic policies we need." It's not surprising that the people of Beaconsfield ignored his volte-face.

Mr Blair also praised his Conservative predecessor's Brexit intervention, telling a pre-election rally: "Thank God for John

Major." He went on to say: "To John (Major), to Michael (Heseltine), for years I have stood against you, tonight it is an honour to stand with you." He also said: "Mr Johnson does not deserve to win a majority and suggested a hung parliament would be a better outcome than a country hung for want of leadership." He also said that he would vote for the Labour Party, under the dubious leadership of Jeremy Corbyn, which effectively means he would rather have an extreme Marxist government, seeking to destroy capitalism, than leave the European Union and reclaiming our independence, democracy and freedom, from the threat of a federal United States of Europe!

These comments about leadership, from former Prime Minister Tony Blair, suggest that our political leaders can ignore the will of the people, as he did, when he took us into the disastrous Iraq War, against the will of the people, and the Middle East went up in flames and millions of innocent people were killed or seriously injured or displaced as vulnerable refugees. This was an example of our political masters disrespecting the will of the people. However, we are not yet a dictatorship, we are still a liberal western democracy, and those we elect to represent us in the corridors of power must respect the will of the people.

There's no doubt, that had he listened to the reasonable voice of the people, the wisdom of the crowd, and had he not taken us into the disastrous Iraq War, alongside the Afghan War, which was later compounded by the Syrian War, there would not be a refugee crisis and the world would be a much safer place.

Prime Minister Blair, and his compliant Cabinet colleagues and the British parliamentarians, who supported his reckless decision to support President George W. Bush (USA) and raze Baghdad to the ground, should be held to account for the dire consequences suffered by millions of innocent people.

Remember the words of Robin Cook (2004), now deceased, who wrote in his book entitled *The Point of Departure*: "I left because I could not support a war based on a false prospectus and waged without any international authority."

Remember the words of Clare Short (2005) who wrote in her book entitled *An Honourable Deception*: "I am afraid that I still find it impossible to brush aside what has happened. I believe the deceit profoundly dishonours Tony Blair and makes him unfit for office or prime minister."

Fifteen years later he has deflected all the criticism and secured his place on the world stage as a proponent of the concept of globalism and an opponent of our escape from Fortress Europe. However, the British people ignored his lectures and voted for independence, democracy and freedom from the European super-state, as it moves towards a United States of Europe, which is the obsession of the European political class. Had he succeeded in his attempt to again ignore the will of the British people and keep us in the European Union super-state, he may have improved his chances of becoming a president of a federal Europe.

Whilst there was a massive pre-general election resistance movement wanting to Stop Brexit, the principal opposition came from former prime minister Sir John Major, former prime minister Tony Blair, former deputy prime minister Lord Heseltine and former deputy prime minister Sir Nick Clegg, who wrote a book entitled *How to Stop Brexit*. How could these former senior statesmen wilfully attempt to overturn the democratic will of 17,410,742 British people?

Furthermore, many of our elected representatives obstructed the withdrawal agreement process through parliament and many voted against leaving without an agreement and many wanted another referendum or a 'people's vote' on the terms of any agreement, which was a direct challenge to the will of the people.

Another member of the Westminster resistance movement, Sir Keir Starmer, a member of the Labour shadow cabinet, when being interviewed on Sky News, 12th November 2018, suggested that 'Brexit could be stopped' and should the deal fail, all options must be on the table, including an option of a 'public vote'. This was a direct challenge to the will of the people by a member of the socialist resistance movement and contrary to the Labour Party general election (2017) manifesto pledge that 'Labour accepts the referendum result.' So, how did his outburst, that 'Brexit could be stopped' and that 'we could have another public vote', affect those people casting their votes at the next general election (2019)?

The Unexpected Result of the General Election (2019)

So, despite the dubious behaviour of our former political masters and many of our elected representatives, the general election took place on Thursday 12th December 2019 and the choice was between the Conservative Party, under the leadership of Prime Minister Boris Johnson, wanting to 'Get Brexit Done', and the Labour Party, under the dubious leadership of Jeremy Corbyn, wanting to renegotiate the withdrawal agreement and have another referendum, and the Liberal Democrats, under the inept leadership of Jo Swinson, wanting to revoke Article 50 and 'Stop Brexit' using the disturbing slogan 'Bollocks to Brexit'!

The decision of the British people was as follows: The Conservatives won 365 seats (an increase of 47 on the 2017 General Election); the Labour Party won 203 seats (a loss of 59 seats); the Scottish Nationalists won 48 seats (an increase of 13 seats); the Liberal Democrats won 11 seats (a loss of one seat) and the Brexit Party got no seats. The people had placed their trust in the Conservative Party to deliver on the result of the Brexit referendum and 'Get Brexit Done'.

It's interesting to note, that none of those parliamentarians who defected from the Conservative Party, over their approach to the leaving process, such as Dominic Grieve, Anna Soubry, David Gauke and Sarah Woolaston, were re-elected by the people. They chose to oppose the will of the people, who had spoken in a referendum or 'people's vote', which is profoundly undemocratic, and they must suffer the consequences and find alternative employment.

It's also interesting to note that the Conservatives got 13,970,000 votes (43.6%), Labour got 10,300,000 votes (32.2%), the Liberal Democrats got 3,700,000 votes (11.6%), the Scottish Nationalists (SNP) got 1,240,00 votes (3.9%) and the Brexit Party got 64,000 votes (2.0%).

It is, however, a matter of public concern that 3,700,000 people voted for the Liberal Democrats, who ignored the result of the referendum or 'people's vote' and wanted to 'Stop Brexit' by revoking Article 50, using the slogan 'Bollocks to Brexit'. They were also in unison with the Europhile MEP Guy Verhofstadt, who promotes a

'United States of Europe' within a 'World Order of Empires'.

It's even more concerning that 10,300,000 people voted for the Labour Party, under the leadership of Jeremy Corbyn, the ultimate protestor, and his neo-Marxist shadow chancellor, John McDonnell, and their aggressive, socialist street-fighters, known as 'Momentum', who want to destroy capitalism and 'keep the red flag flying here' and engineer a socialist United States of Europe.

It's suggested that the Damascene Conversion of the Labour leadership to the European Union (involving many former Eastern European communist states), having been opposed to the Common Market trading group (involving a small number of Western European, democratic countries), is that they could see the possibility of a socialist United States of Europe on the political horizon!

It's also interesting to note that the Beaconsfield constituents, who experienced the pro-remain campaign, 'Vote for a Final Say', fronted by Lord Heseltine, Sir John Major and Tony Blair, ignored their advice and returned the Conservative candidate with 32,477 votes, a majority of 15,712 votes, on a 74.46% turnout. This result was a clear warning to former political leaders, not to disrespect the result of a referendum or 'people's vote', which was profoundly undemocratic.

Incidentally, this was the fifth time that the people had voted to leave the EU. First there was the 2015 general election, won by the Conservatives, with a promise to hold a referendum on our membership of the EU; then there was the result of the 2016 referendum, with a majority of 1,269,501 votes to leave the EU; then there was the 2017 general election won by the Conservatives with a promise to get us out of the EU; then there was the European Parliamentary Elections (2018), won by the Brexit Party; and then the 2019 General Election, with a landslide victory for the Conservatives and melt-down for Labour and the Liberal Democrats. The British people, who are made of stronger stuff, were not prepared to be intimidated by the European political class and the Brussels and Westminster resistance movements and the bogus 'Project Fear' campaigners.

The Scottish National Party (SNP) and the Break-Up of the United Kingdom

It's been so disturbing to watch the leaders of the Scottish Nationalists, who got 45% of the Scottish votes in the general election (2019), demanding another independence referendum, with the intention of leaving the UK and applying to re-join the EU. Incidentally, whilst the Scottish Nationalists got 1,242,380 votes (45%), from those who want Scottish independence, the other three main parties got 1,468,194 votes (53.20%) from those who may not want independence.

Furthermore, the general election results in Scotland (2019), where 45% of the Scottish electorate voted for the Scottish Nationalists and 55% did not vote for the nationalists, on a 68% turnout, are almost identical to the results of the Scottish Independence Referendum (2014), where 44.7% of the electorate voted for independence and 55.30% voted against independence, on an 84.6% turnout.

It's very sad to watch the Scottish Nationalists demanding independence from the United Kingdom, their island 'friends and neighbours', the most successful political union in the history of the world, to become a dependent state of the burgeoning European Union, which is a contradiction in terms. Do they really want 'independence' from the UK to become a 'dependent' state of the EU, which means they would leave the Pound Sterling and the Bank of England and presumably create their own currency under the Bank of Scotland, and apply to re-join the EU and join the Eurozone, and come under the supervision of the European Central Bank? That means they would rather have a subordinate political and economic union, with a multitude of foreign countries, than with their island 'friends and neighbours' on the British Isles, where they already have significant self-determination and are virtually independent.

Incidentally, the state of the Scottish economy, particularly their penchant for over-spending, could mean that they would not meet the entry requirements of the European Union. Scotland's annual budget deficit is currently circa 8% of their Gross Domestic Product (GDP), when it should not exceed 3% of GDP.

Furthermore, Scotland and England united, to form the Kingdom of Great Britain, in 1707 and throughout three centuries the people have become deeply integrated and assimilated. It's also rather ironic that the English are considered to be xenophobic, for wanting independence from the European Union, which the United Kingdom joined in 1992 (The Maastricht Treaty), yet the Scottish are not considered to be xenophobic for wanting their independence from the United Kingdom, which they both joined in 1707! The Scottish Nationalists are concerned that they are dominated by an elected Westminster government and parliament, of which they are an integral part, when they also have their own regional government and parliament, yet they want to be run by an unelected European Commission and a remote European Parliament, based in Brussels!

It's difficult to believe that the Scottish people really want to leave the United Kingdom, their largest trading partners by a country mile. They exported £49.8 billion of goods to the rest of the United Kingdom (2015), which is circa four times more than their £12.3 billion of exports to the European Union. Scotland's largest overseas market, outside of the EU was the USA at £4.6 billion, which is more than any single EU country. Within the EU, Netherlands was their biggest market at £2.3 billion (which includes goods to the port of Rotterdam, destined for another country), then £1.8 billion with France and Germany. They do a significant 63% of their trade with the rest of the UK and 16% with the EU!

According to Wikipedia, the economy of Scotland had an estimated nominal gross domestic product (GDP) of up to £170 billion in 2018. Since the Acts of Union 1707, Scotland's economy has been closely aligned with the economy of the rest of the United Kingdom (UK) and England has historically been its main trading partner. Scotland conducts most of its trade within the UK. In 2014, Scotland's exports totalled £76 billion, of which £48.5 billion (64%) was with the other constituent nations of the UK and £11.6 billion with the other member states of the EU and £15.2 billion with other parts of the world.

So far as the Scottish Independence Referendum (2014) is concerned, according to a post on Democratic Audit UK (www.democraticaudit.com) by Richard Berry, Research Associate at Democratic Audit, and Craig Berry, Research Fellow at the Sheffield Political Economy Research Institute, the franchise for the referendum did not include Scottish citizens overseas or those living in the rest of the United Kingdom and they argue that the exclusion of these voters is not justified and violates established democratic principles. The post said that there were 3,570,000 Scottish citizens resident in Scotland and able to vote in the independence referendum; 474,000 residents from the rest of the United Kingdom; 121,000 residents from the rest of the European Union; and 89,000 residents from the Commonwealth. There were, however, 620,000 Scottish citizens living in the rest of the United Kingdom and 286,000 Scottish citizens resident overseas, who could not vote in the independence referendum.

The Scottish Parliament and the United Kingdom Parliament both voted to agree the terms of the independence referendum, which included a register to include 16- and 17-year-olds on the franchise but the Scottish Government proposed to exclude Scottish voters, resident elsewhere in the United Kingdom.

The report concluded: "There is little justification for excluding Scots living in the rest of the UK on a decision of such magnitude, which directly affects them and is being taken by a political community to which they belong. Although we cannot know for certain which way this group would have voted, it seems likely most would want to keep the union together; equal to about 15% of the resident Scottish population, votes from this group could have been decisive."

Another report by Nick Eardley of BBC News, on 7th August 2014 said: "It might sound surprising but according to the latest census figures, there are about 750,000 people born in Scotland who live south of the border. That's more than the population of Edinburgh or Glasgow." The report showed the people born in other parts of the UK, who were resident in Scotland, and were eligible to vote on Scottish independence, as follows: England 422,386. Northern Ireland 35,123 and Wales 16,186. (Total: 473,695). The report also showed the people born in Scotland who were resident elsewhere in the United Kingdom, who were not eligible to vote on Scottish independence, as follows: England 681,406. Wales 23,095. Northern Ireland 14,074. (Total 718,575). Source: 2011 Census; National Records of Scotland (NRS), Office of National Statistics (ONS), Northern Ireland Statistics and Research Agency (NISRA).

It's clearly a policy of the Scottish Nationalists to include 16- and 17-year-old voters, resident in Scotland, who are likely to vote for independence, in the franchise, and exclude the 718,575 Scottish-born people, living south of the border, many of whom may want to remain in the United Kingdom.

It's also their policy to allow 473,695 people born elsewhere in the United Kingdom, who are resident in Scotland, to vote on independence, but exclude 718,575 people born in Scotland, who are living elsewhere in the United Kingdom. It's also their policy to allow 121,000 citizens from elsewhere in the EU and 89,000 Commonwealth citizens, resident in Scotland, to vote on independence, whilst excluding 718,575 people born in Scotland, living in the rest of the United Kingdom, mentioned in the Democratic Audit UK report.

The author believes that, despite the bellicose rhetoric of the populist Scottish Nationalists, the Scottish people will never vote to leave the United Kingdom, their island 'friends and neighbours' and biggest trading partner, with whom they are deeply integrated, but any future Scottish independence referendum must include Scottish-born people living elsewhere in the United Kingdom.

The Pro-Brexit Conservative Party Landslide Victory

Incidentally, whilst the Conservatives had a landslide victory with 365 seats, as opposed to Labour with 203 seats, it has been suggested by the pollsters that they could have taken twenty more seats, had it not been for the intervention and competition of the Brexit Party, which got 2% of the vote but no seats.

According to *The Times* on Wednesday 18th December 2019, Paul Hilder, Chief Executive of the polling firm 'Datapraxis' said: "According to our analysis there are at least twenty Labour-held seats, where the Brexit Party likely cost the Tories victory… In seats such as Hartlepool, Rotherham and Barnsley Central and East, between 70 and 90 per cent of Brexit Party voters said they would have voted Conservative in a two-horse race, with a maximum of 6.5 per cent choosing Labour instead." Without the Brexit Party, which got 64,000 votes but no seats, the Conservatives could have got a majority of circa 100 seats, which, perhaps, reflects the mood of the people to 'Get Brexit Done'!

In Hartlepool Labour got 15,464 votes, the Conservatives got 11,869 votes and the Brexit Party got 10,603 votes. That's 15,464 votes for Labour and 22,472 votes for the Conservatives and the Brexit Party. In Rotherham, Labour got 14,736 votes, the Conservatives got 11,615 votes and the Brexit Party got 6,125 votes. That's 14,736 votes for Labour and 17,740 votes for the Conservatives and the Brexit Party. Labour won Barnsley Central with 14,804 votes, the Brexit Party got 11,233 votes and the Conservatives got 7,892 votes. That's 14,804 for Labour and 19,125 for the Conservatives and the Brexit Party. In Doncaster North, Labour got 15,740 votes, the Conservatives got 13,370 votes and the Brexit Party got 8,294 votes. That's 15,740 votes for Labour and 21,664 votes for the Conservatives and the Brexit Party. In Doncaster Central, Labour got 16,638 votes, the Conservatives got 14,360 votes and the Brexit Party got 6,842 votes. That's 16,638 votes for Labour and 21,202 for the Conservatives and the Brexit Party. In Normanton, Pontefract and Castleford, Labour got 18,297 votes, the Conservatives got 17,021 votes and the Brexit Party got 8,032 votes. That's 18,297 votes for Labour and 25,053 for the Conservatives and the Brexit Party, yet the pro-remain member of parliament retained her seat.

It was a similar story in Barnsley East, Hull East, West and North, Easington, Wigan, South Shields, Washington and Sunderland West, Jarrow, Wentworth and Dearne, Makerfield, Blaenau Gwent, Cynon Valley and Rhonda.

Hull East is another example of the adverse effect the Brexit Party had on the result of the election. Labour got 12,713 votes, the Conservatives got 11,474 votes and the Brexit Party got 5,764 votes. That's 12,713 votes for the 'pro-remain' Labour Party and 17,238 votes for the pro-leave Conservative and Brexit Parties, a majority of 4,525, but Labour won, and the Conservatives lost.

Incidentally, Normanton, Pontefract and Castleford voted decisively to leave the European Union, and is an example of a majority of the electorate voting for a leave party, the Conservatives and the Brexit Party (25,053), and a minority voting for a remain party, Labour and the Liberals (21,444), yet the prominent pro-remain

Labour member of parliament, Yvette Cooper, retained her seat!

It's also interesting to consider the general election result of the Wakefield constituency (which voted 67% to leave the EU in the Brexit referendum), which destroys the allegation that leavers were racist. This West Yorkshire constituency, with a mainly Northern European and Christian electorate, ousted their pro-remain, Labour Member of Parliament, Mary Creagh, and voted for an Asian, Muslim, Conservative Member of Parliament, Ahmad-Khan. This was a decisive victory for the Brexiteers, with the Conservatives polling 21,283 votes (47.27%) and the Brexit Party with 2,725 votes (6.05%), a total of 24,008 votes (53.32%), against the Labour Party with 17,925 votes (39.81%).

An obvious loser in the general election was the new leader of the Liberal Democrats, Jo Swinson, with an anti-democratic policy to 'Stop Brexit' and a disgusting t-shirt slogan 'Bollocks to Brexit'. The result was that the Liberal Democrats won eleven seats and she lost her Dunbartonshire East constituency, to the Scottish Nationalists, with a swing of 5.29%, and she resigned as leader of the Liberal Democrats, having been in office for just 144 days.

Whilst the biggest winner in this general election campaign was Prime Minister Boris Johnson, with his clear message to 'Get Brexit Done' getting 365 seats (an increase of 47 on the 2017 general election), the biggest casualty was the dubious Labour leader, Jeremy Corbyn, with 203 seats (a reduction of 59 on the 2017 general election), who declared that he would not lead the party into the next general election but would remain as leader until a suitable replacement was elected. This means that he would remain at the helm during the leadership contest, which would be influenced by his militant, socialist, or even Marxist Momentum street fighters, which could result in the selection of another extreme socialist leader and deputy leader, both determined to 'keep the red flag flying here' but may never get near the steps of 10 Downing Street!

The conclusion of the Brexit debate, was that the people had spoken for the fifth time and it was imperative that the Conservatives kept their manifesto campaign pledge to 'Get Brexit Done' under the assertive leadership of Boris Johnson, who confirmed that we would leave the European Union on 31st January 2020.

Independence Day: 31ˢᵗ January 2020

The first hurdle on the final straight of the 'Brexit Sweepstakes' was to leave the European Union, on 31ˢᵗ January 2020. The current Conservative majority of 80 seats in the House of Commons made that achievable and they passed the second reading of the Withdrawal Agreement on Friday 20ᵗʰ December 2019 by 358 votes (mainly Conservatives) to 234 votes (mainly Labour). We were told that the outgoing leader of the Labour Party, Jeremy Corbyn, had whipped his members to oppose the Withdrawal Agreement, which means that he had not learned any of the lessons from the thrashing they got at the general election.

The Liberal Democrats, under the inept leadership of Jo Swinson, with their 'Stop Brexit' mantra, and their disgusting slogan 'Bollocks to Brexit', had betrayed the British people and destroyed the notion of a liberal democracy and they suffered the negative consequences from those who believe in democracy.

The Labour Party, under the socialist leadership of Jeremy Corbyn, promised a fantasy renegotiation of the second withdrawal agreement and then to put a third withdrawal agreement to the people in a second referendum or 'people's vote', and campaign to remain in the European Union, and ignore the decisive result of the first referendum, which would have been a betrayal of the 'will of the British people' and the virtual destruction of our liberal western democracy.

Incidentally, the hypocrisy of Jeremy Corbyn, is breath-taking. He has always been opposed to our membership of the EU, yet he accepted a manifesto pledge to renegotiate the second withdrawal agreement and then put a third withdrawal agreement to the people in a 'people's vote'. This would have further extended the tortuous withdrawal process and ignored the result of the first referendum, which would have raised the ridiculous prospect of any plebiscite being decided on a principle of the 'best of three'! This is a man who encouraged the Irish to vote against the Lisbon Treaty (2009) and said: "if you succeed in getting a no vote here, that will be such a boost to people like us, all over Europe, who do not want to live in a

European Empire of the 21st century, I'm pleased you're having a referendum, I wish we were having one in Britain." Hypocrisy is the ultimate sin and honesty is the ultimate virtue of our politicians. When those we select and elect to the corridors of power are found to be strangers to the truth and are comfortable with pretence, they must be removed from office.

The Conservative Party, under the leadership of Prime Minister Boris Johnson, emerged from this debacle with the most credit, because they accepted the will of the British people and pursued a campaign promise to 'Get Brexit Done' and they achieved a landslide electoral victory from the weary British electorate!

As we approached 2300 on Friday 31st January 2020, 'Independence Day', preparing for the transition period, to negotiate our future relationship, there was a suppressed feeling of euphoria. We were warned by the liberal media not to be too triumphalist! Whilst the prime minister made an address to the nation there was a resistance to flag-waving, which may have upset those who voted to remain. In his message to the nation, he said: "Quitting the EU was a moment of real national renewal and change. I know we will succeed. We have obeyed the people. We have taken back the tools of self-government. Now is the time to use those tools to unleash the full potential of this brilliant country."

The Negotiation of a Mutually Beneficial Free Trade Agreement

So, the final hurdle on this release from Fortress Europe, the playground of the European political class, is to negotiate a trade deal with the European Union, before the end of the transition period, 31st December 2020, which many believe cannot be achieved. However, Prime Minister Boris Johnson intends to set the date in stone with legislation, which means that we'll leave the European Union on 31st December 2020 with or without a trade deal, and, if no deal is agreed, trade under World Trade Organisation (WTO) rules, which is in accordance with the legal terms of Article 50 of the Lisbon Treaty (2009), which the United Kingdom parliament approved by a significant majority.

Whilst the doom-mongers suggest that we'll not get an acceptable trade deal with our European partners, the optimists believe that it's in both our interests to do so, and these are the warm words of the Ursula von der Layen, on 16th July 2019, when she was campaigning to be President of the European Commission:

"I cannot talk about Europe without I talk about our friends from the United Kingdom. For the very first time in 2016, a member state decided to leave the European Union. This is a serious decision. We 'regret' it but we 'respect' it. Since then… the EU has worked hard to organise an orderly departure… The withdrawal agreement… provides certainty, where Brexit created uncertainty… However, I stand ready for a further extension of the withdrawal agreement, should more time be required for good reason. In any case the United Kingdom will remain our ally our partner and our friend."

It's also important to consider the terms of the revised political declaration and withdrawal agreement, which sets out the framework for our future relationship, agreed at a European Council summit meeting on 17th October 2019. It provides a commitment to an ambitious goods trading relationship, and free trade deal or agreement, with deep regulatory and customs co-operation and fair competition.

The agreement proposes that negotiations will start as soon as possible, making the best endeavours to conclude by 31st December 2020. Both parties will start preparatory work, including drawing up a full schedule of the most challenging areas, and they will convene in June 2020 to take stock of progress.

Incidentally, it's important to remember the positive wording of Article 4a of the original 'Agreement on the Withdrawal of the United Kingdom from the European Union', under the heading 'Good Faith', which said: "The parties shall in full mutual respect and good faith, assist each other in carrying out tasks, which flow from this agreement. They shall take all appropriate measures to ensure fulfilment of the obligations arising from this agreement and refrain from any measures which could jeopardise the attainment of the objectives of this agreement… particularly the principle of sincere co-operation."

Consequently, now that the British people have reinforced their decision to leave Fortress Europe, with a landslide victory for the Conservatives, which should derail the Westminster and Brussels resistance movements, the two parties should work together in a spirit of mutual respect and good faith and sincere co-operation, to negotiate a mutually beneficial free trade deal.

Incidentally, whilst the wording of the original Withdrawal Agreement and the Political Declaration, included the words mutual respect and good faith and sincere co-operation, the obdurate negotiator for the European Commission, Michel Barnier, announced that the British would only get a basic trade deal or agreement before the end of the transition period of 31st December 2020.

However, 'good things come to those who wait'. In response to the determined approach of our prime minister, to leave the European Union on 31st January 2020, and to complete a mutually beneficial free trade deal before the end of the transition period on 31st December 2020, Michel Barnier appeared to have had a refreshing change of mind. In his New Year (2020) address, he sent a message to Britain, insisting that the European Union wants to 'build a new, strong and fair partnership' in trade talks with its 'close friend and ally'!

In a spirit of optimism, the *Daily Express*, leader column, 1st January 2020, said: "Britain will begin a thrilling new chapter in its magnificent story as a global force for good in 2020. The country is led by a prime minister who is ablaze with optimism about our nation's future and he has the electoral mandate and the parliamentary majority to drive forward his exciting vision of change…"

In support of this media optimism, *The Daily Telegraph*, Business Section, 21st January 2020, said: "Chief Executives from around the world are poised to unleash a wave of investment in Britain, as forecasts show that our economy will outperform the eurozone in the two years after Brexit." And, "The United Kingdom is the fourth most important nation for business growth plans, behind the US, China and Germany, according to a Price Waterhouse Cooper report, launched at the World Economic Forum's annual conference in Davos. The report suggested that Britain was an increasingly stable place to do business, in a world beset by political and economic turmoil, despite previous claims that its international standing would be undermined by Brexit."

A Beacon of Light in the Darkness

Despite the deep divisions of the past few years, since the people voted to leave the European Union, it is hoped that we can now come together in a spirit of optimism and enterprise and inspiration and create an independent nation, trading with Europe and the world. We could become an example to many of our 'friends and neighbours' on the Continent, who may also be concerned about the movement of the European Union towards its ultimate destination of a federal United States of Europe, as part of a 'World Order of Empires'.

It's also hoped that many Scottish people, at home and abroad, are proud of their beloved homeland and want greater self-determination, but, unlike the bitter leaders of the Scottish National Party, can see an exciting future as an integral part of an independent United Kingdom, these island nations, rather than a subordinate and dependent state of a federal United States of Europe.

If we all work together in a spirit of inspiration and aspiration and co-operation and celebrate our release from the shackles of the European Union, we could become a beacon of light in the darkness to many of our European friends, and become a successful, independent nation-state, trading on the world stage.

The main question is, however, not whether the United Kingdom will survive as an independent country, these island nations, but whether the European political elite can continue with their discreet journey towards a federal United States of Europe, and have the support of the people of Europe, particularly the Germans, the French and the Italians (and others), the net-contributors, who pay the bills.

The British people gave the European political elite the opportunity to reconsider the direction of their grand project, particularly their obsession with 'ever-closer' union and the 'free movement of people'. Sadly, they ignored our genuine concerns and turned their backs and they must now face the prospect of scaling back their grand project, towards the safe haven of a Common Market, rather than the creation of a federal United States of Europe. However, whatever they decide, it must be done with the approval and support of the people of Europe.

In the meantime, the leaders of the European Union are faced with a significant budget shortfall, because of the departure of one of their biggest net-contributors. The United Kingdom's withdrawal from the European Union has left a huge £62 billion (£62,000,000,000) hole in their budget, over the period 2021 to 2027. The consequence of the budget shortfall is that they need to reduce their expenditure, or some member states will have to pay more. The need for reduced expenditure will be recognised by the many net-contributor member states, but any reduction in 'cohesion funds', the money dedicated to supporting the poorer member states, will be resisted by the beneficiaries, known as the 'Friends of Cohesion', which includes the Czech Republic, Hungary, Poland, Slovakia, Estonia, Croatia, Malta, Slovenia, Bulgaria, Cyprus, Lithuania, Latvia, Romania, Portugal and Greece.

We must now call a spade a spade and accept that the European Union is very much a multi-national welfare state, which takes from the 'richer' member states and gives to the 'poorer' member states, and it is in the interests of the, mainly East European, 'Friends of Cohesion' to keep the show on the road and they are very unlikely to see the departure of the United Kingdom as a beacon of light.

However, the European political class have ignored the British 'master-class' on independence, democracy and freedom, and it's not in their interests to facilitate the departure of one of their major net contributors. They will probably make the negotiation of a free trade deal as difficult as possible, to warn other renegades that they can't desert the cause without damaging their economies. They should have listened to the voice of the great British people and realised that they cannot continue on their discreet journey towards a federal United States of Europe, as part of a 'World Order of Empires', without the will of the European people. The European political class must now seriously consider a return to the European Economic Community (EEC) or the Common Market or take a lead from the Russian Federation and create a Commonwealth of Independent States (CIS)!

The Future of the European project

A Commonwealth of Independent States

The respected columnist, Bill Carmichael, had this to say in the *Yorkshire Post* on Friday 3rd January 2020, under the heading 'EU will only survive Brexit if it reforms': "If the EU is to have a future, it is not as a 'United States of Europe' but as a friendly association of free independent countries, co-operating on trade, security and other matters, but in terms of tax and spending, domestic and foreign policy, subject to the democratic will of their own citizens. If such an organisation eventually emerged from the wreckage of Brexit, the people of Europe may be grateful - once again - to the British for securing their liberty and who knows - perhaps a few decades down the line - the UK will decide to re-join?"

Perhaps, they should emulate the Commonwealth of Independent States (CIS), founded by Russia, Belarus and Ukraine (1991), which is an alliance of independent countries, which have signed agreements for economic and foreign policy and defence co-operation and other matters but they have managed to trade with each other without the need for a common currency, which would have led to a central bank, a finance minister and a controlling federal government. This would be a 'friendly association of free and independent countries, co-operating on trade, security and other matters', as envisaged by Bill Carmichael. However, dismantling the monolithic institutions in Brussels and Strasbourg, which service the burgeoning European Union conglomerate, is much easier said than done. This enormous bureaucratic, political, economic and trading structure, has been designed to maintain the creation and operation of an empire and would need ruthless surgery to return to a Common Market, trading group, or a European Economic Community (EEC) or a Commonwealth of Independent States (CIS).

Furthermore, wouldn't it have been refreshing if the European political elite had listened to the perceptive British people, the so-called 'Eurosceptics', who were happy with the Common Market or the European Economic Community (EEC) but not happy with the move towards 'ever-closer' union and the 'free movement of people' and the ultimate clandestine destination of a United States of Europe?

The liberal elite may support the 'free movement of people' and 'ever closer' union, but they must get the ordinary people on board, as they steam towards a federal United States of Europe. The adverse reaction of the Liberal Democrats towards the result of the Brexit referendum was profoundly undemocratic. When our more liberal-minded people are prepared to ignore the will of the people and attempt to overturn the inconvenient result of a people's vote, using the disgusting t-shirt slogan 'Bollocks to Brexit', our liberal democracy is under serious threat.

However, despite the obdurate resistance of the liberal-minded democrats, and the socialist-minded Labour movement, the Conservatives got the withdrawal agreement through parliament and started our great escape from Fortress Europe.

The third reading of the EU (Withdrawal Agreement) Bill, which documents the arrangements for the withdrawal process, was passed by the House of Commons on Thursday 9th January 2020 by 330 to 231 votes. The President of the European Commission, Ursula von der Layen and the President of the European Council, Charles Michel, signed off the Withdrawal Agreement on 24th January 2020 before ratification by the European Parliament. On 24th January 2020, Prime Minister Boris Johnson said: "Today I have signed the Withdrawal Agreement for the UK to leave the EU on 31st January 2020, honouring the democratic mandate from the British people. This signature heralds a new chapter in our nation's history." Her Majesty the Queen gave the Royal Assent to the legislation on Thursday 23rd January 2020 after it cleared the Commons and the Lords.

The Attitude of the European Political Elite Towards our Future Relationship

The new President of the European Commission, Ursula von der Leyen, gave a speech at the London School of Economics, 8th January (2020), which included the following comments about our future relationship with the European Union: "Before the end of the month, I expect both the British and European Parliaments to ratify the agreement and… on 31st January (2020) the UK will spend its last day as a member state… This will be a tough and emotional day but when the sun rises on 1st February, (we) will still be the best of friends and partners. The bonds between us will be unbreakable… We will still share the same challenges from climate change to security. We will still be allies and like-minded partners in NATO, the United Nations and other international organisations. We will still share the same values and the belief that democracy, freedom and the rule of law must be the foundation of our societies… So as one door will unfortunately close, another door will open. Now is the time for us to look forward together. It's time for the best and the oldest of friends to build a new future together, but… I want to be honest about what lies ahead… The European Union is ready to negotiate an ambitious and comprehensive new partnership with the United Kingdom… We will go as far as we can, but our partnership cannot and will not be the same as before, because with every choice comes a consequence… Without the free movement of people, you cannot have the free movement of capital, goods and services. Without a level playing field on environment, labour, taxation and state aid, you cannot have the highest quality access to the world's largest single market. The more divergence, the more distant the partnership… The European Union's objectives in the negotiation are clear, we will work for solutions that uphold the integrity of the EU, its Single Market and its Customs Union. There can be no compromise on this, but we are ready to design a new partnership… that goes beyond trade and is unprecedented in scope. Everything from climate action to data protection, fisheries to energy, transport to space, financial services to security. We are ready to work, day and night, to get as much of this done within the timeframe. None of this means it will be easy, but we start from a position of certainty, goodwill, shared interests and purpose and we should be optimistic… Brexit does not only mark the end of something, it marks a new phase in an enduring partnership and friendship… I know the last few years have been difficult and divisive. I hope that by being constructive and ambitious in the negotiations, we can move forward together. There will be tough talks ahead and each side will do what's best for them, but I can assure you that the United Kingdom will always have a trusted friend and partner in the European Union."

Whilst the new President of the European Commission, Ursula

von der Leyen, who apparently supports a United States of Europe, used the warm words of partnership, friendship and goodwill, she warned that without the 'free movement of people', you cannot have the free movement of capital, goods and services, which really takes us back to the main reason why the people voted to leave!

The 'Free Movement of People' Principle!

The European political elite need to reconsider their obsession with the four pillars of the European Union constitution, which includes the 'free movement of people'. Surely, they must realise that the uncontrolled 'free movement of people', which may include dependent, vulnerable and disadvantaged people and those who indulge in criminal behaviour, with a multitude of foreign languages, is a recipe for chaos in the receiving countries, which cannot plan for their arrival.

The arrival of an unknown number of dependent, vulnerable and disadvantaged European Union citizens, besides the arrival of refugees and 'asylum seekers' from elsewhere in the world, places an enormous burden on the essential public services of the receiving country, and can only cause disruption and often chaos.

Surely, it was not beyond the imagination of the European political elite to ensure that those who decide to move to another member state, are self-sufficient and not immediately dependent on the essential public services or welfare support of the receiving country. However, those citizens who are employed and can find accommodation, still need education services for their children (who may not speak English) and medical services for their families (who may need urgent medical treatment). None of our public services can cope with the unplanned arrival of thousands of people, which puts the service providers under increased pressure and reduces the availability of the service for the indigenous population.

Many of our public services suffer from the persistent challenge of 'limited resources (such as teachers, nurses and police) chasing unlimited demand'.

Furthermore, the flawed 'free movement of people' principle includes the free movement of those who indulge in serious criminal behaviour. How can the criminal justice system, particularly the police service, of any receiving country, cope with the free movement of serious criminals, particularly those who don't or won't speak the language of the receiving country and can evade the criminal justice authorities by non-communication and moving from one state to another.

Just to confirm that we have a problem of the free movement of serious criminals, the number of foreign criminals in our prisons from other member states (2018) according to the Home Office, include 822 from Poland; 720 from Ireland; 644 from Romania; 382 from Lithuania; 253 from Portugal; 167 from the Netherlands; 125 from Latvia and 108 from Slovakia. However, the problem goes much deeper than those who are sent to prison; what about the less serious crimes committed by those from other member states who are not sent to prison?

To give some idea of the extent of the challenge, *The Guardian* newspaper reported on 15th January 2020, that: 'Britain had failed to pass the details of 75,000 convictions of foreign criminals to their home EU countries' (since 2012). This raises the question, as to whether the authorities of any member state are aware of their own criminals, who leave their country and arrive in another country, which is very unlikely. These criminals are free to move across member states, without the authorities in their home member state being able to track their movements, which is a 'recipe for disaster' for the unsuspecting law-enforcement agencies and the unsuspecting law-abiding people of the receiving member states.

The problem created by the free movement of criminals, across the many member states of the European Union, goes much deeper than the minority of criminals who end up in our prisons or even those who are prosecuted and not incarcerated, it includes the serious social damage to our communities, caused by the antisocial and criminal behaviour of many foreign criminals, who are not caught and not prosecuted by the authorities, who may not even know that they are in the country.

As a former senior police officer, the author knows the difficulties of keeping track of the movements of our own serious criminals, when they are free to roam across the four nations of the United Kingdom, despite their criminal and vehicle records being immediately available from the Police National Computer (PNC). However, monitoring the movements of serious criminals from other member states of the European Union, besides immigrants from elsewhere, who indulge in criminal behaviour, and not having direct access to their homeland criminal or vehicle records, makes law enforcement and crime prevention extremely difficult.

The author suggests that the concept of the 'free movement of people', which includes the free movement of serious criminals, across the borders of so many member states, is deeply flawed and counter-productive to the diligent work of the multitude of law enforcement agencies across the wider European Union.

However, the new President of the European Commission, Ursula von der Leyen, has already stated that if we do not accept the 'free movement of people' we cannot have the free movement of capital, goods and services, which will damage our trade negotiations and our future relationship. The British authorities must inform the European authorities, that the 'free movement of people' principle, which includes the free movement of serious criminals, is a serious risk to internal security and cannot be managed effectively in any liberal democratic society.

Those responsible for the continued development of the European Union, must accept that the unplanned 'free movement of people', across so many member states, may be necessary when creating a federal country called Europe or the United States of Europe, but it is a serious challenge for the provision of public services in the receiving member states and the free movement of serious criminals is a serious risk to their internal security. So, the free movement of capital, goods and services, may be a viable proposition across member states but the 'free movement of people', including the free movement of serious criminals, is unacceptable in a free society. The uncontrolled free movement of independent, law-abiding citizens and their families, seeking employment and housing and access to essential public services, despite the shortage of work and affordable housing and our over-stretched essential public services, is probably manageable, but the uncontrolled free movement of serious (and other) criminals, and the damage they do to our society, and the increased pressure on the criminal justice system, particularly the police service, is unmanageable in a free society.

If the European political elite were not prepared to acknowledge the concerns of the British people, regarding the challenges of the 'free movement of people' principle, together with the free movement of refugees and asylum seekers from elsewhere in the world, they could face a similar backlash from other member states, such as Germany, Italy and Greece, which have suffered unprecedented numbers of immigrant arrivals and a similar adverse reaction from their people.

Incidentally, the 'free movement of people' principle would be workable if it was not for the dramatic economic differences between the member states. It is not unreasonable to expect that the citizens of 'poorer' member states want to move to 'richer' member states to improve their economic circumstances. Conversely, we would not expect large movements of migrants from 'richer' western European member states to 'poorer' eastern European member states. To put the matter into some perspective, according to 'The World Factbook' produced by the Central Intelligence Agency (CIA), the following are the net migration rates of European Union, member states, which are the difference between the people entering and leaving a member state during the year (2017) per 1,000 population.

The net migrants per 1,000 population in western European member states were as follows: Luxembourg 15.5; Cyprus 8.7; Spain 7.8; Belgium 5.4; Sweden 5.3; Austria 4.8; Ireland 4.0; Italy 3.7; Finland 2.9; United Kingdom 2.5; Portugal 2.5; Greece 2.3; Denmark 2.1; Malta 2.0; Netherlands 1.9; Germany 1.5; France 1.1. In contrast, the net migrants per 1,000 population in eastern European member states were as follows: Czech Republic 2.3; Slovenia 0.4; Slovakia 0.1; Serbia 0; Romania -0.2; Bulgaria -0.3; Poland -0.4; Croatia -1.7; Estonia -3.2; Lithuania -6.1; and Latvia -6.1. Clearly, there have not been many economic migrants heading towards the former 'poorer' communist states of Eastern Europe, but they've had a virtual diaspora of people leaving the Eastern Europe countries to take advantage of the more successful enterprise economies of Western Europe.

So, where do we go from here?

So, where do we go from here to secure our future relationship and a 'mutually beneficial' free trade deal, with our European friends and neighbours? We left the European Union on 31st January 2020, 'Independence Day', and we have started to negotiate our future relationship and a future trade deal, to be completed by the 31st December 2020. The optimists feel that we can complete the substance of a free trade deal within the limited time frame, but the pessimists fear the opposite.

We are told that the City of London's access to Europe's financial markets, worth circa £26 billion in annual exports, will be one of the first to be negotiated. Our banks and insurance and financial services will lose their automatic right to operate in the European Union at the end of the transition period. The government will be asking the EU to make an 'equivalence' ruling to allow the banks and insurance and financial services to continue to trade after the transition period.

So far as fishing is concerned, the government intends to take back control of our coastal waters but the EU will seek to ensure that the French, Spanish, Belgium, and Dutch fishermen, can continue to fish in our coastal waters. Britain will have the right to exclude European fishermen from our coastal waters to protect and renew our troubled fishing industry, but the solution is not straight forward. Incidentally, we are told that we export 80 per cent of our catch and we import two thirds of our fish from European fishermen, which is nonsense. Surely, as an independent nation, we must support the renewal of our devastated fishing industry and we must buy the fish caught by British trawlers, to avoid the extra cost of importing fish caught in our coastal waters by European trawlers?

So far as farming and food is concerned, food safety standards are paramount, and the European Union farm regulations are the gold standard in global trade. If the UK departs from present and future food safety standards, set by the European Union, there will be significant new trade barriers, particularly at the Northern Ireland border with Southern Ireland. Surely as an independent nation, we must support our own farmers and increase our own standards and buy British produce.

So far as our trade in goods is concerned, the negotiations will be concerned with 'regulatory alignment'. Whilst the UK will want divergence from EU regulations, especially when setting new standards in sectors such as artificial intelligence and technology, the EU will want to hold us in close regulatory alignment and retain a level playing field. The more we want to diverge from close regulatory alignment or a level playing field the more barriers and tariffs will be imposed.

Whilst the negotiations about our future relationship and future trade deal will be controversial and held in the full glare of the media headlights, our prime minister is prepared to walk away without a trade deal at the end of the year (2020) and he has made it abundantly clear that there are no circumstances under which the British Government will extend the transition period beyond 31st December 2020.

Under the terms of the Withdrawal Agreement both sides have the option of requesting an extension of up to two years to the current trading arrangements. We are told that some trade experts have questioned whether it will be possible to conclude an agreement, covering all sectors of the economy, before the deadline but the British Government has not ruled out a series of 'interim agreements' that could be concluded afterwards, to preserve elements of existing trade and co-operation, while a more comprehensive agreement is negotiated.

The Eurosceptic Reaction to the Brexit Referendum

As we extricate our country from the European Union, rules and regulations, and become an independent nation, trading with Europe and the world, our enterprise economy could go from strength to strength. We could become an inspiration to many of the people of the other member states, who may be concerned about the momentum towards a federal country called Europe or a United States of Europe.

Whilst their views may be dismissed as nationalist or populist or xenophobic or Eurosceptic, the following comments by the radical French politician, Marine Le Pen, leader of the nationalist party –

National Party – previously known as the National Front, and by the outspoken Laura Huhtasaar, Member of the European Parliament for Finland, need to be taken seriously by the European political elite.

Marine Le Pen is one of the most prominent critics of the European Union and was delighted to see the vote to leave in the 2016 Brexit referendum. She said: "This was a victory for freedom" and "We must now have the same referendum in France and other European Union countries" and "The United Kingdom has started a movement that can't be stopped" and "Brexit was the beginning of the end for the European Union." Shortly after the referendum she said: "This is the beginning of the end of the European Union and I hope the birth of the 'Europe of Nations', a Europe of co-operation, that we've been propounding for years."

It's worth repeating that the French people were consulted on the Maastricht Treaty (1992), which discreetly changed the Common Market trading group into the European Union, and they ratified the treaty by a slender margin of 50.8% in favour and 49.2% against. It would not take another French Revolution for them to vote against a federal United States of Europe, of which they would be a major net contributor, and that would be the beginning of the end for their grand project.

The Finnish MEP Laura Huhtasaar, also showed her support for Brexit in the European Parliament, when she said: "On Friday it will be a glorious day for the UK. Brexit is the victory of the common British people, against multi-national corporations, special interests and other elites. The 2020's are the decade when the national state makes the ultimate comeback in Europe. The super-national, unaccountable, bureaucracy, will be rolled-back in favour of real democracy at a national level. Britain will triumph outside of the EU. The island nation has begun a shining movement, that can't be stopped. Farewell to the Brexit Party."

The Prospects for the United Kingdom Outside the European Union

As we negotiate a mutually beneficial free trade deal with the

European Union and free trade deals with the rest of the world, our government wants to create an environment in which our enterprise economy will flourish and will produce the taxation revenues to finance world-class public services for the British people.

On Thursday 23rd January 2020 a study by the Confederation of British Industry (CBI) reported the biggest surge in confidence on record among manufacturers, with companies planning to increase investment after years of austerity measures.

This is what the CBI report had to say about our prospects for the future, as an independent country, which contradicts the warnings of 'Project Fear', during the post-referendum negotiations, to produce a withdrawal agreement and a political declaration about our future relationship and future trading arrangements: "The CBI's quarterly gauge of manufacturing optimism in the UK rose to +23 in the first quarter of 2020, its highest level since the second quarter of 2014. Export sentiment and investment intentions also improved, with a record proportion of firms expecting to authorise capital expenditure in order to expand capacity…"

As we debate the chances of our economic and commercial success, as an independent nation trading on the world stage, we should revisit the wise words of Roger Bootle, winner of the Wolfson Economic Prize, in his book entitled *The Trouble with Europe*, published by Nicholas Brealey Publishing (2016), as follows: "The EU hasn't delivered the prosperity and growth it promised, the euro has turned out to be a disaster and the EU's share of GDP is set to fall. Moreover, no one is clear what the EU is for or how ever-closer union can be matched with expanding borders and huge disparities of income and culture. The EU is the most important thing that stands between Europe and success. Prime Minister David Cameron's renegotiation produced nothing of substance. It now looks like the EU cannot and will not willingly embrace fundamental reform… Brexit could provide the spur for the EU to either reform or break-up (and) the Brexit vote can lead the way to a better Europe." However, judging by the reaction of the European political elite, our departure has brought the remaining member states closer together, as they continue their political journey towards a United States of Europe, without the informed consent of the unsuspecting European people.

Proposed Immigration Control from 1ˢᵗ January 2021

The new government intends to introduce immigration controls, effective from 1ˢᵗ January 2021, which will limit EU nationals without a visa to a maximum of six months in the country; prevent all new migrants, including EU nationals, from claiming income-related benefits; require all migrants, including those from the EU, who come to work, to contribute towards the cost of the NHS; exclude more Europeans who have criminal records and much more. The announcement could, of course, cause a rush of EU migrants before the end of the year as any EU citizen living in Britain by the end of 2020 can live and work here under the current rules. The Home Secretary has also said: "We will choose who comes here based on the skills they can offer to benefit our country. They must speak English – so they can integrate into our communities. They must have a job offer – so they can make a genuine contribution to our country. They must be paid a salary that does not undercut local workers and ensures that they can support themselves." There have been complaints from business leaders that there will be a shortage of 'low-skilled' foreign labour, particularly on our farms, but the government has said they should use people from our own 'unemployment pool'.

In support of the demand to use our own pool of unemployed people, rather than people from abroad, we are told that in the 16 to 24 age group, there are 800,000 so-called 'NEET's'; that's young people who are not in education, employment or training, which is very concerning. The government must find ways to get these vulnerable young people to take some form of education or training (including government-sponsored apprenticeships) as the first step towards employment, or alternatively take offers of low-skilled seasonal work, particularly on our farms.

The following information about 'unemployment' and 'economic inactivity' was released in a 'Labour Force Survey' by the Office for National Statistics (ONS) on 18ᵗʰ February 2020: There was an estimated 1.29 million people unemployed and an estimated 8.48 million people (16 to 64) were not in the work force and classified as 'economically inactive', between October and December 2019.

Incidentally, Jo Faragher, *Personnel Today*, 6th January 2020, reported that according to the Resolution Foundation 'think-tank', just over 8% of working age people (16 to 64) or 3.4 million people have never had paid employment!

Furthermore, according to the Office for National Statistics (ONS), the following are the reasons why our people are classed as 'economically inactive' (October to December 2019): Students > 2 million (27%); Sick > 2 million (26%); Carers, circa 1.9 million (22%); Retired, circa 1.2 million (13%) and Other, circa 1 million (not started looking for a job or awaiting result of a job application or say they don't need work). They also (apparently) suggested that of those 8.48 million people who are 'economically inactive', as many as 6.61 million do not want a job and 1.87 million would like a job but may not be currently looking for a job!

Whilst this may be a complex subject, the welfare system must ensure that our able-bodied young people are required to participate in education, training or employment, rather than receiving a cheque in the post and being free to roam. These 'economically inactive' young people cannot be abandoned to survive on welfare, they must be required to participate in some form of education or training or take low-skilled work, such as working on our farms, as a platform to a better future.

Incidentally, coming from a low-income, single-parent household, the author left grammar school early, to work as an underground miner for five years, which was an excellent springboard to a very successful professional and business career.

The Road to Independence, Democracy and Freedom

However, regardless of whether we create a successful enterprise economy or whether we employ more of our own people, rather than people from abroad, the main result of the referendum was to regain our independence, democracy and freedom from the European Union, which is moving towards a federal United States of Europe, and requires individual member states to cede their sovereignty.

If the Europhiles are dismissive of the suggested movement towards a United States of Europe, we should revisit the 'Schuman Declaration', on 9th May 1950, made by the French Foreign Minister, Robert Schuman, the architect of European integration, which said: "Europe will not be made all at once or according to a single plan... The coming together of the nations of Europe... The pooling of coal and steel production should... provide for the setting-up of common foundations for economic development as a first step in the federation of Europe."

Furthermore, if the Eurocrats attempt to conceal their intended destination of a federal European Union super-state, we should revisit the words attributed to the French economist Jean Monnet, one of the founding fathers of the European Union, on 30th April 1952, who said: "Europe's nations should be guided towards the super state, without their people understanding what is happening. This can be accomplished by successive steps, each disguised as having an economic purpose, but which will eventually and irreversibly lead to federation."

It's clear that the European people have been deceived from the beginning of this clandestine project of the European political elite and we should remind our political masters of the words of Thomas Jefferson, President of the USA (1801-1809) who said: "The will of the people is the only legitimate foundation of any government and to protect its free expression should be our first objective."

If that's not enough to confirm that democratic power must be vested in the people, we should remind the European political elite of the words of President Abraham Lincoln (USA), in his 'Gettysburg Address' (1863) that: "The nation was conceived in liberty and dedicated to the proposition that all men are equal and that the future of democracy in the world would be assured that government of the people, by the people, for the people shall not perish from the earth."

The vision of Thomas Jefferson and Abraham Lincoln was grounded in the idea that the 'will of the people' is the foundation of democracy, and that our elected representatives, are meant to work on behalf of the people and not get carried away with their own importance, while consumed in an academic discourse about multi-nationalism or globalism. Consequently, we should revisit the words of Prime Minister Theresa May, when she said: "Too many people in positions of power, behave as if they have more in common with international elites than with the people down the road… but if you believe you are a citizen of the world, you are a citizen of nowhere, you don't understand what citizenship means."

The people of Europe are standing at the bar of the last chance saloon and they must heed the concerns of the British people, expressed through a 'people's vote', and they must now hold their political masters to account, before they lead them into the autocratic wilderness, where their calls for freedom will not be heard!

Whatever the outcome of the negotiations on our future relationship and future trade deal, they must not water-down our hard-won independence, democracy and freedom, which is what the people voted for in the referendum. Whatever the discussions around close regulatory alignment with their rules and regulations, we must remain an independent country and negotiate a trade deal, very similar to the trade deals negotiated with other independent countries around the world.

Furthermore, we should reject the concept of 'associate citizenship', being floated by Sadiq Khan, Mayor of London, in discussion with Guy Verhofstadt, which could reverse our release from the 'free movement of people' principle, which was one of the main reasons why the people voted to leave. It has been reported that the influential Guy Verhofstadt said: "The Maastricht Treaty created the concept of European citizenship and I am in favour of using this as a basis for people who want to keep their link with Europe." Incidentally, Guy Verhofstadt is in favour of a 'United States of Europe', as part of a 'World Order of Empires', so we must insist on a clean break from the control of the European Union.

A Final Message to our 'Friends and Neighbours' Across the Channel

A final message to the people of the European Union. The great British people voted to leave the European Union, this project of the European political elite, as it moves inexorably towards a federal United States of Europe, but they did not vote to leave our European 'friends and neighbours' and our trading partners.

Incidentally, those citizens of the European Union who are living and working in our country, and contributing to our economic success, must be assured by the government and the people, that they are welcome in our country, as we re-establish ourselves as an independent nation, trading with Europe and the world.

The British people were, of course, an independent seafaring and trading nation, over many centuries, and only recently joined the European Union political, economic and social construct, when it emerged from the European Economic Community (EEC) or the Common Market of western European trading nations.

The European political elite changed a small group of western European trading nations (Common Market) into a greater European political, economic and social construct (European Union), and when the British people realised that they had lost their independence, democracy and freedom and voted to leave, they were immediately confronted with a Brussels and Westminster resistance movement.

The adversarial approach of the European political class, our political masters, towards the people of a member state wanting to leave their grand project, is a warning to the people of Europe, that they've surrendered their independence, democracy and freedom to a dominant multi-national super-state, which Mikhail Gorbachev thought was the 're-creation of the Soviet Union in Western Europe.' For the sake of the unsuspecting people of the European Union, as it transitions into a United States of Europe, it is hoped that the much-respected Mikhail Gorbachev, who oversaw the collapse of the brutal Soviet Union, was mistaken!

Furthermore, whilst her views about the result of the Brexit referendum may be dismissed as extreme, the people of Europe must note the pragmatic words of Marine Le Pen, when she said: "This was a victory for freedom" and "We must now have the same referendum in France and other European countries" and "The United Kingdom has started a movement that can't be stopped" and "This is the beginning of the end of the European Union" and "I hope the birth of the 'Europe of Nations', a Europe of co-operation, that we've been propounding for years."

The people of Europe must consider the radical decision of the

British people to leave the European Union super-state, as it moves inexorably towards a United States of Europe, and demand a 'people's vote' on whether they want to be part of this grand project of the European political elite, which effectively means that their proud countries will surrender their independence, democracy and freedom!

This enormous leap in the dark from an independent, democratic nation-state, to a dependent member of a multi-national super-power, must be a decision of the people and not their elected representatives, and the people must be made aware that they are actually surrendering their independence, democracy and freedom.

Assuming that the citizens of some other member states demand a 'people's vote' on their future relationship with the European Union, and assuming that some of the member states vote to leave the grand project, the current leaders of the European Union must reconsider their raison d'être, which according to Jean Monnet and Robert Schuman, was the creation of a federal European super-state.

Before they reach such an impasse, which could see the collapse of their European Empire, the leaders must consider a return to the European Economic Community (EEC) or the Common Market or even a Commonwealth of Independent States (CIS), which was created by the Russian Federation, Belarus and the Ukraine (1991) as an alliance of independent nation-states, with formal agreements on economic and foreign policy and defence co-operation and many other matters.

However, the European political elites have created monolithic, bureaucratic institutions, in Brussels and Strasbourg and beyond, which are designed to govern a monumental United States of Europe, and there's no easy return to a European trading group of independent nation states. The shock British departure must, however, be a warning to the European people, that they must take back control from their political masters, who are not leading them towards the promised land!

Printed in Great Britain
by Amazon